LIBERATING REFORMED THEOLOGY

Liberating Reformed Theology

A South African Contribution to an Ecumenical Debate

John W. de Gruchy

WILLIAM B. EERDMANS PUBLISHING COMPANY
GRAND RAPIDS, MICHIGAN

DAVID PHILIP PUBLISHERS
CAPE TOWN

First published 1991 by Wm. B. Eerdmans Publishing Co.
255 Jefferson Ave. S.E., Grand Rapids, Mich. 49503
and David Philip Publishers (Pty) Ltd
208 Werdmuller Centre, Claremont 7700, South Africa

ISBN 0-8028-0536-1 (Eerdmans)
ISBN 0-86486-202-4 (David Philip)

Printed in the United States of America

Library of Congress Cataloging-in-Publication Data

De Gruchy, John W.
    Liberating Reformed theology: a South African contribution
to an ecumenical debate / John W. de Gruchy.
        p.   cm.
    "Expanded and edited version of the Warfield lectures . . .
April 1990" — Introd.
    Includes bibliographical references and indexes.
    ISBN 0-8028-0536-1
    1. Reformed Church — Doctrines. 2. Sociology, Christian
(Reformed Church). 3. Reformed Church — South Africa.
4. Liberation theology. I. Title. II. Title: Warfield lectures.
BX9422.2.D44   1991
230′.4268 — dc20   91-7867
                                                                                CIP

To
Joseph Wing
Douglas Bax
Jaap Durand
and to
Alex Boraine

Theologians, Pastors, and a Politician
who have demonstrated
the liberating power of the gospel

In gratitude
for years of friendship

Contents

Contents

Acknowledgments

I have dedicated this volume to four close friends and colleagues who exemplify the best in the Reformed tradition, (even though one is a Methodist!): Joseph Wing, former general secretary of the United Congregational Church of Southern Africa, and more recently the president of the Federal Theological Seminary; Douglas Bax, the minister of the Rondebosch United Church (Congregational and Presbyterian), and, during 1989–90, moderator of the Presbyterian Church of Southern Africa; Jaap Durand, a former Dutch Reformed missionary and member of the Dutch Reformed Mission Church, professor of theology, and presently vice-rector of the University of the Western Cape; and Alex Boraine, a former president of the Methodist Church in Southern Africa, member of Parliament, and presently executive director of the Institute for Democratic Alternatives in South Africa. Each in his own way has helped to keep hope alive in the dark days of struggle and has helped to facilitate the changes we are now experiencing in South Africa. In doing so, each has demonstrated the integral connection which Reformed theology makes between Christian faith, working for social justice, and relying on God's liberating grace in shaping the future of society.

I wish to express my thanks to President Thomas Gillespie of Princeton Theological Seminary, David Willis-

Watkins, the Benjamin B. Warfield Professor of Systematic Theology, and the faculty of Princeton Theological Seminary for the invitation they extended to me to give the Warfield Lectures, as well as for their friendship, support, and generous hospitality during the week they were delivered. I am also most grateful to them and to the seminary community more generally for the gracious and positive response they gave to the lectures, and especially for those critical comments that have helped to clarify certain ideas and improve what I have attempted. I also wish to thank Larry Rasmussen, Elsie Anne McKee, Christopher Morse, Nicholas Wolterstorff, and Mark Taylor, who kindly read earlier drafts of the manuscript, as well as my son Stephen, with whom I discussed much of it at various times, for all their helpful comments and suggestions. As always, Bill Eerdmans and Jon Pott have been most supportive and encouraging, and a joy to know as good friends as well as publishing professionals. Finally, I am indebted to the University of Cape Town for enabling me to take research and study leave during 1989 to work at this task; to the Human Sciences Research Council which enabled me to do some of my research at Union Theological Seminary in New York; to my colleagues in the Department of Religious Studies for their friendship and support; to Nan Oosthuizen, for her enthusiastic secretarial help; and to my wife, Isobel, for her love and encouragement, but also for reminding me from time to time that writing books is not necessarily the most important thing in life.

Cape Town   John W. de Gruchy
Pentecost 1990

Introduction

This book is an expanded and edited version of the Warfield Lectures that I gave at Princeton Theological Seminary, New Jersey, at the end of April 1990. The terms of the Warfield Lectures, established by the distinguished Reformed theologian Benjamin B. Warfield in honor of his wife, Annie Kinkead Warfield, require that they be on some aspect of the Reformed tradition, but the specific choice of theme is left to the designated lecturer. By "Reformed tradition" is meant, of course, that Christian tradition which derives from the sixteenth-century Protestant Reformation, especially as this found expression in Switzerland under the powerful influence of John Calvin.

My choice of theme, expressed in the title "Liberating Reformed Theology," arises out of the conviction that Reformed theology is best understood as a liberating theology that is catholic in its substance, evangelical in principle, and socially engaged and prophetic in its witness. At the same time the title intentionally reflects an ambiguity in Reformed theology and the Reformed tradition more broadly. For while they may well be liberating in intent, they have also been guilty of legitimating oppression in practice. Thus they need to be liberated in order to fulfill their liberating potential and role. One way of doing this is for Reformed theology to enter into dialogue with the various forms of liberation theology at work in the contemporary church. This is the substance of what I attempted in the Warfield Lectures.

It might appear a little odd that we should be engaged with a theological tradition that is rooted in sixteenth-century Switzerland while seeking to do theology in an African—albeit South African—context. Benjamin Warfield did, of course, maintain that Calvinism was the more modern term for Augustinianism, and seeing that St. Augustine was a North African we could perhaps claim that Calvinism is not a total stranger to the African continent. But Calvinism remains a product of sixteenth- and seventeenth-century Europe rather than Africa. What could be more remote from the vibrant worship and nonintellectual spirituality of the African church than the somewhat austere theology and practice of the church in Geneva? They are literally worlds apart. If, after all, John Calvin's theology is a return to the biblical gospel, why do we have to approach Jerusalem via Geneva, especially if we need the help of liberation theologians to do so? Why not simply be a liberation theologian?

The first answer to that question is personal, deriving from the fact that every Christian belongs to some ecclesial tradition which, for good or ill, influences his or her understanding of the Christian faith. As an ordained minister of the United Congregational Church of Southern Africa, I belong to one branch of the Reformed family of churches, though not one as dogmatically tied to that tradition as some others. So it has been important for me to try to understand that tradition better in order to appreciate both its strengths and its weaknesses in our contemporary context, and especially in the struggle for justice in South Africa. As a professor of theology I have taught courses and done research on the Protestant Reformation, and on John Calvin in particular. Though I can claim no particular expertise in either field, what I have attempted here has been simmering beneath the surface of my theological consciousness for some time. It was particularly stimulated during a sabbatical year at Princeton Theological Seminary in 1983, when I was privileged to participate in Professor Edward Dowey's doctoral seminar on the structure of Calvin's theology. So when the invitation came to give the Warfield Lectures, I immediately knew what it was I would like to do.

A second reason for engaging in the task is the fact that for many black Reformed Christians in South Africa, Reformed theology and especially Calvinism is regarded as in some significant way responsible for their oppression. Black Congregationalists and Presbyterians hesitated to use the name "Reformed" when a title for a proposed united church was under debate between their respective denominations because of its associations with apartheid and oppression. But this profound suspicion and reservation about the Reformed tradition also means that it cannot be ignored. Moreover, and conversely, some black and white Reformed Christians in South Africa have begun to discover that there is another side to their tradition, one both prophetic and liberating, which needs to be reclaimed as part of the struggle for liberation and justice and as a contribution to the ecumenical church.

In a recent collection of essays on *Reformed Theology in America*, George Marsden has commented that it "is ironic that 'Reformed' has so little meaning in America today when in fact the culture has been so shaped by that heritage."[1] This is not only ironic but also tragic, because the Reformed tradition truly understood witnesses so powerfully to the transforming power of the gospel. Yet Reformed Christians have only themselves to blame for this state of things, a development that could in all likelihood also eventuate in South Africa in the decades to come. Our task is not, however, to attempt to bolster the Reformed tradition so that it may in some way regain its former glory. Our task is to make a small contribution to ecumenical debate which may help ensure that the Reformed witness to the gospel is not lost but rather is able to make a contribution to the shaping of the church and of the world in the closing and critical years of the twentieth century and the beginning years of the twenty-first.

1. George Marsden, "Reformed and American," in *Reformed Theology in America: A History of Its Modern Development*, ed. David F. Wells (Grand Rapids: Eerdmans, 1985), p. 4.

Reformed theology is by no means confined to, nor necessarily best expressed in, church denominations bearing that name. A great deal of Anglican theology, for example, can be traced back to the Reformation and to Calvin, and the "father of Methodism," John Wesley, while not a Calvinist, was strongly influenced by Reformed theology.[2] Reformed theology and Calvinism are not necessarily the same. Moreover, much contemporary theology of virtually all traditions has been profoundly influenced by Karl Barth, a Reformed theologian standing firmly, albeit critically, in continuity with Calvin. Indeed, one of the surprises I had in working on this project was the discovery of the extent to which the reforming labors of Calvin in sixteenth-century Geneva correspond to those of some Catholic theologians, not least Catholic liberation theologians in Latin America. On reflection this should not be surprising, because Calvin was not a Protestant in the first instance but a Catholic lay theologian committed to the renewal of the Catholic church and its witness. Certainly I have found that contemporary Roman Catholic theologians who have studied and written about Calvin generally have an insight into his thought not always apparent in the writings of later Protestants.

There is, of course, a vast historical gap between the sixteenth and late twentieth centuries. Calvin was a man of his times, so it would be foolish to try to make him out as our contemporary. Quite apart from anything else, we are separated by the far-reaching changes in human consciousness that have resulted from the eighteenth-century Enlightenment and subsequent developments which continue in ever new ways to shape our understandings of ourselves and the world. We cannot ignore such developments. At the very least we must keep them in mind as we proceed. Yet in a profound sense Calvin, like others before the dawning of the modern era, straddles the centuries and speaks directly to us and the human condition. If I have erred, then, in bringing Calvin closer to our time than

2. John T. McNeill, *The History and Character of Calvinism* (New York: Oxford University Press, 1954), p. 371.

some might feel appropriate, it is not because I am unaware of the gulf separating him from us, but because I have purposefully sought to highlight the connections and continuities.

The fact that I have extensively used material derived from Afrikaner Calvinism in what follows should not be misconstrued. However, because Afrikaner Calvinism has too often been misunderstood, I have taken care to try to define it more precisely than is commonly found. Not all Afrikaners are Calvinists; neither is the theology of the Dutch Reformed Church to be equated with Afrikaner Calvinism. Afrikaner Calvinism is a particular ideological blend of various sources that emerged within the Dutch Reformed Church in the late nineteenth century, and that dominated its life during the heyday of Afrikaner nationalism and apartheid in the twentieth. While it is an aberration of Calvinism and is repudiated by many Dutch Reformed theologians today, Afrikaner Calvinism remains a potent force within right-wing Afrikanerdom, where it is still evoked to give apartheid and Afrikaner nationalism divine sanction.

Afrikaner Calvinism provides a case study for much of what has gone wrong in the Reformed tradition, and as I am most familiar with its history and character I have not hesitated to refer to it. But similar illustrative material could have been culled from other sources as well, and, indeed, from traditions other than Reformed. In using Afrikaner Calvinism in the way I do I am certainly not attacking white Afrikaners, nor do I wish to suggest that white English-speaking South Africans are paragons of virtue. White South Africans of whatever variety are not very different from whites elsewhere in the world—at least that is my experience and the experience of others. Racism runs deep in the European psyche and in most European Christian traditions. One of the most promising aspects of contemporary South Africa is the extent to which many Afrikaners have, in fact, begun to break decisively with apartheid and its sanctioning by Afrikaner Calvinism. Indeed, one of the problems in preparing these lectures for publication has been the rapidity with which change is beginning to take place in South Africa.

As the Warfield Lectures and the manuscript for this volume were completed early in 1990, it has proved impossible to incorporate much comment on the significance of the events which followed the unbanning of the African National Congress, the Pan African Congress, and the South African Communist Party, as announced in Parliament by State President de Klerk on February 2, 1990. Nothing that has since happened, however, fundamentally alters the substance of what follows; indeed, if anything, the discussion is perhaps more relevant for such an era of transition.

At least some theologians within the Reformed tradition have been positively and creatively engaged in responding to the challenge of contemporary forms of liberation theology for some time, and much that we will explore was anticipated by Karl Barth earlier this century. As a result, many of the insights and issues which liberation theology has placed on the contemporary theological agenda are already part and parcel of Reformed theological thinking. This can be seen not only in the writings of individual theologians, but also in some more representative documents, not least those emanating from the World Alliance of Reformed Churches. In pursuing the theme of these lectures we will endeavor to show that while Reformed theology is a liberating theology, it cannot simply be equated with any particular contemporary liberation theology. In certain respects the two must be in critical tension with each other, even though they are complementary and not antithetical. Thus, just as it is possible to be a Catholic liberation theologian, so it is possible to be a Reformed one as well, and to be one not only in countries of obvious oppression but also in situations where the oppression may be more subtle, even if very real for those who are dehumanized and oppressed.

We turn then to examine the challenge that liberation theology presents to the Reformed tradition and its theology. But we do so mindful that the challenge will not be one way. Reformed theology, as an evangelical and prophetic theology, has, as it were, been in the field much longer than liberation theology. Moreover, it has certain insights into the nature of

Christian faith and obedience that it rightly treasures and brings to the dialogue. Thus, whatever its failings, and however much it may need to be liberated from its various forms of captivity, it has both a critical and a constructive contribution to make to the liberating and prophetic witness of the church today.

1. A Ferment Nourished by the Gospel

Almost a century ago the Dutch statesman and theologian Abraham Kuyper gave his famous Stone Lectures on Calvinism.[1] In them he claimed that Calvinism not only embraced "the Christian idea more purely and accurately" than other forms of Christianity, but that it was "the only decisive, lawful, and consistent defence for Protestant nations against encroaching, and overwhelming Modernism."[2] By "Modernism" he meant the forces of atheistic revolutionary change unleashed by the Enlightenment and the French Revolution. By "Calvinism" he meant more than a particular set of doctrines or denominations; he meant a comprehensive "life-system" or worldview. "Calvinism," he declared,

> is rooted in a form of religion which was peculiarly its own, and from this specific religious consciousness there was developed first a peculiar theology, then a special church-order, and then a given form for political and social life, for the interpretation of the moral world-order, for the relation between nature and grace, between Chris-

1. Abraham Kuyper, *Lectures on Calvinism* (Grand Rapids: Eerdmans, 1931). The lectures were delivered in 1898 under the auspices of the L. P. Stone Foundation, Princeton Theological Seminary, New Jersey.
2. Ibid., pp. 17, 12.

tianity and the world, between church and state, and finally for art and science.[3]

The world has changed dramatically since Kuyper gave his lectures in 1898. Few if any of us would perceive the struggle of our time as one between Calvinism and Modernism, nor would we be satisfied with the precise way in which Kuyper understood the Reformed tradition. Yet we cannot but be impressed by his neo-Calvinist attempt to relate Christian faith and theology to the world in which he lived: its philosophy, art, science, and politics. Christianity, and more especially Calvinism as Kuyper understood it, was engaged in a historical, ideological struggle for the soul and conscience of individuals and the true liberation of the nations.

The Protestant Reformation in the sixteenth century was an integral part of a monumental upheaval in the social, cultural, and spiritual life of Western Europe. Generated by a new experience and understanding of the gospel, it was also a product of diverse social, political, and economic forces. Focused on the renewal of the church and the salvation of the individual, it made a decisive contribution to the transformation of society. While Martin Luther pioneered the way and gave powerful, existential expression to evangelical doctrine, it was John Calvin, a second-generation Reformer, who consciously and with some determination related evangelical theology to the structures and conflicts of church and society.

Yet it was even more Calvin's successors who, passionately latching onto elements of his legacy, made Calvinism a potent social force within the political struggles and ferment of sixteenth- and seventeenth-century Europe. In the process, Calvinism brought into being what Ernst Troeltsch called a new "type of humanity."[4] This "type of humanity" had an overwhelming sense not only of God's providence in history, but also of its own calling to participate in the shaping of that

3. Ibid., p. 17.
4. Ernst Troeltsch, *The Social Teaching of the Christian Churches*, vol. 2 (London: George Allen & Unwin, 1956), p. 528.

history. Thus, in Michael Walzer's words, Calvinism became an "ideology of transition" in the revolutionary developments of the post-Reformation era—in France, Holland, Scotland, and England, and subsequently in New England, South Africa, and elsewhere.[5]

Walzer's description of Calvinism as an "ideology of transition" is undoubtedly open to criticism,[6] yet there is no denying that Calvinism in the sixteenth and seventeenth centuries contributed significantly to social movements that managed to turn a theology of evangelical salvation into a program of political transformation. In the case of Holland, Britain, and their colonies, the impact was far-reaching. In the celebrated instance of France, Calvinism as embodied within the Huguenot movement almost succeeded in the Protestant reconstruction of society, but finally failed to achieve its goal as a result of Catholic repression and inner contradictions. In many respects the French Revolution of 1789 became necessary and inevitable as a result.[7]

Calvinism as perceived by Kuyper and Troeltsch, then, was not confined to a set of doctrines or denominations; it was a life system contributing in a decisive way to the social construction of reality. In the process, however, "it gave way to other social and intellectual forces which sustained something of its achievement but not everything."[8] Part of this achievement was a significant contribution to social democracy and human freedom, but there have been more ambiguous and less noble achievements as well.[9] Along with the rest of Christendom, Calvinism contributed to the legitimation of colonial con-

5. Michael Walzer, *The Revolution of the Saints* (Cambridge, Mass.: Harvard University Press, 1965), p. 312.

6. See David Little, "Max Weber Revisited: The 'Protestant Ethic' and the Puritan Experience of Order," *Harvard Theological Review* 59 (1966): 415ff., especially p. 426 n. 37.

7. See Henry Heller, *The Conquest of Poverty: The Calvinist Revolt in Sixteenth Century France* (Leiden: E. J. Brill, 1986).

8. Walzer, *Revolution of the Saints*, p. 300.

9. See Robert M. Kingdon and Robert D. Linder, eds., *Calvin and Calvinism: Sources of Democracy?* (D. C. Heath and Co., 1970).

quest, and it was subsumed in secularized versions of the kingdom of God, thus contributing to the rise of nationalist doctrines of manifest destiny. For example, as Ernst Troeltsch put it, Calvinism "merged with and to some extent produced that political and social way of life which may be described as 'Americanism'."[10] In a similar way, it contributed to what has been described as Afrikaner civil religion in South Africa[11] and, in a convoluted manner, to the sanctification of the ideology of apartheid.

Calvinism, Catholicism, and Apartheid

In his searing critique of apartheid, *Naught for Your Comfort*, published in 1957, Trevor Huddleston, who was then an Anglican priest serving in Sophiatown, Johannesburg, virtually blamed Calvinism for the ideology of apartheid.

> The truth is that the Calvinistic doctrines upon which the faith of the Afrikaner is nourished contain within themselves—like all heresies and deviations from catholic truth—exaggerations so distorting and powerful that it is very hard indeed to recognise the Christian faith they are supposed to enshrine. Here, in this fantastic notion of the immutability of race, is present in a different form the predestination idea: the concept of an elect people of God, characteristic above all of John Calvin.[12]

Huddleston wrote those words almost a decade after the National Party came to power in South Africa on the ticket of apartheid. While he was careful not to blame Calvin directly for apartheid, there is no denying that he regarded Calvinism as heretical and guilty. In the light of Troeltsch's understanding

10. Troeltsch, *Social Teaching*, p. 577.
11. T. Dunbar Moodie, *The Rise of Afrikanerdom: Power, Apartheid, and the Afrikaner Civil Religion* (Berkeley: University of California Press, 1975).
12. Trevor Huddleston, *Naught for Your Comfort* (London: Collins, 1957), p. 50.

of the social role of Calvinism in history, it is difficult to deny some validity in Huddleston's indictment, and that in certain respects Calvin may himself be held ultimately responsible. Yet students of Calvin's theology, as well as those who know the Reformed tradition well, may be forgiven for raising some critical questions about the too easy identification of Calvin and Calvinism with apartheid that is popularly held both inside and beyond the borders of South Africa.[13] The issues are far more complex than caricatures allow.

The notion of Calvinism as the heresy responsible for Afrikaner nationalism and apartheid predated Huddleston. After a conference on Christian Reconstruction held at the University of Fort Hare in 1942, where church leaders in anticipation of the end of the Second World War tried to lay the foundations for a new society, the editor of the Anglican newspaper *The Watchman* summed up the challenge facing Christians in South Africa by declaring:

> The issue that confronts us is between Catholicism and Calvinism. When we are capable of an understanding of these two faiths which form our dual ancestry we shall be equipped to see our more immediate problems in their true perspectives.[14]

How ironic this sounds when placed alongside Kuyper's perception that the struggle for liberty in his time depended upon Calvinism winning against what he called Modernism. Looked at from our present perspective, it is equally impossible to conceive how the issue facing the future of South Africa could have been formulated as a struggle between Catholicism and Calvinism. But it was, and by both parties. Not only did Roman and Anglo Catholics perceive Calvinism as a heresy that created such monsters as apartheid, but Afrikaner nationalists

13. See, for example, the caricature of Calvin and Calvinism in Ivor Wilkins and Hans Strydom, *The Super-Afrikaners: Inside the Afrikaner Broederbond* (Johannesburg: Jonathan Ball, 1978), pp. 292-93.

14. Quoted by Alan Paton, *Apartheid and the Archbishop* (New York: Charles Scribner's Sons, 1973), p. 113.

placed *die Roomse-gevaar* (the "Roman danger") on a par with communism and liberalism. For many it was an even greater danger than the threat of the black majority.[15]

Pondering on the vagaries of South African history, a Roman Catholic historian in the 1950s was tempted to think that all would have turned out for the better if the balance between Calvinists and Catholics had been different. Little did he anticipate that the day would come when black Catholics would outnumber white Calvinists, as is presently happening.

> It is tempting to wonder how far the history of South Africa might have been different, and whether the approach in these recent years to the critical problem of racial relationships might not have been different, if from the first the Dutch population in South Africa had been a true projection of the population in the Netherlands, with Catholics a minority of at least a third among the Boer farmers, numerous enough to establish a tradition in contrast to that which is in fact so deeply entrenched and which is grounded in Calvinist theology.[16]

What are we to make of this Catholic indictment of Calvinism as the source of apartheid? Was it more than part of a traditional anti-Catholic or anti-Protestant polemic in which both sides have engaged for centuries? Perhaps it was that to some extent, but it was undoubtedly more than that. As in Northern Ireland, so in South Africa the traditional theological polemic was inseparable from political realities and policies—namely, those of Afrikaner nationalism and apartheid, or, if you happened to be an Afrikaner Calvinist, internationalism, liberalism, and communism.

The relationship among Afrikaner nationalism, apartheid, and Calvinism has been the subject of much scholarly discus-

15. See John W. de Gruchy, "Catholics in a Calvinist Country," in *Catholics in Apartheid Society*, ed. Andrew Prior (Cape Town: David Philip, 1982).

16. W. E. Brown, *The Catholic Church in South Africa* (London: Burns & Oates, 1960), p. 5.

sion.[17] Afrikaners in South Africa have been equated with the Puritans of seventeenth-century New England,[18] and it has been argued, as Huddleston did, that some of the values popularly associated with what Troeltsch called "primitive Calvinism"[19]—for example, those derived from its stress on the doctrines of original sin or predestination and election—have so permeated Afrikaner culture that they have taken on a life of their own in the shaping of society. This is of course a variant on Max Weber's argument regarding the relationship between Calvinism and capitalism.[20]

The debate is important both in terms of understanding the role of the Reformed tradition in South Africa and in clarifying what we mean by Calvinism. In doing so it also helps us to debunk the mythology that uncritically assumes that Calvin and Calvinism are responsible for Afrikaner nationalism and apartheid, and, in doing so, to rediscover both the catholic substance of Calvin's own theology and the liberating power of the gospel as he understood it. We shall do this in two stages: first by looking briefly at the original Dutch settlement at the Cape in comparison with the Catholic colonization of Latin

17. See, inter alia, T. Dunbar Moodie, *The Rise of Afrikanerdom;* Irving Hexham, *The Irony of Apartheid: The Struggle for National Independence of Afrikaner Calvinism against British Imperialism* (New York: Edwin Mellen Press, 1981); Johann Kinghorn, ed., *Die NG Kerk en Apartheid* (Cape Town: Macmillan, 1986); J. Alton Templin, *Ideology as a Frontier: The Theological Foundation of Afrikaner Nationalism* (Westport, Conn.: Greenwood Press, 1984); A. J. Botha, *Die Evolusie van 'n Volksteologie* (Ph.D. thesis, University of the Western Cape, 1984); André du Toit, "Puritans in Africa? Afrikaner 'Calvinism' and Kuyperian Neo-Calvinism in Late Nineteenth Century South Africa," *Comparative Studies in Society and History* 27 (April 1985).

18. See W. de Klerk, *The Puritans in Africa* (London: Rex Collings, 1975).

19. Troeltsch, *Social Teaching*, pp. 581ff.

20. Max Weber, *The Protestant Ethic and the Spirit of Capitalism* (New York: Scribner's, 1930). See Jan J. Loubser, "Calvinism, Equality, and Inclusion: The Case of Afrikaner Calvinism," in *The Protestant Ethic and Modernization*, ed. S. N. Eisenstadt (New York: Basic Books, 1968); Randall G. Stokes, "Afrikaner Calvinism and Economic Action: The Weberian Thesis in South Africa," *The American Journal of Sociology* 81 (1975).

America, and then, in a later section, by considering the evolution of Afrikaner Calvinism in the nineteenth and early twentieth centuries. In between the two sections we shall seek to clarify what we understand by Calvinism and the Reformed tradition.

A brief comparison of the role of the first European conquistadors and colonists in Latin America with that of their counterparts in South Africa is instructive. In much the same way as the sixteenth-century colonists in Latin America were Roman Catholic by tradition, so the first Dutch settlers at the Cape in the seventeenth century were members of the established Reformed Church of the Netherlands, supplemented by a small but significant group of French Huguenots who came to the Cape in 1688. The conquistadors in Latin America pursued their task of conquest and colonization in tandem with the missionary endeavor to spread the Catholic faith and establish the Catholic Church on the continent. Hispanic colonization and Catholic evangelization were regarded as integrally related.[21] Likewise, the "founding father" of the Dutch settlement at the Cape, Jan van Riebeeck, whose mission in 1652 was to establish a halfway house for Dutch ships engaged in trade with the East Indies, prayed shortly after his arrival that the "true reformed religion" would be spread among the peoples of the new colony.[22]

While it is true that the conquistadors were Roman Catholic, some more devout than others, it is perhaps as true, if not more so, that they were soldiers of the crown and of fortune who often found themselves at serious odds with those missionaries committed to the gospel. In like manner, the Dutch and French settlers at the Cape were adherents of the Reformed Church brought up on the Bible and the Heidel-

21. See Enrique Dussel, *A History of the Church in Latin America: Colonialism to Liberation* (Grand Rapids: Eerdmans, 1981), pp. 37ff.; H. McKennie Goodpasture, *Cross and Sword: An Eyewitness History of Christianity in Latin America* (New York: Orbis, 1989), pp. 6-7.
22. See J. du Plessis, *A History of Christian Missions in South Africa* (London: Longmans, 1911), p. 23.

berg Catechism, the doctrinal standard of most immigrant European Reformed communities in their various colonies. But to regard them as ardent, well-informed Calvinists like the Puritans in New England, committed to the establishment of a holy commonwealth and the evangelization of the heathen, would be a serious exaggeration. Many were nominal in their membership of the church, as was true of their peers in Holland itself.[23] By far the majority were petty officials, artisans, and farmers struggling to establish themselves on foreign terrain, often at the expense of the indigenous San and Khoi, rather than people theologically informed and committed to a holy cause.

Like the Roman Catholic Church in Latin America, the Dutch Reformed Church played an important and prominent role in the life of the fledgling colonial Cape community. Despite some missionary protest to the contrary, both were largely captive to colonial needs and interests, and all were under the control of ecclesial authorities in their respective mother countries. The Dutch Reformed Church's status as the established state church meant, among other things, that the church was subservient to colonial policy and its ministers were in the pay of the Dutch East India Company. Little wonder, then, as Giliomee and Elphick conclude on weighing the evidence, that "it was not Calvinism's distinction between the elect and reprobate, but the Company's distinctions among legal status groups, which initially structured Cape society." It was not Calvinism, but the "attitudes and institutions inherited from earlier Dutch experience in Europe and the Indies" that shaped life at the Cape.[24] Likewise, subsequent to the Cape and then Natal becoming British colonies at the turn of the nineteenth century, it was not Calvinism, but British colonial policy, settler interests, land hunger, and imperial greed that

23. Alistair Duke, "The Ambivalent Face of Calvinism in the Netherlands, 1561-1618," in *International Calvinism 1541-1715*, ed. Menna Prestwich (Oxford: Clarendon Press, 1985).

24. Richard Elphick and Hermann Giliomee, eds., *The Shaping of South African Society, 1652-1820* (Cape Town: Longman, 1982), pp. 364-65.

determined attitudes and government policies and helped lay the foundation for apartheid.[25]

It is not surprising, then, that the histories of South Africa and many Latin American countries are remarkably similar in regard to discrimination against other races and the oppression of indigenous peoples and cultures. This does not mean that there were no differences. But such differences were determined more by local context and culture, and by the European background and social context of the colonizers, rather than by their theology. The conquistadors came out of a European feudal society,[26] whereas the settlers at the Cape were products of the new bourgeois and mercantile world of those nations that had espoused Protestantism. Insofar as they thought of their role as extending the kingdom of God, and thought of themselves as an elect people of God, which was probably not very often, it was to legitimate their enterprise in a way common to all European colonizers, irrespective of whether they were Protestant or Roman Catholic. The sense of being an elect people of God with a divine mission to save the world was, after all, the foundation of Hispanic politics as much as, and perhaps even more than, the Dutch.[27] This certainly did not make them Calvinists. What was crucial in European colonization was not whether the colonists were Calvinist or Catholic, but whether they had sufficient power to dominate the indigenous peoples and further their own colonial interests, whether Dutch or Hispanic.[28]

That later colonial Roman Catholics in Mozambique and Angola—to come nearer to South Africa—were neither paragons of nonracial virtue nor great defenders of human rights confirms the fact that the issues we are considering can by no means be reduced to a conflict between Calvinist and Catholic

25. See David Welsh, *The Roots of Segregation: Native Policy in Natal, 1845-1910* (Cape Town: Oxford University Press, 1971).

26. Dussel, *History of the Church in Latin America*, p. 38.

27. Ibid.

28. See Heribert Adam and Hermann Giliomee, *The Rise and Crisis of Afrikaner Power* (Cape Town: David Philip, 1979), p. 92.

theologies and values. Calvinism did not lay the foundations for apartheid any more than Catholicism laid the foundations for oppression in Latin America. The real struggle in South Africa is not, and never has been, between Calvinism and Modernism, or Calvinism and Catholicism, but between injustice and justice, between colonial or neo-colonial domination and democratic equality, between economic greed and the just distribution of resources, and therefore between a Christianity, irrespective of its confessional form, that is captive to the sectional interests of the dominant white culture and a Christianity identified with the struggle for justice and equity.

In this struggle all European Christian traditions—including Presbyterianism and Congregationalism, two other traditions of Calvinist orientation with British origin—have been trapped by their cultural ties with colonialism and the material interests of the white settler community, even when they have sought to serve the interests of their black constituencies.[29] Indeed, it was none other than David Livingstone, the famous missionary-explorer of the London Missionary Society and opponent of the slave trade, who apparently first introduced into southern Africa the notion that the European, and specifically the Afrikaner, colonizers were an "elect People of God."[30] This notion was much later applied by Afrikaner neo-Calvinists to Afrikaner history in order to give legitimacy to, as well as empower the struggle for, national identity and political power against British hegemony. But neither the Dutch settlers nor the later Trekkers interpreted their experience in theological, let alone Calvinist, terms. In André du Toit's words: "The theory of an authentic Calvinist tradition going back to a primitive Calvinism nurtured in the isolated *trekboer* society on the open frontier, and ultimately derived

29. See James Cochrane, *Servants of Power: The Role of English-Speaking Churches, 1903-1930* (Johannesburg: Ravan, 1987); Charles Villa-Vicencio, *Trapped in Apartheid* (New York: Orbis, 1988).

30. See André du Toit, "No Chosen People: The Myth of the Calvinist Origins of Afrikaner Nationalism and Racial Ideology," *American Historical Review* 88 (1983): 939ff.

from the golden age of 'seventeenth-century Calvinism', is an historical myth."[31]

Recent studies on the origins of Afrikaner political development reject any simplistic equation between the origins of apartheid and Calvinism.[32] This does not mean that Calvinism or the Reformed tradition is let off the hook, though it does change our understanding of their relationship with apartheid. Rather than being the origin of Afrikaner nationalism, racism, and subsequently apartheid, as we shall see, Calvinism was later adapted to further their cause and legitimate them.[33] In this way, Calvinism was not only co-opted by Afrikaner nationalism, becoming instrumental in its transition to power, but was itself transformed into Afrikaner Calvinism, a religious ideology sufficiently Calvinist to be recognized as part of the Reformed tradition, but also sufficiently deviant to seriously undermine and damage its witness. Afrikaner Calvinism's legitimation of apartheid became the heresy, not Calvinism as such. This was the heresy to which Huddleston was really pointing, a heresy that has in more recent times, though tragically not before, been condemned and rejected by churches within the Reformed tradition itself.[34]

From our latter-day perspective it is almost impossible to believe that any responsible Christian theology, Reformed or not, could have become party to such a travesty of the biblical message. Yet our focus on Afrikaner Calvinism as a case study should not prevent us from recognizing similar instances in other contexts where Christianity, in whatever form, has been party to the sanctification of oppression. We could, for example, have chosen case studies for this volume from North America and elsewhere to describe the ambiguities and captivities of Calvinism and other forms of colonial Chris-

31. du Toit, "Puritans in Africa?" p. 234.

32. See André du Toit and Hermann Giliomee, *Afrikaner Political Thought: Analysis and Documents, 1780-1850*, vol. 1 (Cape Town: David Philip, 1983), p. xvi.

33. Adam and Giliomee, *Rise and Crisis of Afrikaner Power*, p. 92.

34. John W. de Gruchy and Charles Villa-Vicencio, eds., *Apartheid Is a Heresy* (Grand Rapids: Eerdmans, 1983).

12

tianity.[35] Afrikaner Calvinism as a case study should remind us of and alert us to all such socially destructive and dehumanizing movements and moments legitimated by Christian theology both past and present. The fact of the matter is that Calvinism and the Reformed tradition more generally, like many other religious movements, is an ambiguous tradition that continually needs to be critically examined and liberated in order to be faithful to the gospel of Jesus Christ.

Catholic, Evangelical, and Prophetic

The title of this book, *Liberating Reformed Theology*, reflects the ambiguity inherent in Calvinism, or what we prefer to call the Reformed tradition. Read in one way, it suggests the need for liberation; read in another way, it suggests a potential for liberation. The Reformed tradition, when it is faithful to its original vision of the gospel of the kingdom of God, most truly exists only in the process of being re-formed in relation to the struggles and issues facing it in its various historical contexts. Yet the Reformed tradition, like any other, can be seduced by social and cultural forces that undermine its witness and keep it captive. It therefore needs liberating from reactionary elements in its legacy in order to fulfill its transformative promise in each generation. In order to understand this legacy better, we need to clarify certain terms, and, in the process, begin to reflect on the influence of John Calvin.

By *Reformed tradition* we mean that tradition within the Christian movement, diverse as it may now be, that has grown out of the sixteenth-century Protestant Reformation associated chiefly, though by no means only, with the life and work of John Calvin.[36] While we must acknowledge the important role played in the shaping of the Reformed tradition by others—

35. See Preston N. Williams, "Calvinism, Racism and Economic Institutions," in *Reformed Faith and Economics,* ed. Robert L. Stivers (New York: University Press of America, 1989), pp. 49, 54.

36. See John T. McNeill, *The History and Character of Calvinism* (New York: Oxford University Press, 1954).

13

notably the Zurich Reformers Huldrych Zwingli and Heinrich Bullinger; Martin Bucer in Strasbourg, from whom Calvin learnt so much; and Calvin's own successor in Geneva, Theodore Beza—Calvin is, as James Gustafson has described him, the "decisive generating source" for the identity of the Reformed tradition.[37] This means that any interpretation of the tradition wishing to retain its identity must take Calvin seriously, even if this requires, as Karl Barth once declared, going against him.[38] For this reason much of our discussion will take Calvin as a point of departure for understanding and also for critically evaluating the tradition.

There has been much debate on the relationship between Calvin's theology and the various forms of Calvinism that developed after his death.[39] In the process, the extent to which Calvin himself was or was not a Calvinist as defined by Protestant orthodoxy and Puritanism during the seventeenth century has become increasingly clear. We shall have reason to refer to this relationship on several occasions in what follows. For the moment a few comments and a definition must suffice. *Calvinism* may be broadly defined as coterminous with the Reformed tradition or narrowly used to refer specifically to the scholastic development of Calvin's theology that took place in the late sixteenth and seventeenth centuries. It may also be applied, as it was by Kuyper and Troeltsch, with appropriate qualifications, to the sociopolitical movements which that the-

37. James M. Gustafson, *Theology and Ethics* (Chicago: University of Chicago Press, 1981), p. 163.

38. "Die Neuorientierung der Prot. Theologie in den letzen dreisig Jahren," in *Kirchenblatt fur den ref. Schweiz, 1940*, vol. 7. See G. C. Berkhouwer, *The Triumph of Grace in the Theology of Karl Barth* (London: Paternoster, 1956), p. 15 n. 15.

39. Holmes Rolston III, *John Calvin versus the Westminster Confession* (Richmond: John Knox, 1972); R. T. Kendall, *Calvin and English Calvinism to 1649* (Oxford: Oxford University Press, 1979), and its review by Paul Helm, "Calvin, English Calvinism and the Logic of Doctrinal Development," *Scottish Journal of Theology* 34 (1981): 179ff.; Richard A. Muller, *Christ as the Decree: Christology and Predestination in Reformed Theology from Calvin to Perkins* (Durham, N.C.: Labyrinth Press, 1986).

ology helped generate and nourish during those post-Reformation centuries.

We will generally use *Calvinism* in its more narrow or precise sense. Even so, several variations in Calvinism thus understood will become apparent as we proceed, not least, for example, the Puritanism of England and New England, the neo-Calvinism of Kuyper, and the subject of our own case study, Afrikaner Calvinism. While there are basic connections between these forms of Calvinism, we must keep in mind at the outset that the character and development of Calvinism is far more complex than is generally assumed.[40] Moreover, we should also be mindful at the outset that Calvin cannot be held responsible for everything which developed under the name of Calvinism, a term he would have rejected as odious, even though there are obviously continuities between him and the movement bearing his name.[41] We must also keep in mind that while Calvinists have always regarded themselves as Reformed, not all of those who have claimed to be Reformed have been Calvinists or relished the title when applied to them.

Reformed theology is more inclusive than *Calvinism*, and means first what those within the Reformed tradition more broadly have commonly believed and confessed. Reformed theology would include theologians as different as Friedrich Schleiermacher, Charles Hodge, Emil Brunner, and Reinhold Niebuhr, to name but a few of the well known.[42] However, there is a second meaning we will give to *Reformed theology*, a meaning more consonant with its original intention. Reformed theology is properly not a generic title but the attempt to understand and interpret the biblical message in relation to the life and witness of the Christian church as a whole within the world. Its original intention was not the establishment and service of another tradition within Christendom, but the refor-

40. Prestwich, *International Calvinism 1541-1715*, pp. 13-14.
41. Ibid., p. 2.
42. See John Leith, *An Introduction to the Reformed Tradition: A Way of Being the Christian Community* (Atlanta: John Knox Press, 1978), pp. 127-28.

mation of the Catholic church, the transformation of society, and the redemption of men and women. Understood in this way, Reformed theology stands in a critical yet empathetic relationship to the Reformed tradition—indeed, to the Christian tradition as a whole—serving them best by continually challenging them to be faithful to the gospel. When Reformed theology does this, it becomes a liberating theology both for the Reformed tradition and within the ecumenical church. When, however, Reformed theology becomes captive to the Reformed tradition, and especially to the self-interests of the tradition's adherents, then it has sold its birthright, forgotten its original intention, and is in dire need of liberation.

Calvin has regularly been read from the perspective of Protestantism in general and Calvinism in particular. While this is understandable, it can easily result in a failure to appreciate important elements in his theology, and thus result in misunderstanding. Writing to his friend Eduard Thurneysen in 1924, in the midst of preparing lectures on Calvin's theology, Barth rhetorically asked: "Is it not possible that that which delights us in the young Luther and in Calvin is *not* the specifically Protestant element but in the best sense the Catholic element in them?"[43] After all, Calvin began his reforming career as a Catholic lay theologian who, with the help of Luther, had rediscovered the evangelical core of the Bible. It is not surprising, then, that some of the best exponents of Calvin's theology are contemporary Roman Catholics imbued with the renewing spirit of Vatican II. Nor should it be surprising to detect a remarkable resonance between elements within Calvin's reforming project and Catholic liberation theology in Latin America in our day. This is one reason why reading Calvin from the perspective of such Catholic theology opens up new possibilities for understanding both him and the Reformed tradition, as well as discerning their liberating and renewing potential.

43. James D. Smart, ed., *Revolutionary Theology in the Making: Barth-Thurneysen Correspondence, 1914-1925* (London: Epworth Press, 1964), p. 168.

Reflecting on the theology of the "young Calvin" from a Roman Catholic perspective, Alexandré Ganoczy, writing at the time of Vatican II, highlighted the positive contribution Calvin made, and still can make, to the ecumenical church.[44] Calvin's positive gift to the ecumenical church, Ganoczy stated, is that his theology

> represented a recollection and a living witness of the transcendence of God, of the absolute sovereignty of the Word, of the unique priesthood of Christ and the place of the Mediator, of the nature of the ministry as service, of its Christ-centred collegiality, and of the role of the laity which is at the heart of the priesthood of the people of God.[45]

These "few major examples," Ganoczy maintained, "introduced and still maintain in Christianity a ferment nourished by the complete Gospel." What Ganoczy here identified corresponds with the major themes, loci, or symbols of Reformation theology which Protestants abbreviate as "grace alone," "Christ alone," and "Scripture alone," and the ecclesial consequences that derive from such affirmations. This, rather than its popular meaning, is what we mean when we use the term "evangelical" to describe Reformation theology. It is surely striking that Ganoczy went on to claim that nothing in principle "prevents the Roman Catholic Church today from recognizing and assimilating this ferment in order to profit from it in its own perpetual, contemporary inner reform."[46] We are here at the nerve center of the liberating and transforming potential not

44. It should be noted that Ganoczy's understanding of Calvin developed considerably during the years of Vatican II, when he came to a greater appreciation for the dialectical and dynamic character of his theology. His dissertation, *Calvin, théologien de l'Eglise*, published in Paris in 1964, predates the Council, whereas *Le jeune Calvin* (Wiesbaden, 1966) was written during and published afterwards. More recent work indicates a growing appreciation for Calvin's hermeneutics.

45. Ganoczy, *The Young Calvin* (Philadelphia: Westminster Press, 1987), p. 311.

46. Ibid.

only of Reformed theology and spirituality but of the Christian gospel.

There is, however, as Ganoczy perceived, also a negative side to Calvin's legacy that we need to take into account and that helps us understand the origins of the ambiguity inherent in the Reformed tradition. Ganoczy reminds us that although Calvin "was initially 'open,' he became the 'Calvin of Geneva,' always 'prophetic' and 'pastoral,' but also more and more intolerant. Thus, Calvinism was born." A "militant Protestantism," Calvinism became known for its "rigorous organization, austere morality, and conquering dynamism in spiritual and temporal affairs."[47] For Ganoczy, then, a clear distinction can be drawn between the positive, evangelical, liberating theology of the "young Calvin" and the negative, dominating Calvinism derived from the "older Calvin." In making this distinction, Ganoczy rightly highlighted what has been widely recognized and rejected by many within the Reformed tradition itself: that "imperial Calvinism" which is reactionary, dominating, and constrictive, a movement "fearful of spontaneity, openness, equalities, and diversities."[48] Here we see the origin of later Calvinism's tendency, especially pronounced in Afrikaner Calvinism, to identify with group self-interest and dominant powers in the belief that this represents the will of God for God's own people. The Reformed tradition's world-formative impulse can, indeed, become "a world-repressive compromise with established orders."[49] As a result, Nicholas Wolterstorff writes, sometimes

> one is . . . confronted with that most insufferable of all human beings, the triumphalist Calvinist, the one who believes that the revolution instituting the holy common-

47. Ibid.
48. Max L. Stackhouse, *Creeds, Society, and Human Rights: A Study in Three Cultures* (Grand Rapids: Eerdmans, 1984), p. 56.
49. Mark Kline Taylor, "Immanental and Prophetic: Shaping Reformed Theology for the Late Twentieth Century Struggle" (unpublished paper, Princeton Theological Seminary, 1983), p. 11.

wealth has already occurred and that his or her task is now simply to keep it in place.[50]

Ganoczy's distinction between the positive and negative elements in Calvin enables us to discern, then, the origin of the fundamental ambiguity in the Reformed tradition, its evangelical and transformative witness on the one hand, and its dominating imperialism on the other. But there is a danger in the distinction if it is made without further reflection and qualification. This is especially so with regard to what we shall call the prophetic dimension, even though Calvin would not have used the word *prophetic* in the way we commonly do so today.[51] By *prophetic* we mean a theology that is socially critical and "world transformative," that is, one that explicitly relates the Word of God to the social and political context within which it is proclaimed.[52] Ganoczy recognizes the validity of this prophetic dimension in Calvin,[53] but his discussion, at least in *The Young Calvin*, concentrates on Calvin's early years as a reformer and does not discuss in any depth his later reforming theology and ministry. The resulting lack of nuance leaves the impression that Calvin's, and later Calvinism's, world-transforming commitment must simply be rejected as unevangelical and negative.

There can be no doubt that much of what Ganoczy labels negative is negative, not least the provincialism, closed-minded intolerance, and severe moralism of imperial Calvinism. No

50. Nicholas Wolterstorff, *Until Justice and Peace Embrace* (Grand Rapids: Eerdmans, 1983), p. 21.

51. But see David Willis-Watkins, "Calvin's Prophetic Reinterpretation of Kingship," in *Probing the Reformed Tradition: Historical Studies in Honour of Edward A. Dowey, Jr.*, ed. Elsie Anne McKee and Brian G. Armstrong (Louisville: Westminster/John Knox Press, 1989), pp. 116-17.

52. Perhaps the closest to our use of the word *prophetic* among the Reformers was its use by Zwingli, for whom the prophetic proclamation of the Word of God to society was central to his understanding of the ordained ministry. See W. P. Stephens, *The Theology of Huldrych Zwingli* (Oxford: Clarendon Press, 1986), p. 8.

53. Ganoczy, *The Young Calvin*, p. 238.

apologia for such is warranted or possible, even though much of the popular, negative image of Calvin is without foundation. Yet it has been rightly said that what was negative about Calvin "was simply the other side of what was essentially positive."[54] Calvin's "imperialism," or the "militant Protestantism" to which he gave birth, with all its negative connotations and reprehensible consequences, nevertheless embodied something essentially biblical. Whatever sociopsychological reasons may be found for his imperialism, theologically it derived from his vision of the kingdom of God and the concomitant calling and responsibility of the church to proclaim God's rule within and over the world.

The prophetic, socially active, world-formative impulse derived from a vision of the kingdom of God is almost, if not equally, as characteristic of Calvin and the Reformed tradition as is the evangelical impulse, though both need each other. In Wolterstorff's words:

> Restless disciplined reformism, or guilt for not being restlessly reformist: these are the characteristic components of the Calvinist social piety. When these are missing, one can reliably surmise that one is confronted with a person who has some other understanding of his or her social role than that characteristic of early Calvinism.[55]

It is inevitably a risky business taking prophetic responsibility seriously because it entails consciously taking sides, eschewing neutrality, and making value judgments. Calvin perceived, in continuity with Augustine in the fifth century, that just as human sin creates conflict within the world, tearing its social fabric apart, so the gospel, in seeking its remedy, creates a ferment for transformation not only within the church but also within society. Prophetic responsibility is thus not avoiding conflict but participating in it in a way consonant with God's

---

54. Ronald S. Wallace, *Calvin, Geneva, and the Reformation* (Edinburgh: Scottish Academic Press, 1988), p. 299.
55. Wolterstorff, *Until Justice and Peace Embrace*, p. 21.

kingdom. All of this means, as the Hebrew prophets knew so well and as Dietrich Bonhoeffer articulated in the context of the Third Reich, speaking the word of God here and now, concretely and with authority. In doing so it is always possible to fall off the knife-edge of genuine prophecy and become the equivalent of an insufferable, imperial Calvinist in whom the grace of God which produces the evangelical virtues of love, forgiveness, and humility are absent.

Despite the risky possibility, however, that reshaping the world according to the justice of God may degenerate into self-righteous triumphalism, the truly Reformed cannot avoid their social, prophetic responsibility without denying both their biblical commitment and their tradition. But they have to ensure that their prophetic ministry is grounded in the gospel and resolutely struggle to prevent their theology from becoming a closed, sectarian ideology masking reality in the interests of a particular social program.

Theology is, of course, inescapably ideological in the sense that it is a human enterprise through which we relate Christian faith to social reality. The critical question is whether the ideological expression of faith, be it Reformed or not, serves the interests of the gospel or the self-interests of a particular group, race, gender, or class in ways contrary to the gospel. We turn, then, to consider the way in which Afrikaner Calvinism evolved in order to discern how one subset within the Reformed tradition became a closed ideology giving legitimacy to apartheid and racist oppression.

The Evolution of Afrikaner Calvinism

Until the Cape became a British colony the Dutch Reformed Church—or, to use its official Afrikaans title, the Nederduitse Gereformeerde Kerk—was the only church in the emergent country. The advent of British colonial rule at the turn of the nineteenth century meant that other denominations gained a foothold, both as churches of the English-speaking settler community and as missions to the indigenous peoples.[56] Among these were two denominations with strong Calvinist roots and affinities, the Presbyterians and the Congregationalists, and their respective missionary societies, notably the Church of Scotland Mission and the London Missionary Society. In fact, the first Calvinist Society was formed in Cape Town in 1800 under the leadership of James Read, a Congregationalist working for the London Missionary Society.[57] Other Reformed missionary societies, such as the Swiss Mission, the Paris Evangelical Mission, and the American Board Mission, soon joined them, though as a result of comity agreements they worked among different tribes. The Calvinism of these other churches and missionary societies, undoubtedly different in many respects from that of the Dutch Reformed Church, not only came out of different ecclesiastical and cultural contexts, but was also shaped by different historical forces—those let loose by the Enlightenment, the French Revolution, and the Napoleonic wars.[58]

At the same time, the Calvinism of the Dutch Reformed Church at the Cape was not static, for it too felt something of the impact of the Enlightenment, and there were many Afrikaners inspired with the spirit of Republican France. However, the Dutch Reformed Church, which was constitutionally separated from the control of the state church in the Netherlands in 1827, reacted negatively to those ministers imbued with liberal theological notions. As a result, it became firmly committed to the Calvinist theology of the sixteenth- and seventeenth-century Reformed confessions: the Belgic Confession (1561), the Heidelberg Catechism (1563), and the

56. See John W. de Gruchy, *The Church Struggle in South Africa*, rev. ed. (Grand Rapids: Eerdmans, 1986), chaps. 1 and 2.
57. See D. Roy Briggs and Joseph Wing, *The Harvest and the Hope: The Story of Congregationalism in Southern Africa* (Johannesburg: United Congregational Church of Southern Africa, 1970), p. 29.
58. For an overview of Calvinism in South Africa see Gideon Thom, "Calvinism in South Africa," in *John Calvin: His Influence in the Western World*, ed. W. Stanford Reid (Grand Rapids: Zondervan, 1982).

ultra-Calvinist Canons of Dort (1619). Of crucial importance in countering the liberal eroding of the faith, but from a somewhat different perspective, was the influence of Scottish evangelicalism and Dutch pietism. The former was injected into the Dutch Reformed Church with the arrival of many Scottish Presbyterian ministers who came to serve the Cape church, which in the early nineteenth century found it increasingly difficult to get pastors from Holland.

A series of revivals in the mid-nineteenth century, largely under the leadership of the famous holiness preacher and Dutch Reformed leader Andrew Murray, Jr. (of Scottish descent but influenced by Dutch pietism while a student in Holland), paralleled similar revivals in Calvinist New England and ensured that evangelical piety had a decisive impact upon the church. While some orthodox Calvinists questioned Murray's adherence to the Canons of Dort, a charge he denied,[59] there is no doubt that Murray's Reformed evangelical pietism has dominated the spirituality of the Dutch Reformed Church in South Africa ever since. As a result, two distinct traditions, two spiritual worlds, continue to coexist in the Dutch Reformed Church: the Reformed—or more precisely, *die Gereformeerde*—and what W. D. Jonker refers to as the "evangelical-methodist" counterbalance each other, often to the detriment of the former.[60]

Evangelicalism sought to be politically neutral. For the most pietistic, all that counted was personal salvation and the spiritual well-being of the church. For the bulk of evangelicals, piety also led to a commitment to missionary work, education, and social philanthropy.[61] Yet it was under the dominance of such evangelicalism, rather than the strict Calvinism of Dort, that the Dutch Reformed Church agreed at its Synod of 1857

59. See J. A. du Plessis, *Life of Andrew Murray* (London: Marshall Bros., 1919), pp. 248-49.
60. W. D. Jonker, "Die Eie-Aard van die Gereformeerde Spiritualiteit," *Nederduitse Geref. Teologiese Tydskrif* 30 (July 1989): 291.
61. See J. J. F. Durand, "Afrikaner Piety and Dissent," in *Resistance and Hope: South African Essays in Honour of Beyers Naudé*, ed. Charles Villa-Vicencio and John W. de Gruchy (Grand Rapids: Eerdmans, 1985), pp. 42-43.

that congregations could be divided along racial lines. Thus began the process of developing separate mission churches, the first of which, the NG Sendingkerk (Dutch Reformed Mission Church) for "coloureds" or people of mixed race, was constituted in 1881.

Despite the fact that this development went against earlier synodical decisions that segregation in the church was contrary to the Word of God, it was rationalized on grounds of missiology and practical necessity. Missiologically it was argued that people were best evangelized and best worshipped God in their own language and cultural setting, a position reinforced by German Lutheran missiology and somewhat akin to the church-growth philosophy of our own time. Practically, it was done in response to the interests of the white community and was nothing less than a capitulation to colonial interests and pressure. Thus the foundation was laid for apartheid in the church and its subsequent theological justification. It was precisely this legitimation that was later rejected by the Dutch Reformed Mission Church and others as a heresy.[62]

Although the evangelical pietistic tradition within the Dutch Reformed Church was not consciously committed to a political program, it was from within its ranks that the idea of a *volkskerk* emerged during the Anglo-Boer War (1899-1902). This was not an attempt to reestablish the Dutch Reformed Church as a state church, but an effort to relate it more directly to the needs of the Afrikaner people who had suffered so severely during the war, and who were reduced to poverty thereafter. However, this concern for the social needs of the people stopped with the poor white Afrikaner. There is no evidence of any concern for the blacks who were far worse off than the whites and even more devastated by the effects of the war, political developments, and the later years of economic depression.[63] There is nothing wrong with the idea of a church

62. See the essays by Allan Boesak, Chris Loff, and David Bosch in de Gruchy and Villa-Vicencio, *Apartheid Is a Heresy*.
63. Durand, "Afrikaner Piety and Dissent," p. 44.

for the people, but a major problem arises when "the people" is confined to a particular race, class, or *volk*, especially when this is done at the expense of others, for then the church denies not only its universal or catholic identity, but also the gospel.

The presence of other Calvinist churches and missions notwithstanding, the Dutch Reformed Church (Nederduitse Gereformeerde Kerk) remained the dominant church in the land and thus the major bearer of the Reformed tradition. During the nineteenth century, however, the church split twice, thus making the character of the Reformed tradition in South Africa even more complex, and, looked at overall, very similar to the development of the tradition in North America.[64]

The first division, which led to the establishment of the Nederduitsch Hervormde Kerk in 1853, was a product of the Great Trek, an event not officially supported by the Dutch Reformed Church in the Cape. As a result, the Nederduitsch Hervormde Kerk became the established church of the Transvaal Republic, whose constitution discouraged churches which did not adhere to the Heidelberg Catechism. Not only were blacks excluded from political representation in the Republic, but there was also a concerted effort to prevent non-Calvinists from participating as well. The second division, which had its roots in Holland, led to the formation of the Gereformeerde Kerk (popularly referred to as the "Dopper" church), a church committed to the restoration of the strictly orthodox Calvinism of the Synod of Dort and therefore opposed to Calvinism's dilution through evangelical pietism. Of particular importance in the development of the Gereformeerde Kerk's theological identity was the influence of the Dutch statesman-theologian Abraham Kuyper.

Kuyper's understanding of Calvinism as an all-embracing "life-system" and especially his teaching that God exercised his sovereignty through autonomous spheres (culture, education, church, politics) were particularly influential towards the

64. See George M. Marsden, "Reformed and American," in *Reformed Theology in America: A History of Its Modern Development*, ed. David F. Wells (Grand Rapids: Eerdmans, 1985), pp. 1-2.

end of the nineteenth century and the decades following the Anglo-Boer War at the beginning of the twentieth. Indeed, Kuyper's neo-Calvinism soon spilled over into other Afrikaner circles beyond the boundaries of the "Dopper" church,[65] not least through the work of the Rev. S. J. du Toit, an ardent Afrikaner patriot and a founder of the Afrikaner Bond.[66]

Alongside this development, and in concert with it, was the reinterpretation of Afrikaner history as "sacred history." President Paul Kruger of the Transvaal Republic, a founding member of the "Dopper" church, had made powerful rhetorical use of this theme and its symbols in his speeches in the years leading up to the Anglo-Boer War.[67] Later, especially during the 1920s and 1930s, the notion of Afrikaner history as "sacred history" became the only hermeneutic filter through which Afrikaner history was to be read and interpreted by all true Afrikaners. It was during this period that the architects and ideologists of Afrikaner nationalism made capital out of the mythology of Afrikanerdom as the Chosen People. The Great Trek was the Exodus from the bondage of British rule at the Cape which led, in turn, to the years of struggling in the Wilderness against all odds, en route to the Promised Land of the Boer Republics.[68]

These biblical notions cannot simply be equated with Calvinism, as though no other tradition in Christianity had ever made similar use of them, or as though the mythmakers were all devout Calvinists and not also, and often more so, ideologists imbued with the spirit of racial superiority and romantic nationalism at that time engulfing much of Europe. The myths and symbols drawn from the Old Testament became "Calvinized" largely because the vast majority of Afrikaners belonged to one of the three Reformed churches, and because

65. See especially Hexham, *The Irony of Apartheid*.
66. See du Toit, "Puritans in Africa?" pp. 228-29.
67. Moodie, *The Rise of Afrikanerdom*, pp. 22-23.
68. F. A. van Jaarsveld, *The Afrikaner's Interpretation of South African History* (Cape Town: Simondium Publishers, 1964); Moodie, *The Rise of Afrikanerdom*, chaps. 1-2.

of the role which Dutch Reformed Church ministers played in fostering the spirit of Afrikaner nationalism.

The neo-Calvinist editors (all Dutch Reformed, Hervormde, or Gereformeerd ministers, theologians, or philosophers) of the several volumed programmatic *Koers in die Krisis,* published in the 1930s as Afrikaner nationalism was reaching new heights of fervor in anticipation of gaining power, not only used this mythology but made it clear that they were reinterpreting Calvinism for a new and different context—that of South Africa with its distinct cultural, racial, and political problems.[69] In doing so they drew heavily on Kuyper and at significant points adapted and distorted his ideas in the interests of Afrikanerdom. Of crucial significance in this respect was the elevating of the Afrikaner *volk* to a "separate sphere." Kuyper's theology shunned any idea of a *volkskerk,* but his notion of the "sovereignty of spheres" was adapted to give the Afrikaner nation an independent status under God with a special calling.[70] By the same inference, other ethnic groups were seen as separate nations created by God even though they all coexisted within the same geographical boundary. Kuyper's ideas were also harnessed in the development of what was referred to as "Christian National" education, which, contrary to its origins in Holland, became a crucial aspect of apartheid policy.[71] In effect, neo-Calvinism was co-opted to legitimate the separate development of racial groups as "nations." The blending of Afrikaner "sacred history" with the Afrikaner *volk* as a "chosen people" and neo-Calvinism with its "sovereignty of spheres" thus provided a powerful ideological base for Afrikaner nationalism and apartheid. Given the fact that Afrikanerdom was virtually coterminous with the Dutch Reformed Church and its sister churches, and that its ideologists were often highly in-

69. H. G. Stoker and F. J. M. Potgieter, eds., *Koers in die Krisis,* vol. 1 (Stellenbosch: Pro Ecclesia, 1935).

70. Moodie, *The Rise of Afrikanerdom,* pp. 65-66.

71. For a discussion of the issues see Irving Hexham, "Religious Conviction or Political Tool? The Problem of Christian National Education," *Journal of Theology for Southern Africa* 26 (March 1979).

fluential dominees, it was almost inevitable that the Dutch Reformed Church gave Afrikaner nationalism and its policies its blessing.

The attempt to give theological legitimation to the emerging racial policies of the National Party thus predated the advent of apartheid as government policy in 1948. But from then onwards, in document after document, the Dutch Reformed Church attempted to justify apartheid on biblical and theological grounds within the framework of neo-Calvinism as adapted by Afrikaner ideologists.[72] The Nederduitsch Hervormde followed suit; the Gereformeerde Kerk did likewise, though with more reservation than the former two. In fact, this process continued within the Dutch Reformed Church right up until 1987 when the General Synod acknowledged that there were no biblical or theological grounds for apartheid. In the case of the Nederduitsch Hervormde Kerk, blacks were still excluded from membership by the church's general assembly in 1989, even though, as the church hastened to add, this did not mean that they were excluded from worship!

The synodical decision of the Dutch Reformed Church in 1987 meant the end of official Dutch Reformed attempts to give apartheid biblical and theological sanction.[73] But it also meant a withdrawal from taking political sides on issues that were increasingly dividing Afrikanerdom and which had split the National Party, first in the 1970s, then more significantly in 1983 when the Conservative Party was launched in an attempt to maintain pristine apartheid. This new spirit of pragmatism in the Dutch Reformed Church, so unlike the principled position

72. See de Gruchy, *The Church Struggle in South Africa*, pp. 53ff.; Johann Kinghorn, ed., *Die NG Kerk en Apartheid*.

73. For a discussion of recent developments within the Nederduitse Gereformeerde Kerk, see Douglas Bax, "The Vereeniging Consultation: A Perspective on What Happened," *Journal of Theology for Southern Africa* 68 (Sept. 1989), and Johann Kinghorn, "On the Theology of Church and Society in the DRC," *Journal of Theology for Southern Africa* 70 (March 1990): 21-22. At its General Synod in October 1990, the Dutch Reformed Church declared apartheid to be sinful.

it had previously taken on political issues, reflected a church increasingly divided by Afrikaner politics in a period of uncertainty and transition.

In light of all this we may now define Afrikaner Calvinism more precisely. It is the product of an uneasy amalgam of nineteenth-century evangelical piety and an adapted Kuyperian neo-Calvinism forged in the fires of the Afrikaner struggle for cultural identity and political and economic power. In the process it drew its symbols and inspiration from the Old Testament struggles of the people of God, but it appropriated them in the interests of the *volk* and thus gave them a character and significance different from their original intention. Indeed, it is significant that throughout the process of attempting to legitimate apartheid and Afrikaner nationalism, the Dutch Reformed Church made no appeal to Calvin or the historic Reformed confessions of faith. In a devastating critique, Douglas Bax has shown how the arguments used were not only based on bad exegesis of Scripture, but were contrary to the teaching of Calvin as well.[74] There was, in fact, little self-critique in the light of Scripture, and, in the righteous republican euphoria of achieving power and restructuring society, an almost total lack of critical consciousness of the oppression which Afrikaner Calvinism was legitimating in the name of Christian faith.

A Cry for Life

Calvinism's influence in South Africa may be overrated, as has been suggested by friend and foe,[75] just as we may exaggerate the Reformed tradition's potential for enabling social transformation today. But we can hardly underestimate the effect of its failure to curb racism, and, in the form of Afrikaner Calvinism, the effect of its sanctioning of apartheid. Moreover,

74. Douglas Bax, "The Bible and Apartheid 2," in de Gruchy and Villa-Vicencio, *Apartheid Is a Heresy*, pp. 112ff.
75. Thom, "Calvinism in South Africa," p. 362.

the damage done to human life by apartheid and its "Christian" legitimation has also hurt the cause of the Christian gospel and more especially the Reformed tradition. Given this history, it is not surprising that a black Dutch Reformed theologian, Lekula Ntoane, could express his gut feelings towards Afrikaner Calvinism by saying:

> Wallowing in it, as Black christians in the South African existential reality already do, they are soul defiled, physically raped and dehumanized.[76]

So, Ntoane asks, "Is 'Calvinism' truly and genuinely representative of the Calvinian tradition? Are the views espoused in it a reflection of the teachings and intentions of its initiator? Are the views expressed in both 'Calvinism' and Calvinian tradition reconcilable with the message of Jesus Christ? Is it worthwhile for black Christians who have adopted and embraced this tradition to remain loyal to it?"[77] These questions are not just academic ones; for Ntoane and many others they are, as he describes his quest, "a cry for life."

In describing his reaction to Afrikaner Calvinism as a "cry for life," Ntoane went to the heart of what liberation is truly about. Liberation refers to the redemption of men and women, as well as societies and nations, from those tyrannies and powers that enslave them and prevent them from knowing the fullness of life God intends for all humanity. Liberation is about the bestowal and renewal of life in all its dimensions. In Gustavo Gutiérrez's words, "the process of liberation is a global one" that "affects every dimension of the human."[78] Liberation properly understood thus includes and integrates the redemption and renewal of the whole of life, whether personal, psychological, and spiritual, or social, political, and environmental.

---

76. L. R. Lekula Ntoane, *A Cry for Life: An Interpretation of "Calvinism" and Calvin* (Kampen: J. H. Kok, 1983), p. 124.

77. Ibid.

78. Gustavo Gutiérrez, *We Drink from Our Own Wells* (New York: Orbis, 1985), pp. 29-30.

Nothing could be more fundamental to the biblical message of the kingdom of God. For this reason, if for no other, Reformed theology cannot avoid the challenge presented to it both by the various forms of liberation theology that have emerged in our time and especially by the challenge of the cry for justice and life that has produced them.

In reflecting on the role of Afrikaner Calvinism in legitimating apartheid, it is too easy to argue that this was simply a distorted version of the Reformed tradition. Of course it was. But that only begs the further question: Why did the tradition allow itself to be misused in this way? Indeed, why did it not prevent slavery, combat racism, and oppose colonial racial policy and the selfish material interests that eventually led to apartheid in the first place? Its failure was not simply that of commission—what it did do to legitimate power and oppression; its failure was even more a sin of omission—what it failed to do. The Reformed tradition in South Africa is thus guilty of a twofold sin: it failed to prevent apartheid and it succeeded in sanctifying it. It aligned itself with an ideology of group interest. It failed to set an agenda for society consonant with biblical norms, to align itself with the interests of the disadvantaged, and therefore to hear their "cry for life." This does not gainsay the witness of other Reformed denominations in South Africa, or the often courageous witness of members of the Dutch Reformed Church itself, or even the latter's extensive philanthropy, which has been far more than any other Christian denomination. But the "cry for life" is a cry for justice and equity, for the dignity that comes from equality as children of God, and not from dependency on the care of others.

It has often been remarked that Afrikaners, as a result of their long struggle against British imperialism, should have been well placed to understand the aspirations and struggles of black South Africans. But somehow there has been a blind spot in Afrikaner Calvinist group consciousness that is only now beginning to change as the twentieth century draws to a close. If and when Afrikaner Calvinists do begin to see reality from the perspective of those who cry out for life, then the change is often dramatic, far-reaching, and radical. But for the majority, along with many other whites in South Africa, the "cry for life" which should awaken self-critical awareness and existential change has yet to be heard, let alone accepted, in a way that leads to personal and social transformation.

For several reasons this "cry for life" was and still is not heard within Afrikaner Calvinism. We may refer first to that tendency in Calvinism, appropriated by Afrikaner Calvinism, to become imperialistic and dominant on the grounds that "we know what is best for others because we know the will of God." While Kuyper himself avoided such self-righteousness, neo-Calvinism, with its understanding of Calvinism as a total way of life based on a specific worldview, combined with a sense of national calling, sacred destiny, and racial superiority, led to the rationalization of apartheid as God-willed, and to the implementation of the policy of "separate development" as the only solution to the problems of the country. Tragically, it can now be seen how much the *bantustan* or "homelands policy" has not only failed, but has exacerbated the problems facing South Africa and made their resolution far more difficult than they might have been.

Second, Afrikaner Calvinism failed to hear the "cry for life" because it went contrary to the material and cultural interests of Afrikanerdom. It was not heard because no one wanted to hear it. A central part of the problem has been that Afrikaner Calvinism as a historical movement of social change has been wedded, as its name implies, to the interests of a particular social group, race, and culture, and increasingly to a comfortably middle-class constituency. In this respect it has reflected what has happened to Calvinism more generally in previous centuries and other contexts.

Although the Reformed tradition has always included people within its ranks who were poor and socially disadvantaged, its ethos has usually reflected the values of the middle class rather than the kingdom of God, when the two were at odds. Hence it is not surprising that workers and aristocrats alike reacted strongly and negatively to its bourgeois system of

32

values in post-revolutionary England in the seventeenth century. Similarly, Henry Heller describes the Huguenot movement in sixteenth-century France as a "protest against poverty,"
but it was a protest of a developing Calvinist middle class.
While both artisans and aristocrats were part of the Huguenot
movement, what brought them together was not only religious
conviction but "the threat of impoverishment and declining
social mobility experienced in the first place by artisans and
later by the well-established, viz., wholesale merchants and
notables."[79] Afrikaner Calvinism has served a similar ideological function. It welded together the "poor white" working class
in the years of the Depression, and the better-educated
Afrikaner elite, in the struggle for economic and political
power. But it did so primarily for the sake of Afrikanerdom
and thus at the expense of the black population.

A final reason why Afrikaner Calvinism failed to hear the
"cry for life" stems from the refusal to be truly Reformed and
apply the radical critique of the biblical message to Afrikaner
and white power and privilege and their religious justification.
This again has precedent in the history of the Reformed tradition. In the struggle for liberty, democracy, and human rights
Calvinism has proved a powerful, liberating credo in legitimating the cause and providing the symbols of empowerment. But
this has invariably served the interests of persecuted, exiled, or
oppressed middle-class Calvinists themselves, rather than
other oppressed groups or the poor. Reformed theologians of
the seventeenth and eighteenth centuries, whether in Europe,
New England, or South Africa, gave their energies largely to
matters of doctrinal and ecclesiastical controversy and purity.
A critical awareness of the social role of the tradition or of their
own endeavors was beyond their frame of reference. Indeed,
Reformed theology from the seventeenth to the twentieth century, within South Africa as elsewhere, seldom had the interest,
let alone the critical tools, with which to examine such ambiguities. Hence the need is crucial for a self-critical and prophet-

79. Heller, *The Conquest of Poverty*, p. 258.

ically critical Reformed theology which can keep the tradition always on the side of the powerless, even when its own advocates have achieved power.

The problem in South Africa has not been Calvinism but rather, with some notable exceptions, the absence of a truly Reformed theology, one in which prophetic critique and evangelical transformation combine to serve the liberation of those crying out for life. Precisely for this reason, Reformed theology in South Africa as elsewhere needs to face the challenge of liberation theology in its various forms. For only in taking this challenge seriously will the Reformed tradition serve the interests of the kingdom of God and therefore the interests of all people: the poor and oppressed as well as its traditional middle-class, white constituency.

A Self-Critical Consciousness of Oppression

Although there remains considerable resistance to, misunderstanding of, and apathy towards liberation theology in its various forms, many of its insights are now almost taken for granted in other forms of theological discourse. Recent Vatican documents, for example, while critical of some aspects of liberation theology, affirm many of its central tenets.[80] Likewise, many Reformed theologians and communities have accepted the validity of its critique and have embodied key elements. This is true not only of the members of the World Alliance of Reformed Churches, but even within some theologically conservative circles.[81] This does not mean that its challenge has

80. See, for example, the Instruction on Christian Freedom and Liberation, *Libertatis Conscienta,* the second Vatican Instruction on liberation theology; and John Paul II's letter to the Brazilian Episcopal Conference, *L'Osseratore Romano,* 28 April 1986; see also Paul E. Sigmund, *Liberation Theology at the Crossroads* (New York: Crossroads, 1990), chap. 9.

81. See the essays of Stephen C. Knapp and Harvie M. Conn in *Evangelicals and Liberation,* ed. Carl E. Armeding (Presbyterian and Reformed Publishing Co., 1977); J. Andrew Kirk, *Liberation Theology: An Evangelical View from the Third World* (Atlanta: John Knox, 1979).

been uncritically received or fully met, nor does it deny that in some instances it has been rejected out of hand or simply domesticated.[82]

Whatever the reception or reaction, our contention is that liberation theologies present a challenge to the Reformed as well as other traditions that has to be taken seriously for the sake of the gospel in the modern world. Liberation theologies are, in Cornel West's words, "the predominant forms of critical consciousness within the Christian church that respond to the dangers of class, racial, and sexual privilege, and project the possibility of class, racial, and sexual equality."[83] Hence the varieties of liberation theology, such as black and feminist theologies, as well as varieties of Latin American liberation theology. Hence, too, the increasing difficulty of speaking about liberation theology in generalized terms.

Whatever their similarities, each type of liberation theology presents a challenge to the Reformed tradition that is distinct and specific. Within the South African context the two most significant types of liberation theology are black and prophetic theologies, the latter being expressed most powerfully in *The Kairos Document*.[84] Their specific contextual challenge lies behind much of our discussion. But we have also specifically chosen to concentrate on the challenge of certain Catholic Latin American liberation theologians because of the similarity we have already suggested between their project today and Calvin's project in his day. Each liberation theology is, however, a response to a particular form of human and social oppression glaringly apparent in the so-called Third World but by no means confined to it, and each must be taken seriously. The

82. See Arthur F. McGovern, *Liberation Theology and Its Critics* (New York: Orbis, 1989), p. 18. For an overview of North American critiques, see Sigmund, *Liberation Theology at the Crossroads*, p. 134. Sigmund's own treatment is sharply critical but fair.

83. Cornel West, *Prophetic Fragments* (Grand Rapids: Eerdmans, 1988), p. 197.

84. *The Kairos Document: A Challenge to the Church*, 2d ed. (Grand Rapids: Eerdmans, 1986).

challenge we face is not only to become critically conscious of oppression in all its forms, but to become self-critically conscious of the role the Christian church has played and should play in that regard. If we are at all sensitive to human suffering and need, to say nothing of the ethical imperatives of the gospel, those of us who are within the Reformed tradition cannot avoid this challenge. We may disagree with the way in which a particular form of liberation theology addresses certain issues. But it is unfaithfulness to the gospel, socially irresponsible, and escapist to think that because a liberation theology may be faulty in its analysis or prognosis the issues themselves do not exist, or that Reformed theology is exempt from dealing with them, and doing so better itself.

At the same time as there are varieties of liberation theology, and therefore different challenges facing Reformed theology, there is sufficient consensus within the genre for us to speak about the challenge of liberation theology per se, and to recognize that the challenge is quite fundamental. In this respect it differs qualitatively from the challenge presented to the Reformed tradition by other historic confessional theologies, such as Roman Catholic and Lutheran. Liberation theology is equally challenging to all the historic traditions because it radically questions the social location, material interests, and consequences of those traditions and their theologies, and not simply their intentions. In this respect, the Reformed tradition stands together with the other historic traditions under the searchlight of liberation theology's critique.

Reflecting on the emergence of one form of liberation theology, namely black theology, Helmut Gollwitzer makes this trenchant observation:

> Whether Rome, Wittenberg, or Geneva prevailed, whether justification before God occurred through works or through faith, whether *est* or *significat* was correct, whether the Canons of Dort or the declarations of the Remonstrants became accepted church doctrine, whether Cromwell or Charles I won—for the red, the yellow, and

the black all this was irrelevant. It did not change their condition.[85]

Few indictments could be more damning. Black theology emerged because of the irrelevance of dominant Western theology, including Reformed theology, in meeting the social, material, and spiritual needs of black people. Hence, when Gayraud Wilmore describes what it means to be "Black and Presbyterian," he finds it necessary to rework radically his Reformed heritage in relation to black religious, historical, and social experience.[86]

The social relocation of theology does not imply in the first instance a new theology, but a new way of doing theology, which may, in turn, lead to a new theology. The importance of what could be labelled a revolution in methodology is at once evident in the opening pages of Juan Luis Segundo's seminal work, *The Liberation of Theology*, where he makes the distinction between a theology of liberation and theologies that deal with liberation.[87] What distinguishes liberation theologies from others is not the introduction of new dogmatic themes, but the way in which dogmatic and ethical tradition is reinterpreted within the struggle for liberation. Theology then becomes a socially committed discipline on the side of those who are disadvantaged and socially oppressed.

Many traditional theologies deal with justice and liberation as ethical themes arising from theological reflection. They are items on their social witness agenda. But they do not regard engagement in the struggle for justice and liberation as fundamental to their dogmatic concern or way of doing theology. For most it is a consequence rather than a prior commitment.

85. Helmut Gollwitzer, "Why Black Theology," in Gayraud S. Wilmore and James H. Cone, *Black Theology: A Documentary History, 1966-1979* (New York: Orbis, 1979), p. 155.

86. Gayraud S. Wilmore, *Black and Presbyterian* (Philadelphia: Geneva Press, 1983).

87. Juan Luis Segundo, *The Liberation of Theology* (New York: Orbis, 1976), p. 8.

The fundamental reason for this is that traditional theology, and much Reformed theology along with it, remains wedded to a Constantinian worldview which, from the fourth century onwards, aligned the church with the dominant culture. This inevitably meant that the church was primarily concerned about the spiritual welfare of people while sanctioning the authority of the state in its exercise of temporal power.

One historical tradition is less threatened by liberation theology than others, at least when it is true to its origins. The early Anabaptists broke decisively with the Constantinian assumptions about church and state shared by their Catholic and Protestant contemporaries alike. In this respect the Anabaptists anticipated liberation theology's radical break with the dominant political powers and their alliance with the church. Just as the Anabaptists rejected the Constantinian captivity of the dominant church, so Latin American liberation theology rejects as its point of departure the captivity of the church to the powerful regimes of Latin America, which has its roots in Hispanic colonialization. In the same way, the point of departure for the authors of *The Kairos Document* in South Africa is a decisive break with the colonial and neo-colonial captivity of the churches in southern Africa and with the "state" or "church theology" underpinning it.

Some important distinctions must be made, however, for the Anabaptists and liberation theologians do not make precisely the same moves.[88] For traditional Anabaptists the break with Constantinianism is complete. For liberation theologians the break is complete insofar as Christendom is the realm dominated by the powerful, the oppressor, and the privileged. But they allow, in varying ways, for what Gustavo Gutiérrez has called "Constantinianism of the Left," which means eschewing ideological neutrality and taking a clear stand with the oppressed. The church, Gutiérrez argues, does not need to divest

88. See Laverne A. Rutschman, "Latin American Liberation Theology and Radical Anabaptism," *Journal for Ecumenical Studies* 19 (Winter 1982): 53.

itself of every vestige of political power. The best way to achieve the divestment of power is "precisely by resolutely casting our lot with the oppressed and exploited in the struggle for a more just society." The question is not, then, whether the church is going to use political influence (Anabaptists also exert political influence), but how, and on behalf of whom, and from what perspective it is going to do so. Is it going to be used "to preserve the social prestige which comes from its ties to the groups in power or to free itself from the prestige with a break from these groups and with genuine service to the oppressed?"[89]

Reclaiming the Tradition

While a tradition can wither and die—or worse, become an albatross around our necks—it can also be retrieved as a source of empowerment in the present, providing the symbols not only for its own revitalization and renewal, but for society at large. Gregory Baum perceptively reminds us that

> what counts in any reform movement—or any revolu-
> tion, for that matter—is to reinterpret the significant sym-
> bols that people have inherited and thus regain them and
> reclaim them as sources for a new social imagination and
> guides for a new kind of social involvement.[90]

The creative and liberating possibilities latent within the central symbols or loci of Reformed theology are of vital importance not just for the Reformed tradition but for the church as a whole. The problem is setting them free so that they can become once again the transforming, fermenting symbols they origi-nally were rather than captives to myths of racial superiority and oppressive power.

Symbols that have been misappropriated or lost their

---

89. Gutiérrez, *A Theology of Liberation*, rev. ed. (New York: Orbis, 1988), pp. 151-52.

90. Gregory Baum, *Religion and Alienation: A Theological Reading of Sociology* (New York: Paulist Press, 1975), p. 223.

potency in the course of history will only regain their trans-forming power as they are critically examined, redeemed from their ideological captivities, and employed by Christian com-munities engaged in obedient service in the world. This re-quires a critical theology able to retrieve, clarify, and give fresh substance to the symbols in the midst of the struggle for justice and transformation. Lekula Ntoane comments that black Re-formed Christians engaged "actively in the liberation struggle" have a twofold task in their struggle. "Firstly, they have to be very critical about 'Calvinism'. This means subjecting it to con-stant scrutiny. Secondly, they have to engage in an activity, which enables them to identify those aspects of Calvin's the-ology which can contribute to the Black liberation struggle."[91] Or, we might add, to whatever struggle serves the cause of human and social transformation consonant with the gospel and God's kingdom of justice.

Ganoczy's pregnant description of the essence of Calvin's theology as "a ferment nourished by the complete gospel" suggests how the Reformed tradition can be true to itself, but also how it can make both a critical and a constructive con-tribution to contemporary society. For whatever the Reformed tradition's failings in practice, its intended primary commit-ment is to the "whole gospel." This means, as Ganoczy rightly perceives, a commitment to the evangelical doctrines as af-firmed in early catholic tradition and retrieved by the Refor-mation, but also a commitment to the biblical prophetic witness to God's purposes of justice and equity within society. While this latter commitment might sometimes necessarily and justi-fiably erupt in a revolutionary passion for truth and righ-teousness, it seeks to be guided by the evangelical norms of love, forgiveness, and grace. This brings us back to our earlier discussion of Calvin's own contribution to Reformed theology.

The real challenge facing the Reformed tradition has al-ways been how to hold its evangelical center and its world-for-mative dynamism in creative tension in the service of truth and

91. Ntoane, *A Cry for Life*, p. 252.

justice. Only by so doing does it remain politically prophetic and socially responsible in the service of justice without degenerating into religious, moral, or political fanaticism—whether imperial or apocalyptic—or, at the other extreme, into world-denying pseudo-piety. Of crucial importance in this process is an acute sense of human sin and fallibility which should, but does not always, inject into true Reformed theologians a healthy scepticism and suspicion with regard to their own position in the first instance, but also with regard to the structures of power. Hence the need is urgent for a Reformed theology that is critical in the sense that it not only prophetically addresses the power structures of the world, but with equal commitment uncovers those elements of alienation and false consciousness at work within the tradition itself. This can only be done as Reformed theology engages in the struggle for justice on the side of society's victims.

Given the history both of the Reformed tradition and of Calvinism in South Africa in particular, it comes as no surprise that we have more recently witnessed the emergence of a militant, prophetic Reformed theology identified with the black struggle for liberation and justice. Allan Boesak gave expression to this in his response to the Minister of Justice in 1979, after the Minister had attacked him for a speech advocating civil disobedience. Boesak declared: "I am of the opinion that I have done nothing more than place myself fairly and squarely within the Reformed tradition."[92] Likewise, the founding charter of the Alliance of Black Reformed Christians in South Africa (an alliance that includes Dutch Reformed, Presbyterian, and Congregational theologians and church members) made no apologies for being within the tradition; on the contrary, this alliance claimed to represent the truth of the tradition:

> In the light of our rejection of the false interpretation of the Reformed tradition, and in relation to our situation as

92. Allan Boesak, "The Black Church and the Struggle in South Africa," *The Ecumenical Review* 32 (January 1980): 23.

blacks, we commit ourselves to come to a truer understanding of the Reformed tradition and accept the challenge to articulate our faith in terms which are authentic
and relevant.[93]

Yet the revitalization of the Reformed tradition in South
Africa today—if in fact it really achieves its promise—is part
of a much longer historical process. For alongside the imperial
Calvinism of the dominant white Afrikaner culture another
more prophetic and evangelical Calvinism has existed in South
Africa since the beginning of the nineteenth century. Gideon
Thom has rightly remarked that it was the Calvinism of Dr.
John Philip of the London Missionary Society that led him to
take social and political positions contrary to the interests of
the colonial settlers at the Cape.[94] This "alternative Calvinism,"
alternative to the dominant tradition, embraces Afrikaner[95] and
English-speaking, black and white, stretching back as it does
to the missionary labors of Johannes Van der Kemp of the
London Missionary Society at the beginning of the nineteenth
century, shaping the new-found faith of the Xhosa hymn writer,
poet-preacher, and African nationalist Tiyo Soga,[96] and the
more recent political struggles of the African National Congress
leader Albert Luthuli,[97] and reaching forward into the present
in the prophetic yet compassionate witness of Beyers Naudé,[98]

93. Quoted in de Gruchy and Villa-Vicencio, *Apartheid Is a Heresy*,
p. 165.
94. Thom, "Calvinism in South Africa," p. 349.
95. See Jaap Durand, "Afrikaner Piety and Dissent," in Villa-Vicencio and de Gruchy, *Resistance and Hope*, pp. 39ff.; John W. de Gruchy, "The
Revitalization of Calvinism in South Africa: Some Reflections on Christian
Belief, Theology, and Social Transformation," *The Journal of Religious Ethics*
14 (Spring 1986).
96. See Donovan Williams, ed., *Journal and Selected Writings of Tiyo
Soga* (Cape Town: Balkema, 1983).
97. Albert Luthuli, like his father, was a deacon in the Congregational Church; see his autobiography, *Let My People Go!* (London: Collins,
1962), pp. 23-24.
98. See Durand, "Afrikaner Piety and Dissent," pp. 45-47.

the charismatic leadership of Allan Boesak, and the less prominent but no less significant witness of many others, including those to whom this book is dedicated.

A few comments on Johannes Van der Kemp and Beyers Naudé will help us bring this chapter to a fitting close. Despite his failures, there is good reason why Van der Kemp (1747-1811) may be regarded as the forerunner of a Reformed liberation and prophetic theology in South Africa in much the same way as Bartolomé de Las Casas fills that role in Latin America.[99] Van der Kemp was a man of his time, and there can be no doubt that he was in some ways an unwitting but useful agent for the colonial authorities, a pertinent reminder that even those thoroughly committed to the struggle of the poor and oppressed find it difficult to overcome their class or cultural background. But although he won grudging admiration both from some Boers and from British settlers and authorities, he also evoked much anger because of his courageous opposition to slavery and defense of human rights. Remarkably ecumenical in his views, yet evangelical and a convinced Calvinist (he espoused the Canons of Dort), Van der Kemp clearly took what we now refer to as the preferential option for the poor and oppressed. Biographer Ido Enklaar remarks:

> To his last days on earth Van der Kemp remained a crusader, fighting for the oppressed and the under-privileged through the evangelical values of mercy and justice, by which he attempted to live and work. For all coloured[100] people in South Africa Van der Kemp became the powerful symbol of the defence of their political rights and the struggle for social equality.[101]

99. Dussel, *History of the Church in Latin America*, pp. 47-48.

100. Van der Kemp's ministry was chiefly among the Khoi of the Eastern Cape. "Coloured" in South Africa normally refers to people of mixed race, and is a designation which some but not all would regard as derogatory.

101. Ido H. Enklaar, *Life and Work of Dr. J. Th. Van der Kemp, 1747-1811* (Cape Town: A. A. Balkema, 1988), p. 208.

Whatever status we give Van der Kemp, the modern apostle of liberating Reformed theology is undoubtedly Beyers Naudé, whose break with the white Dutch Reformed Church in the 1960s and whose establishment of the Christian Institute with its commitment to a confessing movement modelled on the Confessing Church in Germany has been an inspiration to many and a catalyst for transformation in the church struggle in South Africa. Naudé symbolizes not only the radical break of a white Afrikaner from cultural captivity, but also a Reformed theology captive to apartheid transformed into a liberated and liberating Reformed theology serving the cause of the oppressed.[102] Indeed, Naudé's dogged commitment to the gospel, his personal piety and prophetic courage, as well as his ecumenical breadth and political engagement, demonstrate and gather together the strands which make the Reformed tradition one of personal and social transformation.

It is of paramount importance that this Reformed tradition on the underside of South African history be remembered, for it provides historical models and depth to the present project. But even more, the recalling of the past helps keep alive the "dangerous memory" of the symbols of formative and transforming Calvinism, and so sustains those who seek to embody it today in the interests not only of the Reformed family but of the church and South Africa as a whole. We need, then, to retell the story, so that the symbols of the tradition are not simply reduced to a set of theological principles or cultic acts remote from reality but are also seen to be embodied in the narrative of the community, a narrative etched in flesh and blood, struggle, suffering, celebration, and hope.

The original impulse or ferment that led to the Reformation and to Calvin's interpretation of it was a rejection of human tyranny of all kinds and the proclamation of the liberating power of the gospel of Jesus Christ. This is what first led to Calvin's

102. See Charles Villa-Vicencio, "A Life of Resistance and Hope," and John W. de Gruchy, "A Short History of the Christian Institute," in Villa-Vicencio and de Gruchy, *Resistance and Hope*, pp. 3ff., 14ff.

break with Rome, and it was this which motivated his attempt to create a new, just, and equitable if not egalitarian society. Likewise, this has been the motivation of all those prophetic Calvinists who have taken the side of the oppressed, whether in the past or the present. The fact that this has invariably threatened the dominant culture, whether it claimed the name of Calvinist or not, is indicative of the ambiguity of the tradition. But a theology that is true to the ferment created and nourished by the whole gospel cannot be anything but prophetic.

South Africa, like many other countries, presently stands at a critical turning point in its history, a period of fundamental change and transition. As in the past, so in the present the Reformed tradition has a contribution to make to the process, a contribution catholic in substance, evangelical in its proclamation, and prophetic in its witness, and thus potentially liberating in its mission. There is no reason, then, why the liberating symbols of the past should remain the sole property of those who misuse and abuse them to sanction injustice or tyranny; there is every reason why they should be set free and reclaimed so they might provide direction, vision, and empowerment for transformation in the present. For this reason, it is ecumenically incumbent upon those within the Reformed tradition not to squander their heritage but to retrieve it for the sake of the church and society as a whole. Part of this task will have to be the identification and retrieval of liberating symbols within the Reformed tradition, within its spirituality and theology. This is the task we have set for ourselves in the following pages. But it should be kept continually in mind that such a task is not simply academic but is primarily one that, like the Reformation itself, is undertaken in the struggle for a renewed church and a transformed society. We conclude, then, with words from the Charter of the Alliance of Black Reformed Christians in Southern Africa, 1981:

> In this struggle, which we share with all our people, we take courage and comfort in life and in death from the assurance, given to us by the Belgic Confession, that "the

faithful and elect shall be crowned with glory and honour; and the Son of God will confess their names before God and his Father. . . . All tears shall be wiped from their eyes; *and their cause which is now condemned by many judges and magistrates as heretical and impious will then be known to be the cause of the Son of God. . . ."*

This is our tradition. This we will fight for.

2. *The Liberating Word*

Several years ago, on passing through the security gates at Heathrow Airport outside London, my hand luggage emitted the ominous sound that alerts police to the presence of a hidden weapon. Having been taken aside by a police officer, my luggage was searched, and eventually the officer confronted me with the offending article. It was a Bible with a metal zip. My immediate reaction was to protest, "That's only a Bible," to which the officer with some theological insight replied, "Maybe, but the Bible can be a very dangerous book!" In a more serious situation, the General Secretary of the South African Council of Churches, Frank Chikane, tells how during a period of detention in prison he was refused a Bible because the officer in charge said, "The Bible makes a terrorist of you."[1] The officer can be forgiven for falsely accusing Chikane of being a terrorist, for the propaganda of the state had taught him to regard all who actively struggle against apartheid as enemies of the state. But unwittingly he had, like the security officer at Heathrow Airport, a greater understanding of the socially transformative power of the biblical message than both the secular critics of

1. Reported by Denise Ackermann in "An Unfinished Quilt: A Woman's Credo," *Journal of Theology for Southern Africa* 66 (March 1989): 78.

Christianity and many Christians themselves. This transformative power has led Nicholas Wolterstorff to comment:

> Through all the dark days of its existence, there is one way in which the church has remained the sacrament of, the effective pointer to, a new day: down through the ages it has been the bearer of the Bible—the Word of God which points to him who is the Word of God, Jesus of Nazareth. The church has borne that Word even when the actual bearers were corrupt. And thereby, often to its surprise and its distress, it has sown the seeds of resistance and hope— among the blacks of South Africa, among the peasants of South America, and indeed throughout the world.[2]

Through the centuries blacks in South Africa, like Indians in North and South America, have been systematically deprived of their land, often in the name of spreading Christian civilization. The adage that the colonial powers, together with the missionaries, brought the Bible to the indigenous peoples of South Africa, took their land from them, and left them only the Bible, would be somewhat humorous if it were not so true. In commenting on this, Archbishop Desmond Tutu has made two perceptive observations. The first is that blacks got the better end of the bargain, for they received the life-giving and liberating Word of God; the second is that they took the Bible more seriously than the colonial authorities, the European settlers, and their successors intended.[3]

It goes without saying that Tutu was not justifying the fact that blacks have been systematically deprived of their land, and therefore not only of their birthright and the ground of cultural identity but also of their economic base. He was not suggesting that because men and women do not live by bread

2. Wolterstorff, *Until Justice and Peace Embrace* (Grand Rapids: Eerdmans, 1983), pp. 144-45.
3. Archbishop Desmond Tutu was addressing the twentieth anniversary dinner of the Department of Religious Studies at the University of Cape Town, April 1989.

alone, Scripture alone is able to meet the physical hungers of the poor and deprived. He was affirming, rather, that those who had gained the land had lost their souls in the process, and that those who had lost their land had discovered the liberating Word of life. But he was also affirming the liberating power of the Bible for those who are oppressed, those who, in a profound sense in continuity with the Protestant Reformers, had to struggle against oppression on the grounds of *sola Scriptura,* Scripture alone. What else does Martin Luther's *Ein' Feste Burg* mean?

> God's word, for all their craft and force,
> One moment will not linger,
> But, spite of hell, shall have its course;
> 'Tis written by his finger.
> And though they take our life,
> Goods, honor, children, wife,
> Yet is their profit small;
> These things shall vanish all;
> The City of God remaineth.

Those familiar with Reformation theology will know that the slogan *sola Scriptura* is referred to as the formal principle of theology as distinct from the material principle—that is, the gospel itself to which it bears witness. Adherence to "Scripture alone" meant that it alone, and not ecclesial tradition, contained the truth of the gospel and all that was needed for salvation and the right worship of God. Superficially, this is undoubtedly a different understanding from what we have just considered, namely, that the disinherited in the land have been forced to live by "Scripture alone." Yet there is a relationship with the Reformers' dictum. *Sola Scriptura* was not simply a formal theological principle over against Tridentine Catholicism, but a battle cry which recognized the source of their empowerment, salvation, and hope in the God revealed through his liberating Word.

Freedom from the Tyranny of Tradition

The rediscovery of the living Word of God in Holy Scripture as a saving, liberating Word, and therefore its normative authority for the life, teaching, and witness of the church, was fundamental to the Protestant Reformation. This does not contradict the fact that the process which led to this rediscovery began at least a century earlier, as evidenced by the use of the slogan *sola Scriptura* among the advocates of the Devotio Moderna, as well as its advocacy by earlier reformers such as John Wycliff in England. But Luther, Zwingli, Calvin, and the other leaders of the sixteenth-century Reformation gave a role and status to Scripture and its proclamation that was revolutionary for the time. The Bible—read, studied, and proclaimed as the Word of God—became the two-edged sword dividing truth and error in the struggle against Rome and the papal scholastic theologians, and it provided the believer with direct access to the message of God's saving and liberating grace.

Luther's break with Rome was theologically based on his interpretation of the Bible in relation to his own intensely personal experience of "justification by faith." This led him to reject all church tradition and practice which proclaimed "another gospel" and to take his stand on the witness of Scripture alone. For Luther, the Spirit of God does not work apart from the Word, whether in the tradition of the Catholic church or in the religious experience of "enthusiasts." Through the Word the Spirit witnesses to the gospel; through the Spirit the Word comes alive, bearing witness to Jesus Christ, bringing us to faith, and transforming our lives. For this reason, Scripture as the Word of God became the sole source of authority for the church and the believer.

Calvin followed Luther in affirming the principle of Scripture alone and was indebted to Luther in his general approach to the understanding and interpretation of Scripture as the "mighty, living, active Word of God."[4] Like many Latin Amer-

4. See Thomas F. Torrance, *The Hermeneutics of John Calvin* (Edin-

ican liberation theologians of our day, Calvin was essentially a biblical theologian. The successive editions of his *Institutes* reflect the way in which his own exegetical studies developed. Insisting that we can truly know neither God nor ourselves without the "spectacles of Scripture," he wrote the many editions of his *Institutes* as a guide to the reading and understanding of the message of the Bible.[5] Like Luther, he also knew that unless the Spirit breathed life into the words of Scripture as they were read and proclaimed, they could neither penetrate the heart and transform the soul nor address the church and society. Thus the reduction of the Bible in the life and preaching of the church by making it subservient to tradition and the papal magisterium destroyed its character as a living and contemporary witness to the liberating Word of the gospel. The battle for the Bible did not concern its inerrancy, for that debate had its origin in later Protestant scholasticism; nor was the battle about the authority of Scripture, for neither Roman Catholic nor evangelical denied its authority; rather, it concerned its liberation from captivity to the control of tradition and its subjugation to the decaying, unevangelical scholastic philosophy of the late Middle Ages.

Although Calvin was introduced to scholasticism as a student and was not a little influenced by it,[6] his encounter with Luther's theology, and especially Luther's attack on late scholasticism, radically altered his opinion and approach.[7] In order to appreciate the attack which Luther and then Calvin launched against medieval scholasticism, it is important to rec-

---

burgh: Scottish Academic Press, 1988), p. 156; Ganoczy, *The Young Calvin* (Philadelphia: Westminster Press, 1987), p. 186.

5. Calvin, *Institutes of the Christian Religion* (1559 edition), ed. John T. McNeill, Library of Christian Classics, vol. XX and XXI (Philadelphia: Westminster Press, 1960), 1.6.1.; see also Calvin's "Introduction," pp. 4-5. Unless stated otherwise, all references to Calvin's *Institutes* are from this edition.

6. Kilian McDonnell, *John Calvin, the Church and the Eucharist* (Princeton: Princeton University Press, 1967), pp. 7ff.; Torrance, *Hermeneutics of John Calvin*, pp. 72ff.

7. Ganoczy, *The Young Calvin*, pp. 179-80.

ognize that the scholasticism in vogue at the time and which they opposed was not the "high scholasticism" that prevailed at the height of the Middle Ages, but a scholasticism gone to seed.[8] Calvin's early attacks on scholasticism were based on a polemical reading of the twelfth-century *Decretals* of Gratian and the famous *Sentences* of Peter Lombard. Only much later, notably in the final (1559) edition of his *Institutes*, do we find significant reference to the great Scholastics, such as Thomas Aquinas. But by then the die had been cast, and there was no possibility of really appreciating the deeply spiritual and dynamic character of Thomas' theology even if Calvin had the inclination to do so. Scholastic theology, especially that of the strongly anti-evangelical theologians of the Sorbonne in Paris, was condemned as an "evil idol which must be overthrown," an unbiblical *theologia gloriae* whose main object was to support the claims of the papacy and "the tyranny of tradition."[9]

Calvin's favorite word of abuse in this regard was "custom" rather than "tradition." The tradition he attacked was not the tradition of the ancient catholic church, but the more recent customs of the papal church. With all the skill of a well-trained humanist and jurist, he cut through the "veil of public consent" that gave papal custom the status of divine law.[10] Undoubtedly, his strictures would apply as much to later Calvinist custom and Reformed traditions as they did then to papal custom and Roman traditions. The church and believers needed liberation from such bondage, and they still do. But as Luther would have said, only the living Word can do it.

In affirming *sola Scriptura*, or, to use Ganoczy's phrase, "the sovereignty of the Word," Calvin was not condoning a rampant

8. This distinction is not only of considerable importance for understanding the Reformation, but it is also important for contemporary ecumenical dialogue between the churches of the Reformation and Rome. See *The Condemnations of the Reformation Era: Do They Still Divide?* ed. Karl Lehmann and Wolfhart Pannenberg (Minneapolis: Fortress, 1990), p. 16.

9. Calvin, *Institutes*, 4.10.18.

10. See William J. Bouwsma, *John Calvin: A Sixteenth Century Portrait* (New York: Oxford University Press, 1988), p. 144.

individualism whereby Scripture could mean whatever its hearers believed the Spirit was saying to them. On the contrary, Calvin insisted that knowledge of God was dependent not on any assumptions and experience we might bring to Scripture, but upon the Word alone addressing us, awakening and confirming faith in us, and enabling us to discern the will of God for us. Hence we have the hermeneutical principle that the Bible interprets itself when believers earnestly search the Scriptures, open to the guidance of the Spirit. Calvin's understanding of this "inner testimony of the Spirit," whereby we come to know God through the Scriptures and thus discover the Word authenticating itself in our experience and obedience, was one of his unique contributions to Reformation and ecumenical thought.[11]

Calvin was, in fact, far more careful than Luther in seeking to ensure that the voice we hear in Scripture is not simply our own. In answering his Roman critics, he strongly asserted "the collective, ecclesial nature of hearing the Word."[12] This opened up the way for a local church to discern the Word of God for its own time and place, and thus for the contextual character of the various Reformed confessions that were to follow later. Likewise, Calvin appealed to the ancient Fathers and the ecumenical councils and creeds. He could, in other words, invoke the ancient tradition of the catholic church against the "evil customs" of the papal church. In the letter to Francis, King of France, with which he begins the first edition of his *Institutes*, Calvin calls in the support of the Fathers against the scholastics and the customs of the church:

> All the fathers with one heart have abhorred and with one voice have detested the fact that God's Holy Word has been contaminated by the subtleties of sophists and involved in the squabbles of dialecticians. . . . Why, if the fathers were now brought back to life, and heard such brawling art as these persons call speculative theology,

11. *Institutes*, 1.7.5.
12. B. A. Gerrish, *The Old Protestantism and the New: Essays on the Reformation Heritage* (Chicago: University of Chicago Press, 1982), p. 67.

there is nothing they would less suppose than that these folk were disputing about God![13]

But having called upon the Fathers of old to underwrite the teaching of the Reformation, he was quite convinced that their testimony was only valid insofar as it confirmed the word of Scripture. In his commentary on 1 Peter Calvin declares:

> Therefore the Papists are thrice foolish in thinking that the name of Fathers alone is sufficient defence for all their superstitions, so that they reject whatever is brought forward from the Word of God without regard to the consequences.[14]

Custom, no matter how hallowed by time, could not become a source of authority for the church.

In rejecting the "tyranny of tradition" as embedded in custom, Calvin believed, then, that he was being faithful to an older catholic tradition that bore witness to the meaning of Scripture. In our own day this understanding of tradition as a witness to Scripture has been deeply enriched through ecumenical dialogue, so that Catholic and Protestant alike have come to a less polemical and more profound grasp of the relationship between Scripture and tradition. What we have come to see is that while there is a necessary distinction between Scripture and tradition, they are not logically equal, and therefore the usual dichotomy drawn between them is false.[15] What really divides Roman Catholics and Protestants is two different concepts of tradition, and the way in which tradition functions as a principle in the life of the Catholic church, rather than the affirmation or rejection of the role of tradition

13. Calvin, *Institutes of the Christian Religion, 1536 Edition*, rev. ed., trans. Ford Lewis Battles (Grand Rapids: Eerdmans, 1986), p. 8.

14. Calvin, *The Epistle of Paul to the Hebrews and I and II Peter*, trans. W. B. Johnston, Calvin's New Testament Commentaries, vol. 12 (Grand Rapids: Eerdmans, 1963), p. 248.

15. David H. Kelsey, *The Uses of Scripture in Recent Theology* (Philadelphia: Fortress, 1975), p. 96.

itself.[16] Indeed, while Protestants might affirm Scripture alone as the basis of faith and practice, they invariably call upon some ecclesial tradition to confirm their interpretation—hence the irony yet inevitability of the phrase "the Reformed tradition." To be faithful to *sola Scriptura* does not necessarily mean breaking with the specific ecclesial tradition that has shaped us, but rather being open to the critique that Scripture brings to that tradition, a critique that is often discerned in ecumenical encounter.[17]

While for Calvin the "Word of God" meant Scripture, it was not simply a reference to the Bible but to the kerygmatic witness of the Bible.[18] In other words, Calvin's primary consideration was the witness of the Word and the Spirit to God's redeeming grace in Jesus Christ. This was the chief basis upon which he interpreted the whole of Scripture, his "canon within the canon," the way whereby Scripture interpreted itself. The inner testimony of the Spirit enabled the reader to discover Christ, "the Word which lies hid in the bosom of God," in the Law, the Prophets, and the gospel.[19] In his Preface to Olivetan's New Testament, he writes:

> Our minds ought to come to a halt at the point where we learn in Scripture to know Jesus Christ and him alone, so that we might be directly led by him to the Father who contains in himself all perfection.[20]

All else in the Reformed tradition, when it is true to itself, flows from this. *Sola Scriptura* is not an end in itself, but a means to

16. Heiko A. Oberman, "Quo Vadis? Tradition from Irenaeus to Humani Generis," *Scottish Journal of Theology* 16 (1963): 225ff.; Otto Weber, *The Foundations of Dogmatics,* vol. 1 (Grand Rapids: Eerdmans, 1981), p. 275.

17. Lehmann and Pannenberg, *Condemnations of the Reformation Era,* pp. 24-25.

18. See Ganoczy, *The Young Calvin,* p. 210.

19. Calvin, *Hebrews and I and II Peter,* p. 254.

20. Quoted in *Calvin: Commentaries,* trans. and ed. Joseph Haroutunian, Library of Christian Classics, vol. XXIII (Philadelphia: Westminster Press, 1958), p. 70.

know God the creator and redeemer through Jesus Christ, because he alone is the living, redeeming, liberating Word of God. This is the foundation for all truly evangelical and prophetic theology. But the question remains: How do we hear that Word today in our own context?

Creative Fidelity to the Scriptures

There is an important dialectic encapsulated in the Reformation phrase "Word and Spirit" which the church has sought to maintain through the centuries. On the one hand, the church has struggled to remain faithful to the apostolic testimony to what we might call the historic "facts" of the gospel. The authority of this testimony has been threatened continually by spiritualist movements, such as gnosticism and Montanism, which exulted in the freedom of the Spirit above the authority of the apostolic Word. In combatting such heresy the church closed the canon of Scripture and developed a hierarchical institutional structure to safeguard its interpretation.

On the other hand, the church has been challenged by the apostolic Word itself not to "quench the Spirit" (1 Thess. 5:19) at work in the witness of charismatic leaders, prophets, and reformers who remind the church of the need for renewal and an authentic knowledge of the living God in every generation. In this latter task the church has been less ardent and committed, thus erring more often in conservatively affirming authority, tradition, and continuity rather than freedom, renewal, and discontinuity. "The freaks ascribed to the Spirit," in P. T. Forsyth's words, "arrest far more attention than the frost which settles on the Word."[21] The ultimate consequence was the authority given to the teaching magisterium of the Roman church and the consequential "tyranny of tradition" against which Calvin protested. Despite Calvin's protest, it must be

21. P. T. Forsyth, *Faith, Freedom and the Future* (London: Independent Press, 1955), p. 41.

kept in mind that he himself, especially in his later years, moved in a similar, authoritarian direction, insisting on the special authority of ministers of the Word, and that this new form of clericalism became characteristic more generally of Calvinism. Indeed, it was a development that led the Nonconformist Puritan poet John Milton to reflect that "new presbyters were but the old priests writ large."

Calvin nevertheless always insisted that the Spirit speaks today through the Word, and the Word through the Spirit. Both together make the gospel contemporary and liberating. In this way the living Word accommodates itself to our capacity to hear, assimilate, and understand. Such accommodation was analogous to the Incarnation itself whereby "the Word became flesh," and thus was fundamental to Calvin's approach to the interpretation of Scripture.[22]

Calvin's emphasis upon the need for the Spirit to breathe life into the words of Scripture was a rejection of biblical literalism, not an excuse for changing its meaning.[23] As a skilled humanist scholar, he insisted on the need for a careful grammatical understanding of the text, on the need to avoid reading into the text what is not there and the concomitant need to discover what is there. His commentaries are models of clarity, unlike the work of those whom he labels "theologasters," who, as he says in his commentary on the Fourth Gospel, "harrassed Erasmus so fiercely because he changed a single word [of the Latin versions] for the better."[24] What was impermissible, however, was for the scholar, the individual believer, or the church to assume an authority above Scripture which changed its meaning and prevented people from hearing

22. See Ford Lewis Battles, "God Was Accommodating Himself to Human Capacity," *Interpretation* 31 (January 1977).

23. See the helpful discussion in Hans W. Frei, *The Eclipse of Biblical Narrative: A Study in Eighteenth and Nineteenth Century Hermeneutics* (New Haven: Yale University Press, 1974), pp. 21ff.

24. Calvin, *The Gospel according to St. John, 1-10*, trans. T. H. L. Parker, Calvin's New Testament Commentaries, vol. 4 (Grand Rapids: Eerdmans, 1961), p. 9.

the living, redeeming Word of God. This remains crucial for Reformed theology today, though the hermeneutical issues surrounding this commitment are far more complex than Calvin could have known. Some lie at the center of the challenge that liberation theology presents to Reformed theology.

Although Barth's commentary on Romans is far more existentialist than Calvin's commentaries, Barth was correct in seeing a similarity between what he was attempting in his early twentieth century situation and what Calvin was doing at a previous time and place. In his introduction to his commentary, Barth writes:

> How energetically Calvin, having first established what stands in the text, sets himself to re-think the whole material and to wrestle with it, till the walls which separate the sixteenth century from the first become transparent! Paul speaks, and the man of the sixteenth century hears.[25]

As anyone familiar with Calvin's expositions of Scripture will know, whether in commentary or sermon Calvin did not hesitate to read Scripture in the light of the events and the struggles of his day, and from the perspective of his own commitment to them. He saw the need for what some Latin American liberation theologians, like Clodovius Boff, refer to as "creative fidelity" in interpreting the Scriptures.[26] Commenting on the contest between Pharaoh and Moses, Calvin speaks of the pharaohs of his own day, and while he is more restrained than Luther in equating the struggle of Moses against Pharaoh with that of the struggle against the pope, there can be no doubt that this was continually in his mind as he expounded the story.

Calvin had an acute sense that what was happening in his own day resonated with the experience of Israel in the Hebrew Bible. This is one reason why he gave such prominence to the Old Testament in his teaching and preaching. It was not

25. Karl Barth, *The Epistle to the Romans* (London: SPCK, 1960), p. 7.
26. Arthur F. McGovern, *Liberation Theology and Its Critics* (New York: Orbis, 1989), p. 39.

simply a book of the church witnessing to Christ, but a book about the church struggling to be faithful. Calvin's lectures on the Book of Daniel, which he appositely chose to give in 1560 when the French evangelicals were suffering at the hands of the authorities, clearly even if only implicitly addresses their situation.[27] So likewise in interpreting Jesus' sermon in Nazareth based on Isaiah 61, he comments on the words "Today hath this scripture been fulfilled" by saying: "This is the due and regular way of interpreters to handle Scripture, by applying it to the present occasion."[28] "Preaching good news to the poor" refers to the preaching of the gospel to those within the unreformed church of the day who are longing for liberation. "Thus he calls them poor, and contrite, and captive, and blind, and broken, to whom God promises renewal." But he also recognizes that the promise goes beyond his own context and struggles, and refers more universally to "those who are in all ways to be pitied, and destitute of all hope." Indeed, "those that are full of pride, and do not groan in their bondage, find no discomfort in their blindness." They are simply unable to hear God's liberating Word.[29] Here is a clear indication that for Calvin, as for liberation theologians today, the existential situation and social location of the hearer of the Word plays a vital role in determining what is in fact heard.

For Calvin and the Reformation generally, a large part of the problem in the medieval church derived from the fact that the preached Word was no longer central to the celebration of the Mass, as it had been, for example, in the days of St. John Chrysostom, that great liturgist and preacher of Constantinople from whom Calvin drew so much of his inspiration. Homilies were indeed delivered in abundance at different types of service, not least by the mendicant friars, and the Scriptures were read

27. T. H. L. Parker, *Calvin's Old Testament Commentaries* (Edinburgh: T. & T. Clark, 1986), p. 221.

28. Calvin, *A Harmony of the Gospels Matthew, Mark and Luke, Volume 1*, trans. A. W. Morrison, Calvin's New Testament Commentaries, vol. 1 (Grand Rapids: Eerdmans, 1972), p. 149.

29. Ibid., p. 148.

in the Mass and the monastic offices. But evangelical and prophetic proclamation—whereby people could hear the living Word in their own tongue calling them to true repentance, faith, and obedience and offering them the liberating good news of grace, forgiveness, and transformation—was rare. Preaching this saving Word of life thus became central to the reformation of the church.

The affirmation of *sola Scriptura* was, of course, no guarantee that the resultant theology would be a faithful witness to the Word of God. Nor were the safeguards Calvin insisted on always able to ensure a common or faithful understanding of Scripture. Calvin might insist on objectivity, but polemics, argumentation, and winning points for a position rather than for truth sometimes took precedence, even in his own interpretation. Both Catholics and Protestants could quote Scripture, and Calvin, "despite all his fidelity to the Bible," François Wendel admits, "seems to have been searching the Scriptures more frequently for texts to support a doctrine accepted in advance, than to derive a doctrine from Scripture."[30] William Bouwsma is not entirely fair to the Reformers and Calvin, but he makes a valid point in saying that "the Reformation slogan *scriptura sola* was intrinsically naive; and Calvin's claim that Scripture was his 'only guide,' and acquiescence in its 'plain doctrines' as his 'constant rule of wisdom,' could never have been more than an aspiration."[31]

Subsequently, the problem has been exacerbated for the Reformed tradition by several factors. The first was the failure of Protestants to agree on the meaning of Scripture with regard to controversial issues dividing them from each other. The second was the rise of historical biblical criticism, which not only made biblical interpretation subject to scholarship, but undermined its authority for many and drove the remainder into a reactionary biblical fundamentalism. The third was the notion of the private interpretation of Scripture, traced back in part to

30. François Wendel, *Calvin* (London: Collins, 1965), p. 359.
31. Bouwsma, *John Calvin*, p. 98.

Martin Luther, which allowed each person to make of Scripture what he or she willed. The fourth is the more recent recognition that while objective knowledge may be a goal to strive for, it is unattainable. All interpretation is affected in some measure by the social location and material interests of the interpreter.

Determining precisely what "the Spirit is saying to the churches" through the Word is thus one problem that has exercised Protestants ever since the teaching magisterium of the Roman Catholic Church was replaced by the appeal to Scripture alone. But initially there was an understandable determination on the part of sixteenth- and seventeenth-century Calvinists, like the medieval scholastics before and their soul mates after, to bring such uncertainty to a halt and to determine, once and for all, what the Word of God says for all people, at all times, in all situations. But that by no means resolved the problem for everyone then, and it does so for far fewer within the tradition today who are acutely conscious of the problems surrounding the interpretation and authority of Scripture. The irony is that many who thought they had secured the place of the Bible as the formal principle of Reformed theology actually undermined the Reformers' own reliance on Scripture and led a retreat away from the living Word.

A Retreat from the Living Word

In his portrait of Calvin, Bouwsma describes a tension within the Reformer between the rational, scholastic theologian-philosopher, and the humanist, biblical scholar and preacher.[32] In the former the stress is upon the primacy of the intellect and the objectivity of timeless truth. In the latter the stress is upon responding to the new historical moment and context, the need for communication of the truth in new forms, and the transfor-

32. This tension in Bouwsma's portrait is ably described and analyzed in Philip C. Holtrop's review article, "Between the 'Labyrinth' and the 'Abyss'," *Reformed Journal* 39 (April 1989): 21-22.

mation of persons rather than the conservation of inherited principles. Bouwsma overstates his case in the interests of making it, especially in giving as much weight as he does to Calvin the rational theologian-philosopher, but there is undoubtedly some truth in what he says. Just as there is a tension between Calvin the evangelical and Calvin the prophet, so there is a tension between Calvin the rational thinker and Calvin the biblical theologian and preacher, though the latter usually kept the former under control.

Both of these tendencies have played a major role in shaping the biblical hermeneutics of the Reformed tradition, but they have taken it in very different directions. The one led to the rationalist metaphysical Calvinism of the seventeenth century and contributed in no small measure to the deism of the Enlightenment, which no longer had any need of revelation or the Bible. The other, often in reaction to the first, led to the experiential piety of much English Calvinism or Puritanism, as well as the evangelical piety of the Dutch Reveil and other Calvinist revival movements, but it did not make a break with the scholastic pre-critical approach to the Scriptures. Although deeply influenced by pietism, Friedrich Schleiermacher at the beginning of the nineteenth century contributed to such a break. In Schleiermacher we see the humanist side of Calvin coming to the fore in the establishment of a new hermeneutic that took seriously the challenges of the Enlightenment and especially the historical critical study of the Bible. But before we consider Schleiermacher's role in the liberation of Reformed theology, let us consider Calvinist scholasticism's role in making it captive to rationalism.

Even though it is difficult at times to discern precisely what constitutes an aberration of Calvin's thought and what is authentically his,[33] Calvinist scholasticism in the later sixteenth and seventeenth centuries took a step backwards behind the Reformation. It was in many respects a return to the philosophi-

33. See the discussion in Charles Partee, *Calvin and Classical Philosophy* (Leiden: E. J. Brill, 1977), p. 19.

cal labyrinth out of which Calvin had broken free. Hence the development of a theological system in which the Bible as an infallible text was reduced to rational propositions synthesized with Aristotelian categories and developed with precise logic. Everything in Christian doctrine was now deduced from a first principle—usually the sovereignty of God or predestination—and rationally ordered into a metaphysical system.[34] Thus, while some of the building blocks for the theology of the Canons of Dort (total depravity, unconditional election, limited atonement, irresistible grace, and the perseverance of the saints) can be traced directly back to Calvin, the order in which they were formulated and the system they generated led to consequences that began a process of unbiblical distortion.[35]

In place of a dynamic confession of faith, as found in the early Reformed confessions and catechisms, such as the Scots Confession (1560) and the Heidelberg Catechism (1563), we find the ultra-Calvinism of the Canons of Dort (1619) and the majestic, all-encompassing Westminster Confession (1643). Claiming to be a subordinate standard, the Westminster Confession became, at least for important sections of the tradition, the final arbiter of biblical truth and faithfulness. What Frederick Farrar later called "the terrorism of Formulae" had begun to prevail with its consequential "crushing of spontaneous thought under the dead weight of petrified dogmas."[36] In a manner at once legalistic, categorical, and individualistic the Westminster Confession claimed to be the only true and therefore universally valid interpretation of Christian doctrine.[37]

For post-Tridentine Catholics, as for Lutheran and Calvinist

34. Ibid., pp. 20-21.
35. See M. Eugene Osterhaven, *The Faith of the Church: A Reformed Perspective on its Historical Development* (Grand Rapids: Eerdmans, 1982), pp. 80-81; R. T. Kendall, *Calvin and English Calvinism to 1649* (Oxford: Oxford University Press, 1979), chaps. 1-2.
36. Frederick W. Farrar, *History of Interpretation* (1886; reprint, Grand Rapids: Baker Book House, 1961), p. 360.
37. See George S. Hendry, *The Westminster Confession for Today* (Richmond: John Knox, 1960), pp. 14-15.

scholastics, what became important was not hearing the living, liberating Word for today, but adherence to opposing dogma. "At Wittenberg, as well as at Geneva," wrote Kuyper, "the conviction was unassailable for long years that their own confession bore an absolute and exclusive character. Everything that contradicted this was a falsification of the truth."[38] Each of the classic and more contemporary Reformed confessions of faith is a product of a particular historical moment in the journey of the Reformed community of faith, not the end point. To cling uncritically to them in the present, as though fidelity to them in itself means salvation, is a denial of their intent to point beyond themselves to the gospel. Adherence to a confession cannot be a substitute for hearing and obeying the Word that addresses us in new ways, at new times, and in new places.[39] It can in fact become another form of tyranny, or, indeed, a form of "ecclesiastical narcissism,"[40] which is the permanent temptation of every tradition.

Pastor John Robinson, a Nonconformist Puritan divine, in his celebrated farewell sermon to the Pilgrim Fathers as they set sail from Plymouth for New England in 1620, charged the travellers in his often quoted and historic words:

> that you follow me no further than you have seen me follow the Lord Jesus Christ. If God reveal anything to you by any other instrument of his, be as ready to receive it as you were to receive any truth by my ministry, for I am verily persuaded the Lord hath more truth yet to break forth from his holy word.

Robinson continued:

> For my part I cannot sufficiently bewail the condition of those Reformed Churches which are come to a period in

---

38. Abraham Kuyper, *Principles of Sacred Theology* (1898; reprint, Grand Rapids: Baker Book House, 1980), p. 659.

39. See the discussion in Karl Barth, *Church Dogmatics* (Edinburgh: T. & T. Clark, 1936ff.), I/2, pp. 862ff.

40. D. J. Smit in *Christ's Rule*, Papers of the Reformed Ecumenical Synod Conference (Harrare, Zimbabwe, 1988), p. 113.

religion and will go at present no further than the instruments of their reformation. The Lutherans cannot be drawn to go beyond what Luther saw. Whatever part of His will our God revealed to Calvin, they will die rather than embrace; and the Calvinists, you see, stick fast where they were left by that great man of God, who yet saw not all things. That is a misery much to be lamented.[41]

Although Robinson himself adhered to the theology of the Canons of Dort, he was clearly worried by the strong theological and ecclesiastical currents of his time that were transforming the dynamic theology of the Reformation into the static scholasticism of Protestant orthodoxy. The Word, he believed, could not be held captive to past formulations of the faith, inherited customs, or ecclesial structures unless these reflected the truth of the Word of God addressing us through the Spirit today.

One reason why there is no definitive Reformed theology is precisely because Calvin did not leave us with a closed theological system, nor with a universal and united Reformed church. Indeed, his own theology was not always logically consistent and can certainly not be reduced to a speculative system from which principles can be deduced.[42] Another reason for diversity within the tradition is that the Reformed movement had a variety of leaders, and while Calvin was "the generating source" he did not fulfill the same role as did Luther within Lutheranism. Thus, the Reformed tradition comprises a variety of theologies and confessions that have emerged at different times and places and in response to different challenges and needs during the past five hundred years. As John Robinson was at pains to stress, Scripture, not Calvin's theology or a particular confessional document, is normative for the Reformed tradition, and the Spirit, not the Reformer or later

41. Quoted in Horton Davies, *The English Free Churches* (New York: Oxford University Press, 1952), p. 56.
42. See Hermann Bauke, *Der Probleme der Theologie Calvins* (Leipzig: J. C. Hinrichs, 1922); John Leith, *John Calvin's Doctrine of the Christian Life* (Louisville: Westminster/John Knox Press, 1989), p. 24.

representatives of the tradition, is the ultimate interpreter of the Word. Barth put this succinctly in his *Calvinfeier* lecture in 1936, pointing to the source of Calvin's freedom, the creative freedom that comes from listening to and obeying the Word:

> Calvin did not leave us a theological system. Even the contents of his *Institutes* is something very different from the theological system which preceded and came after him. It was no Calvinism. The austere harshness with which Calvin himself thought through and defended his position has only the appearance of severity, an order to which he subdued it. Within there is only a given freedom, a freedom of listening, but also an obedience, the obedience of the free. Who would want to be a student of Calvin's must become a student of the Holy Scriptures.[43]

Criticism of Calvinist scholasticism should not overlook the significance of what its best exponents were attempting. They were trying to produce the equivalent of a *summa theologia* in the tradition of the great medieval scholastics. They were attempting to do this on the premise of Scripture alone, with the Bible understood as an infallible book of divinely given propositions, rather than on the basis of Roman Catholic tradition. In doing so, they rightly saw the need for a rational, coherent account of Christian faith, something on which the Reformed tradition has always placed a premium. Thus Karl Barth bemoaned the fact that his theological teachers had given him a caricature of the "old orthodoxy,"[44] just as they had failed to introduce him adequately to Calvin. When he later encountered the writings of the older Calvinists he began to appreciate not only their diversity, but also the depth and thoroughness of what they had achieved, preferring that to the shallowness of much liberal theology. But he could not follow

---

43. Karl Barth, "Calvinfeier 1936," *Theologische Existenz heute*, Heft 43 (Munich: Chr. Kaiser Verlag, n.d.), p. 4. My translation.

44. Karl Barth, *The Theology of Schleiermacher* (Grand Rapids: Eerdmans, 1982), p. 264.

them because, as he says, "in their justifiable attempt to adopt the Early and Medieval Church tradition," they "overloaded it with presuppositions which were bound sooner or later to jeopardize Reformed knowledge of God and salvation."[45] Once revelation "in all its mystery" is turned "into something like a handy intellectual principle," then what becomes important is adherence to the principle, not response to the revelation today. In Otto Weber's words: "The more that Orthodoxy tried to secure its position, the weaker it became; it found itself being continuously forced to retreat more and more from the reality of the living biblical Word."[46]

This, incidentally, is not very different from the reasons such Catholic liberation theologians as Gustavo Gutiérrez give in rejecting the debased scholasticism of the pre–Vatican II manuals of theology. When they reject that kind of "academic" theology they are in company with Calvin and all genuinely Reformed theology.[47] Catholic spirituality and rational knowledge are, in Gutiérrez's words, "permanent functions of all theological thinking," and the same is true for a truly Reformed theology. But with Gutiérrez, Reformed theology must go on to say that "both functions must be salvaged, at least partially, from the division and deformations they have suffered throughout history."[48] Reformed and liberation theologies cannot avoid the need for systematic coherence and expression, as well as integration into the theological task of the universal church. But in keeping with the dogmatic spirit of Western theology as a whole, the Calvinist scholastics, like their Catholic predecessors, allowed the rational and systematic concern to control their theology to such an extent that form determined content, and reason sought to control the mystery of revelation.

---

45. Heinrich Heppe, *Reformed Dogmatics*, rev. ed. by Ernst Bizer, trans. G. T. Thompson (Grand Rapids: Baker Book House, 1978), p. vi.

46. Weber, *Foundations of Dogmatics*, vol. 1, p. 119.

47. See Gustavo Gutiérrez, *A Theology of Liberation*, rev. ed. (New York: Orbis, 1988), pp. 3-4.

48. Ibid., p. 5.

A New Way of Theological Discourse

It has become a cliche that liberation theology is a new way of doing theology rather than a new theology. In fact, the way in which liberation theology does theology is very old, for much of the theology in the Bible grew out of the struggles of the people of God to be faithful to their covenantal relationship with God in relation to their sociopolitical journey through history. Theology was worked out in the process of responding to the promises and commands of God within history. Likewise, Paul's letter's are models of doing theology in the same way.[49] Hence, the familiar hermeneutical circle adopted by liberation theology in which "each new reality obliges us to interpret the word of God afresh, to change reality accordingly, and then to go back and reinterpret the word of God again"[50] resonates with what we actually find in much of Scripture, in Calvin, and in much contemporary Reformed theology.

While Calvin would decry any recourse to novelty in doing theology, he was concerned to relate the gospel to new historical conditions. Bouwsma observes that Calvin's "awareness of the need for accommodation to the times was so strong that it drove him to what, for the times, was a new way of looking at theological discourse." Bouwsma even goes so far as to suggest that this points not only to the liberal but "perhaps even the liberation, Christianity of the future."[51] We must avoid the temptation to cast Calvin in the incongruous role of either the pioneer of liberal theology or an early forerunner of liberation theology. Apart from the fact that a gulf separates liberal and liberation theologies, Calvin was a man of his times, and the legacy he left cannot easily be categorized in modern-day terms. But there is, nevertheless, some substance to Bouwsma's surmising that enables us to see the continuity between Calvin

49. See J. Christiaan Beker, *Paul the Apostle: The Triumph of God in Life and Thought* (Philadelphia: Fortress, 1982), pp. 23ff.

50. Juan Luis Segundo, *The Liberation of Theology* (New York: Orbis, 1976), p. 8.

51. Bouwsma, *John Calvin*, p. 232.

and Schleiermacher, and to see a methodological relationship between them and liberation theology.[52]

Schleiermacher, the pioneer of liberal theology, regarded himself as a Reformed, or better (though it may sound strange to modern ears), an evangelical theologian. He regarded his project as in continuity with Calvin's attempt to interpret the Bible in his context, but now in terms of a new theological discourse for a post-Enlightenment world.[53] Indeed, contrary to the neo-Orthodox rejection of Schleiermacher's theology earlier in this century, sometimes based on misrepresentation, it was none other than the neo-Calvinist Kuyper's opinion that Schleiermacher gave "theology back to herself," "lifted her out of her degradation," and "inspired her with new courage and self-confidence."[54] Whatever his critics make of it, what Schleiermacher attempted was summed up in his announcement: "The Reformation still goes on!" In making that assertion he was in continuity with the spirit of John Robinson, and, indeed, with Calvin, who did not stop with but moved beyond Luther.[55] Just as Renaissance humanism enabled Calvin to break free from the constrictions of a decadent late medieval scholasticism and "extricate himself from the labyrinth of philosophy,"[56] so the challenge of the Enlightenment, the insights of Romanticism, and the experience of pietism enabled Schleiermacher to cast off the shackles of a rationalist Calvinism and deism, and do Reformed theology in a new key.

In pursuing his theological task, Schleiermacher laid some of the foundations for modern hermeneutical theory, but he

52. See Terence N. Tice, "Schleiermacher's Theology: Ecclesial and Scientific, Ecumenical and Reformed," in *Probing the Reformed Tradition: Historical Studies in Honour of Edward A. Dowey, Jr.*, ed. Elsie Anne McKee and Brian G. Armstrong (Louisville: Westminster/John Knox Press, 1989), p. 387.

53. See Brian Gerrish, *Tradition and the Modern World: Reformed Theology in the Nineteenth Century* (Chicago: University of Chicago Press, 1978), pp. 13ff.

54. Kuyper, *Principles of Sacred Theology*, p. 676.

55. See Gerrish, *Tradition and the Modern World*, p. 48.

56. Bouwsma, *John Calvin*, p. 113.

also reshaped Protestant theology along lines that led it away from Calvin's biblical theology. The legitimacy of what he attempted cannot be faulted—the Reformation had to continue and theology could not stop with Calvin. A new theological discourse was not only necessary; its pursuit was also appropriately Reformed. Indeed, theology within the Reformed tradition should not only condition but also evoke new theological possibilities.[57] That was how Schleiermacher understood his task, and that is surely how we must understand ours. Theology is not meant to regurgitate the past or simply react to the challenges of new eras, but to point beyond the present to God's future for the world and so enable humanity to break out of its captivities and anticipate now the liberation God seeks for the whole of creation. Such is the creative edge of doing theology, one reason why old confessions lose their liberating power and new ones become necessary. The major question to be faced then is whether such theological creativity is still faithful to the Word of God, or whether it has become captive to culture or subjective intuition. At what point does creative fidelity to Scripture become creative infidelity?

What Karl Barth said about his own situation is still often true of ours: "When we learn to know Schleiermacher we learn to know ourselves."[58] For many of us the reality of religious experience and culture inevitably takes precedence over the Word which is addressed to us from beyond ourselves and which graciously but firmly makes a claim upon our lives. It is perfectly legitimate and necessary that we read the Bible in the light of our experience and needs, and it is inevitable that we do so from the perspective of our own cultural and social location. But if we are to hear the Word that speaks to us in Scripture, then we have to discern a Word which not only confirms our experience, need, and perspective, but more often radically challenges us. Too often we fail to hear the Word that

57. Benjamin Reist, "Dogmatics in Process," *Reformed World* 39 (September 1987): 760-61.
58. Barth, *The Theology of Schleiermacher*, p. xv.

speaks against us in all its strange otherness. Having surrendered the mystery of the Catholic Mass and the Reformation Word, all that is left is the mystery of our own souls or the captivities of our culture. For such reasons, many have found in the theology of Barth a way to hold on to the living, liberating Word and so rediscover the liberating power of the gospel as this was retrieved by the Reformation.

Barth's ongoing "love-hate" relationship and debate with Schleiermacher, as well as his rejection of liberal theology and its hermeneutics, need not detain us as such.[59] With others we recognize the need to go beyond the impasse in much contemporary theology represented by stressing the discontinuities rather than the continuities between Schleiermacher and Barth.[60] At the same time, there are discontinuities and they represent an ongoing struggle or tension within Reformed theology. At the very least we need to affirm Barth's critique of a liberal theology that reduces the Word of God to a reflection of communal, pious, and usually bourgeois experience and interests, just as we must also affirm his critique of rationalist Calvinism. Creative infidelity and sterile fidelity ultimately amount to the same thing—a failure to hear the liberating and life-giving Word in relation to our own historical context.

In a strange way, Afrikaner Calvinism represents a blend of both Calvinist scholasticism and liberal theological methodology. Although it is true that Afrikaner Calvinism was rooted in neo-Calvinism and claimed to stand firmly by the confessions of the Reformed tradition, its failure may be attributed not to its faithful adherence to the Word, but to its reading the Word from the perspective of Afrikaner experience and interests alone, and not listening to the cry for life of those who were being oppressed. The many Dutch Reformed statements on church and society, while claiming to interpret the Bible alone, have

59. See ibid., pp. 261-62. See also Keith Clements, *Schleiermacher: The Pioneer of Modern Theology* (New York: Harper & Row, 1988), pp. 63-64.

60. James O. Duke and Robert F. Streetman, eds., *Barth and Schleiermacher: Beyond the Impasse?* (Philadelphia: Fortress, 1988).

traditionally done so on the basis of a social analysis determined by the norms of Afrikaner communal experience, piety, culture, and politics.[61] Behind that lies a natural theology derived from the "orders of creation," the kind of culture-theology Barth attacked during the German Third Reich. Precisely for this reason Jaap Durand says that "one of the great tragedies in the development of Afrikaner Reformed theology in the three decisive decades of its evolvement (1930-60) was that Karl Barth's criticism of religion and of natural theology was never really heard or given any opportunity to be heard in those Kuyperian circles that needed it most."[62] It is not surprising, then, that some Dutch Reformed theologians in South Africa have discovered Barth as a theologian who has liberated them and enabled them to hear the Word of God as it speaks to their situation.[63]

In struggling to overcome the subjectivity of liberal theology and the cultural, racist captivity of German natural theology, Barth was not without his own personal presuppositions. Like Calvin and the rest of us, he read Scripture in the light of his experience and the historical situation facing him, even though he was profoundly committed to hearing the Word of God alone in all its critical otherness. The objectivity of the Word remained, but it could only be read through human spectacles. The fact was, however, that Barth's socialism and his involvement with the labor movement in his parish of Safenwil enabled him to discover in Scripture that God is on the side of the poor and oppressed. Thus for Barth a theology grounded in the Bible always meant a radical attack not only

61. See the critique in J. J. F. Durand, "Bible and Race: The Problem of Hermeneutics," *Journal of Theology for Southern Africa* 24 (September 1978): 3-4.

62. Durand, "Afrikaner Piety and Dissent," in *Resistance and Hope,* ed. Charles Villa-Vicencio and John W. de Gruchy (Grand Rapids: Eerdmans, 1985), p. 40. See also de Gruchy, *Bonhoeffer and South Africa* (Grand Rapids: Eerdmans, 1984), p. 109.

63. Jaap Durand, "Church and State in South Africa," in *On Reading Karl Barth in South Africa,* ed. Charles Villa-Vicencio (Grand Rapids: Eerdmans, 1988), p. 134. Most of the essays in this volume are relevant to this present discussion.

upon totalitarianism but also upon social and economic oppression. In other words, because Barth read the Bible from this perspective, he was able to discern the Word of God within it as critique and challenge, a Word against human pretension and oppressive power, a Word, in that instance, for the socialist cause of the workers. For this and related reasons Barth provides the link in the chain that relates Calvin and Reformed theology generally to liberation theology.[64]

Yet, despite what Gollwitzer has called the "antibourgeois tendency" in Barth's theology, once Barth was no longer involved in the struggles of the workers in Safenwil but ensconced in the academic milieu of a German university, this "antibourgeois elan lost its force."[65] Like Calvin, Barth could not easily break free from his social and intellectual class and thus hear the Word of God alone. This brings us once again to consider the challenge that liberation theology presents to Reformed theology, and especially its challenge to Reformed theology's claim that it always seeks to do theology in fidelity to the Word of God. To put the question most sharply: Is the Bible always a liberating Word?

Ideological Conflict and the Word

We have in the course of this chapter identified several hermeneutical problems that have become apparent since the time of the Reformation. One of the most recent and far-reaching has resulted from the sociology of knowledge, namely, the awareness that our interpretation of texts is affected by our material interests. Consider the emergence of what is called the "hermeneutics of suspicion" and the rejection of any claim to ideological neutrality and pure scholarly objectivity in the interpretation of the Bible. In Elisabeth Schüssler Fiorenza's words:

64. See George Hunsinger, "Karl Barth and Liberation Theology," *Journal of Religion* 63 (1983): 247ff.
65. Helmut Gollwitzer, "Kingdom of God and Socialism in the Theology of Karl Barth," in George Hunsinger, *Karl Barth and Radical Politics* (Philadelphia: Westminster, 1976), p. 106.

The basic insight of all liberation theologies, including feminist theology, is the recognition that all theology, willingly or not, is by definition always engaged for or against the oppressed. Intellectual neutrality is not possible in a world of exploitation and oppression. If this is the case, then theology cannot talk about human existence in general or about biblical theology in particular without critically identifying those whose human existence is meant and about whose God the biblical symbols and texts speak.[66]

The problem has to be faced at two levels. The one is the ideological position of the interpreter; the other is the ideological perspective of the biblical authors. While the first is not a problem for those who maintain a high view of biblical authority, unless they refuse to acknowledge that they are themselves ideologically constrained or committed, the second does present a major problem.

This latter challenge has been put most sharply recently in South Africa by Itumeleng Mosala. Mosala critically challenges the way in which theologies of the Word of God, including that of black Reformed theologians like Allan Boesak, fail to deal with the ideological conflicts within Scripture itself. The point Mosala makes "is not that Boesak and other black theologians are mistaken in finding a liberating message in the Bible." Rather, Mosala contends, "the category of the Word of God does not help to bring out the real nature of the biblical liberation because it presumes that liberation exists everywhere and unproblematically in the Bible."[67] From this perspective, the Bible itself is now seen as embodying within itself different ideological trajectories in conflict with each other.

Let us begin with the first of the challenges, namely that every interpreter of the Bible comes to the text with presuppositions, acknowledged or hidden. The spectacles of Scripture may be necessary to know God, but we all wear ideological spectacles

66. Elisabeth Schüssler Fiorenza, *In Memory of Her: A Feminist Theological Reconstruction of Christian Origins* (New York: Crossroad, 1983), p. 6.

67. Itumeleng J. Mosala, *Biblical Hermeneutics and Black Theology in South Africa* (Grand Rapids: Eerdmans, 1989), p. 20.

that determine how we understand what we read and hear in Scripture. Such presuppositions, which range from material interests to those of spiritual concern, mean that we do not read Scripture alone any more than the scholastic theologians of Calvin's day, or Calvin himself, despite his struggling to do so. Incidentally, given Calvin's own use of philosophy as a theological resource,[68] it would not be inconsistent with his theological method if we were to argue that today Calvin would not have hesitated to use the social sciences as aids to theological reflection, though he would not have allowed them to determine its substance any more than he allowed philosophy to do so.

The problem we face is that Scripture can be read from different contextual perspectives and with different interests in mind. It can be read from the perspective of the poor and oppressed and thus from the perspective of the struggle for justice and liberation in the world. When read in this way it can become a revolutionary book because it bears witness to God's intent and power to overthrow unjust structures, establish freedom for all, and give life in its fullness to all. But it can and has been read to sanction power, injustice, and oppression. We need little reminder of how the Bible has been used to defend crusades, war, slavery, racism, child labor, the domination of women, rampant capitalism, and apartheid, and that within the Bible there are sufficient texts that—when wrenched from their context, and sometimes when not—provide ammunition for these abuses.

One of the most bizarre illustrations of the misuse of Scripture is the fact that Armscor, the giant para-state arms corporation in South Africa, a few years ago at the height of militarism in the country sponsored a program for the distribution of Bibles among soldiers. This was undoubtedly motivated by several considerations: a very spiritualized understanding of the message of the Bible as one that could help soldiers face death on the battlefield with greater assurance of life after death, an understanding that the biblical message requires uncritical loyalty and obedience to the state, and a desire to promote a public image of Christian legitimacy for the manufac-

68. See Partee, *Calvin and Classical Philosophy*, pp. 19-20.

ture of armaments. It was certainly not based on an understanding of the liberating, prophetic, and transforming Word
that confronts us in Scripture. But Armscor was on safe ground
because the vast majority of the soldiers who would receive the
Bibles would have likewise read them from the same perspective. This explains why it was so traumatic for the young white
South African soldier who discovered a pocket New Testament
on the body of a Swapo guerrilla who had been shot dead in
a skirmish on the Namibia/Angola border.

Leaving aside for the moment the question as to whether
the Bible can be interpreted legitimately in such diametrically
opposed ways, what we have established is that within the
church today, not least in South Africa, there is, underlying
much else, what might be described as a hermeneutical
struggle. In fact, it could be argued that this is the real hermeneutical struggle, the locus where what the scholars talk
about impinges upon harsh reality. That is, the church today,
irrespective of denomination, is divided, often radically, by
fundamentally different understandings of the biblical message, even among those who adhere strictly to *sola Scriptura*
and seek to establish the meaning of Scripture from Scripture
itself. These different interpretations are not simply the product
of diverse theological standpoints, but of very different perceptions of social reality, and the influence of material interests.

The sharpness of this hermeneutical struggle is very obvious in many third-world countries, including South Africa, as
can be seen from *The Road to Damascus* document, an international sequel to *The Kairos Document*.[69] *The Kairos Document*
pointed clearly to such a hermeneutical struggle in making the
distinction between "state," "church," and "prophetic theology." According to *The Kairos Document*, "state theology" is
obviously ideologically committed to the legitimation of an unjust status quo. It is virulently at work in right-wing fundamen-

69. *The Road to Damascus: Kairos and Conversion,* a document signed
by third-world Christians from seven nations: South Africa, Namibia,
South Korea, Philippines, El Salvador, Nicaragua, and Guatemala (Johannesburg: Skotaville, 1989).

talist religious groups, and despite its apolitical claims, it is clearly politically committed. "Prophetic theology" makes no apologies for being politically committed, but it is committed to the struggle for justice on behalf of the oppressed. "Church theology," as defined by *The Kairos Document,* is, however, more problematic, because it is avowedly committed to reconciliation between racial groups. It represents where most of the mainline churches are theologically, whether Afrikaans- or English-speaking. But it is not informed by an adequate analysis of what is happening in South African society; it lacks any specific strategy for change other than at the level of personal relations, and it reveals a spirituality essentially private and individualistic.

The critique of "state theology" in *The Kairos Document* was clearly directed, inter alia, at Afrikaner Calvinism, while the critique of "church theology" was aimed at the more liberal English-speaking churches. Both are therefore challenges to the Reformed tradition in South Africa, but the critique of "church theology" is aimed at the Reformed tradition more generally throughout the world. As a predominantly bourgeois movement, it has tended to affirm reconciliation between classes and races without dealing with the underlying causes that produce social conflict. Sergio Rostagno, a Waldensian pastor within the broad Reformed tradition, has labelled this an "interclass" perspective, which, while undermined by Paul's dialectic in the New Testament, is present in the pastoral letters.

> Masters and slaves are to be of one mind, in the light of their common divine paternity, obeying the same Lord and so on. The poor have one function, the rich another, and the church supplies the needs of the former and offers them to the latter as an opportunity of good works. (1 Tim. 6:17)[70]

Rostagno continues: "This was still acceptable to Calvin, who wrote in this connection, 'When the rich have the wherewithal to do good and the poor thank God for having something to

---

70. Sergio Rostagno, "The Bible: Is an Interclass Reading Legitimate?" in *The Bible and Liberation: Political and Social Hermeneutics,* ed. Norman K. Gottwald (New York: Orbis, 1983), pp. 70-71.

eat, they all glorify God' (commentary on Deut. 16:11)." Indeed, Rostagno maintains that this "interclass approach is interwoven into the history of Protestantism." Its consequence is an individualistic ethic and an approach to charity that not only fails to transform the class structure of society but in fact reinforces it. A new page is turned with the early Barth's rediscovery of the message of Paul, but even Barth, Rostagno argues, qualifies his position in such a way as to suggest that "the interclass illusion is an incurable illness of Protestantism."[71]

We are now in a position to make two proposals in response to the challenge of liberation theology that the Bible is inevitably read from an ideological point of view and that within the Bible itself we find different ideological trajectories. In regard to the first we need to develop a Reformed hermeneutic that recognizes what José Míguez Bonino has called "the epistemological privilege of the poor." Thus, we not only need the spectacles of Scripture in order to know God the creator and redeemer in Christ, but we also need the spectacles of the victims of society in order to discern the liberating Word in Scripture itself. In regard to the second challenge, we need to recognize not only that Scripture interprets itself *(Scriptura scripturae interpres)*, but that this implies that Scripture, precisely because it does witness to the liberating Word of God, also has the power to liberate itself. Thus there is a need to reaffirm but also to retrieve in a new way Calvin's christological "canon within the canon." But first we turn to consider what is meant by the "spectacles of the victims."

The Spectacles of the Victims

Whether or not Rostagno is correct in his scepticism about mainline Protestantism's ability to break out of its middle-class captivity, he has pinpointed a major problem for the Reformed tradition. This tradition is historically wedded to middle-class culture, even though it has always included poor people and other victims of society within its ranks. Thus, one of the most

71. Ibid., p. 71.

challenging and penetrating insights of liberation theology is precisely that the victims of society, and especially the poor, are able to discern the meaning of Scripture in a way in which those of us who are not poor cannot.

Why is this so, especially if we affirm, as we surely must, that material poverty is generally a curse and not a blessing, and that being poor does not automatically bring insight into the meaning of Scripture? It is because in being on the margins of the dominant society, yet inescapably related to its structures, the poor and other social victims can see how the dynamics of society operate contrary to God's purposes of liberating grace, justice, and fullness of life. "The poor," Míguez Bonino writes, "are not morally or spiritually superior to others, but they do see reality from a different angle or location—and therefore differently."[72] This makes it possible for them to discern the liberating Word directly, without it being filtered through the various protective devices such as spiritualizing, which the rest of us use to make the Word more acceptable to our situation.

From a Reformed perspective, the idea that the poor have a special insight into the meaning of Scripture should come as no surprise if we are familiar with Calvin's biblical expositions. The Reformer frequently maintained that God prefers to reveal himself to the poor, the simple, and the humble because they more readily recognize their need of God. In asserting this, Calvin was saying no more than what Jesus himself declared in the Beatitudes. God reveals himself only to those who recognize their need of God, the "poor in spirit" as well as the materially poor (Matt. 5:3; Luke 6:20ff.). If this is true, if God is discerned by those who know their need of God, it follows that the Word of liberating grace and life in Scripture would best be understood by those who are in a position to hear it. Thus the testimony of Scripture corroborates what we are also able to learn from considering the social location of the poor. Scripture itself has ample evidence that the victims perceive most clearly God's liberating and living Word.

72. José Míguez Bonino, *Toward a Christian Political Ethics* (Philadelphia: Fortress, 1983), p. 43.

Several qualifications need to be made at this point. The first is the recognition that while we learn from the Scriptures themselves that the poor are victims in a special sense, and that the way in which we relate to the poor is indicative of our understanding of the gospel, not all the victims of society are necessarily poor. It is precisely for this reason that we have spoken of the spectacles of the victims and not just of the poor. Women, blacks, ethnic minorities, and homosexuals are all victims of society even though they may not be poor, and each may discern in Scripture the liberating Word somehow hidden from others. Many Protestant refugees, we need to be reminded, though their outlook was middle-class, were in fact poor.[73] Calvin himself was a refugee and his "own experience of exile contributed to his understanding of the Gospel as a haven for the dispossessed, a refuge for those quite literally alienated."[74] It is not surprising then that Reformed theology and liberation theology often "express concern for the victims in essentially the same manner,"[75] though they do not always agree on the definition of who are the victims.

The second qualification is the recognition that the liberating Word speaks to all human need, including the desperate need for the conversion of those who oppress others, those who abuse power, and those whose wealth prevents them from "entering the kingdom of God." Jesus made this abundantly clear in his own preaching and teaching, Calvin reinforced it in his, and it has been powerfully stated in our own time in *The Road to Damascus* document, which is essentially a call to conversion to those with power and wealth. Those who are powerful, rich, and privileged need to heed the cry for life of the victims in society in order to discern the liberating Word that can transform their own lives. God wishes all people to be saved, Calvin reminds us, but "shepherds are the first to be

73. See Ronald H. Stone, "The Reformed Ethics of John Calvin," in *Reformed Faith and Economics*, ed. Robert L. Stivers (New York: University Press of America, 1989), p. 36.
74. Bouwsma, *John Calvin*, p. 17.
75. Wolterstorff, *Until Justice and Peace Embrace*, p. 65.

called to Christ; then afterwards come the philosophers; uneducated and despised fishermen hold the most honourable place, but, later, kings and their advisers, senators and orators are received into their school."[76]

The third qualification is that the Bible is only truly understood within a community of faith, even though the living Word does speak directly to individual people and their needs. As Calvin saw so clearly, hearing the living Word in Scripture is a communal, ecclesial experience, and not one confined only to the present. By reflecting on the historic creeds and confessions of the church, on tradition understood as the interpretation of the Scriptures in different historical epochs, the contemporary community of faith discovers rich resources for discerning the liberating Word today. It is as the church gathers around the Word in worship and reads, proclaims, and listens to it in faith and openness to the Spirit that it is enabled to hear, understand, and obey. Thus, when we speak of the ability of the poor or other victims to hear God's Word we imply that they do so as they share a common life together as communities of faith.

The poor in Latin America invariably have been nurtured within the Catholic church, and much of the writing about the ability of the poor to understand the good news of the kingdom within Scripture assumes their involvement in some form of community where the Bible is read and discussed. In like manner, the vast majority of the poor in South Africa are Christians, so when we speak about their ability to understand Scripture we are assuming that they do so not only from the vantage point of their social location but also from the perspective of their faith. Neither the poor nor other social victims automatically understand the Scriptures simply because of their social location or experience. Like anyone else they need both the opportunity to listen to the Scriptures and the faith that precedes understanding. Indeed, we see here another impor-

76. Calvin, *The First Epistle of Paul to the Corinthians*, trans. John W. Fraser, Calvin's New Testament Commentaries, vol. 9 (Grand Rapids: Eerdmans, 1960), p. 44.

tant parallel between the Reformation of the church in the sixteenth century and the liberation of the church in twentieth-century Latin America.[77] The Bible must be accessible to the people in a way that enables them to discover its meaning.

The fourth qualification is that although the God of the prophetic tradition in the Bible takes sides with the oppressed and speaks to their needs, the same tradition indicates that God can also speak against the oppressed. When the Hebrew slaves left Egypt they continually hankered after the "fleshpots" they had left behind. In response, Moses constantly reprimanded them and called them to trust in God and struggle through the wilderness to the promised land.[78] In other words, even though the victims may perceive the message of Scripture more clearly, their "epistemological privilege" is not one of determining or controlling what the Word declares. Gutiérrez puts it clearly when he writes:

> Not only is it legitimate in principle to read the Bible from the standpoint of our deepest and most pressing concerns; this has also in fact been the practice of the Christian community throughout history. But this principle and this fact must not make us forget something I have often said because I am deeply convinced of it: although it is true that we read the Bible, it is also true that the Bible reads us and speaks to us.[79]

Nothing could be more Reformed than this acknowledgment: we stand under the Word, the Word is not ours to control. Gutiérrez's classic description of liberation theology as "critical reflection on Christian praxis in the light of the Word"[80] clearly indicates the normative role Scripture plays in evaluating and

---

77. See Carlos Meester, "The Use of the Bible in Christian Communities of the Common People," in Gottwald, *The Bible and Liberation*, pp. 119ff.

78. Pablo Richard, "Biblical Theology of Confrontation," in Richard et al., *The Idols of Death and the God of Life* (New York: Orbis, 1983), p. 8.

79. Gutiérrez, *On Job* (New York: Orbis, 1987), p. xvii.

80. Gutiérrez, *A Theology of Liberation*, pp. 5-6.

determining faith and action. For this reason, whatever its limitations, the textual and grammatical studies of Scripture on which both Calvin and liberation biblical scholars insist remain indispensable interpretative tools. For even if such historical-critical methods are not without their problems, and even if we need other, additional hermeneutical resources to get at the meaning of the Bible for today, they put a brake on subjectivity running away with itself and they force us to seek clarity and take the text seriously as it stands.

The Liberating Word as Canon

Sola Scriptura does not only mean that the Bible alone is our authority. It also means that the Bible ultimately supplies us with the clue to its own interpretation. At the time of the Reformation, the interpretative key for understanding Scripture or discerning the liberating Word within it was "justification by faith," especially for Luther. This remains important for us as it was for Calvin, for it is at the heart of the gospel message that nourishes ferment. It is, in fact, the core of evangelical faith. But Calvin himself recognized that it is inadequate in providing a "canon within the canon." The main reason for this inadequacy is that it is primarily personal, whatever its social implications may be, reflecting the existential concerns of the German Reformer rather than the message of what Ganoczy called the "complete gospel." Hence, for Calvin and the Reformed tradition the "canon within the canon" became the reign of God in Jesus Christ, and this meant that both the evangelical and the prophetic were crucial for understanding Scripture. In Christ, whom Calvin acknowledged as prophet, priest, and king, the Word of liberating grace and that of prophetic justice were united.

Like Luther before him, however, Barth clearly saw that we cannot simply equate Scripture and the Word of God, that Scripture bears witness to the Word, and that therefore in a profound sense Scripture not only interprets itself but also liberates itself. Not all Scripture is liberating, but Scripture does contain within itself the liberating good news of God revealed in Jesus Christ. That was the powerful message of the Barmen Declaration, which many within the Reformed tradition today would want to claim as a contemporary confession of faith:

> Jesus Christ, as he is attested for us in Holy Scripture, is the one Word of God which we have to hear and which we have to trust and obey in life and in death.[81]

Ultimately for the Reformed tradition, the liberating Word is none other than Jesus Christ. He is the liberating "canon within the canon," the one to whom the Scriptures bear witness, but also the one in and through whom we read the Scriptures. What liberation theology enables Reformed theology to discern is that this christological "canon within the canon" must be understood in relation to the prophetic and liberating trajectory that runs through Scripture and that provides within Scripture its own internal ideological critique.[82] But this prophetic trajectory cannot be separated from the evangelical trajectory of God's gracious redemptive love and mercy, for both belong together and both find their coherence and fulfillment in Jesus Christ. Jesus Christ is the victim, the poor man of Galilee, the despised and rejected man of sorrows crucified by Judaea and Rome, and, as such, he is the Lord of the Scriptures, the gracious, liberating Word through whom we have life and through whom we interpret and evaluate Scripture itself.

The focus of this evangelical and prophetic liberating tradition is what Calvin called the reign of God in Christ, or what is referred to in the Gospels as the kingdom of God. Thus the Reformed tradition, starting with Calvin, has likewise often regarded the reign of God in Jesus Christ as the key that unlocks

81. The Barmen Declaration, Article One. The first English translation of the Barmen Declaration is to be found in Arthur C. Cochrane, *The Church's Confession Under Hitler* (Philadelphia: Westminster, 1962), pp. 238-42.

82. Walter Brueggemann, "Trajectories in Old Testament Literature and the Sociology of Ancient Israel," in Gottwald, *The Bible and Liberation*, pp. 307-8.

the biblical message. This relates well to the twentieth-century rediscovery of the centrality of the kingdom of God as the hermeneutical key for understanding not only Jesus himself but also Scripture as a whole. Moreover, it is precisely the message of the kingdom of God proclaimed and embodied in Jesus that provides the crucial hermeneutical link with liberation theology, opening up possibilities for a common approach to the biblical message.[83] In other words, when we speak of Jesus Christ as the "liberating canon" we are not simply speaking of Jesus of Nazareth, or Jesus the crucified Messiah, but of Jesus the Christ in relation to the universal redemptive and liberating purposes of God in history. Therefore not only is the kingdom of God to be understood in terms of Jesus, but Jesus is to be understood in terms of the kingdom, a kingdom yet to come in its fullness.

Having said this, we have to recognize that within the Reformed tradition the message of the kingdom of God has too often been spiritualized and de-historicized. Largely because of the Platonic residue in his own theology, Calvin himself tended to understand the kingdom of God in this way, despite the fact that he so strongly affirmed the reign of Christ over all reality. In fact, here we see another ambiguity or tension in his theology—between a spiritualized eschatology and an affirmation of the Lordship of Christ over all of history here and now. Hence the suspicion has cropped up that Calvin's Christology has a docetic tendency.[84]

Insofar as Reformed theology has adopted a de-historicized eschatology, it has denied the implications of its primary commitment to the Incarnation of the Word and the reign of God over all reality for our present earthly historical existence and obedience. Liberation theology challenges Reformed theology by calling it back to its biblical roots and insisting that

83. See Jon Sobrino, *Spirituality of Liberation* (New York: Orbis, 1988), pp. 118-19.

84. See the discussion in Jürgen Moltmann, *The Crucified God* (London: SCM, 1974), pp. 259-60.

the reign of God has to do with God's liberation and justice here and now in anticipation of what is to come. While the kingdom of God always remains God's gift that comes to us from beyond ourselves, it is always a gift making a demand upon our obedience in relation to life in the world. Significantly, it was Jürgen Moltmann, a Reformed theologian, who helped both liberation and Reformed theology to rediscover the sociopolitical and historical significance of our hope in the coming of the reign of God, and who grounded that in the evangelical message of the cross.[85] The liberating Word of justification and the liberating Word of justice are thus brought together in Jesus Christ in such a way that while they are not confused, neither are they separated.

Throughout this chapter we have made reference to the various confessions of faith that have marked the historical route taken by the Reformed tradition since the Reformation. These confessions have, in fact, indicated the place reached by the tradition, giving some indication of how the tradition understood itself and the biblical message in different epochs and contexts. They also indicate what Calvin stressed, namely, that the interpretation of Scriptures and the discernment of God's Word for each situation takes place within the community of faith. Hermeneutics, as we have already stressed, is not simply an individualistic or academic enterprise. It is central to the life of the church; it has to do with the church understanding and confessing its faith in Jesus Christ in relation to the discernment of changing reality.

Reformed confessions in recent years indicate a notable shift in theology within the Reformed family of churches brought about by doing theology in this way in relation to the kingdom of God understood in historically transformative terms. One commentator (with reference to the Barmen Declaration, the Nederlandse Hervormde Kerk's *Fundamenten en Perspectiven,* the United States Presbyterian Confession of 1967, the

85. Jürgen Moltmann, *A Theology of Hope* (London: SCM, 1967); *The Crucified God*, pp. 317-18.

New Confession of the Presbyterian Church in Korea, the Reformed Church in America's Song of Hope, the Belhar Confession, and the Christian Reformed Church's Our World Belongs to God) has noted that political issues are now seen from the eschatological perspective of the kingdom of God rather than in terms of providence and predestination.[86] This is why, he argues, the Dutch Reformed Church's document, *Church and Society*, did not find wide acceptance within the Reformed community. It reflects a static, traditional position on order, rather than one more faithfully reflecting biblical teaching on God's rule of justice. Thus we find, in these more recent confessions, that the primary consideration is not support for those in authority, but concern and commitment to the poor and the oppressed.

> The crucial shift in tone and theology in the new confessional statements is such that the priority for stability and patience has been replaced by the urgency of the coming of the kingdom of God. The poor must not be made to wait and the captives must no longer be kept in prison. Prayer is a call for change as well as an act of simple trust.[87]

This change from the old Reformed confessions to the new reflects both a theological as well as a sociological shift within the Reformed community. The theological shift is not so much a movement away from traditional Reformed doctrines but a reworking of those doctrines on a new theological or, better, eschatological foundation. The sociological shift is that the Reformed community, with some exceptions, is no longer comprised only of those who, having achieved power, wish to maintain it, or those who, while affluent and privileged, have

86. Eugene P. Heideman, "Old Confessions and New Testimony," *Reformed Journal* 38 (August 1988): 7ff. See also *Reformed Witness Today: A Collection of Confessions and Statements of Faith Issued by Reformed Churches*, ed. Lukas Vischer (Bern: Evangelische Arbeitsstelle Oekumene Schweiz, 1982).

87. Heideman, "Old Confessions and New Testimony," p. 10.

become more aware of and sensitive to the needs and the just cause of those oppressed; it now includes many who are black, poor, and oppressed. But whatever the confessional shift within the Reformed tradition, the real crunch comes when we accept Jesus' dictum—a dictum strongly affirmed by Calvin and stressed by liberation theology—that it is not the hearers but the doers who really discern the will of God.

The Hermeneutics of Faith, Hope, and Love

The Scots Confession of 1560 summarizes its hermeneutical principles by making three points that should guide any interpretation of Scripture. "We dare not receive or admit any interpretation which is contrary to any principal point of our faith, or to any other plain text of Scripture, or to the rule of love."[88] This is an admirable place to end our discussion. First, as we have seen, there is a canon within the canon (the principal points of faith), which, for us, is Jesus Christ the Incarnate liberating Word; second, Scripture interprets itself, enabling us to see that it is the victims of society who best discern the good news of the kingdom; but finally, the "rule of love," or, for the Heidelberg Catechism, "the rule of faith and love,"[89] is the crux, for it is in doing what God calls us to do through the Word that we really begin to understand it.

In bringing this chapter to a close we want to suggest that another way of expressing this final key to the interpretation of the Bible—one consonant with the Reformed tradition and yet at the same time essentially Catholic—is "faith active in hope and love" (cf. Gal. 5:6; 1 Cor. 13). Indeed, in this formula we bring together not only the conviction that "faith precedes understanding," but also Calvin's insistence that "faith makes love possible,"[90] and the conviction that faith is both christo-

88. The Scots Confession, chap. 18.
89. The Heidelberg Catechism, chap. 2.
90. Calvin, *The First Epistle of Paul to the Corinthians*, p. 283.

logical and eschatological. Faith reaches out and perseveres in hope towards the coming of God's kingdom as revealed in Jesus Christ, and therefore it expresses itself in the evangelical and prophetic struggle for human and social transformation. This struggle in turn is guided and maintained by love or *agape*, a suffering love that includes a commitment to justice as an integral element.[91]

We have already noted that both Calvin and many liberation theologians are biblical rather than speculative or philosophical theologians. Gutiérrez's stress that theology is critical reflection on praxis "in the light of the Word" is highly significant in its clear indication that the Word is not only normative, but that the object of its critical scrutiny is action informed by faith. This was precisely what Calvin himself attempted in his own work as a Reformer. His theology was highly critical of the praxis of the church of his day. He placed, as we have seen, "the tyranny of tradition" under the spotlight of the Word.

The slogan "orthopraxis not orthodoxy," usually but incorrectly attributed to liberation theology as a whole, is based on a false unbiblical dichotomy, for the hermeneutical struggle is certainly not between affirming the evangelical truth and prophetic action. Right belief and right action need and complement each other.[92] The real issue is not whether one has priority over the other, for they are inseparable. Nonetheless, liberation theology reminds us that we cannot know the truth of the Scriptures by somehow objectively standing outside and critically examining them in search of truth. Truth is inseparable from faithful love. We only know the truth as we become engaged in what the living and liberating Word requires of us. We know who Jesus is when we follow him. Ultimately, both Catholic liberation and Reformed theology find their focus in

91. On the interrelatedness of love and justice in Calvin's own thought, see his discussion on the Sixth Commandment in *John Calvin's Sermons on the Ten Commandments* (Grand Rapids: Baker Book House, 1980), pp. 162-63.
92. See Gutiérrez, *A Theology of Liberation*, p. xxxiv.

this spirituality of evangelical discipleship which, as we shall later assert, is inseparable from the struggle for justice and liberation.

Thus, a further important point of correspondence between Calvin and liberation theologians underlies this emphasis on faith in action. Both are practical and pastoral theologians—that is, their work as interpreters of the Bible not only takes place within the context of the community of faith, but it is engaged in with the expressed purpose of awakening faith, stirring hope, and enabling love. For this very reason they engage in doing theology, they reflect on praxis in the light of the Word. The motivation for their careful biblical exegesis and exposition is to enable the people of God to know and do the will of God. This does not mean that action is placed above truth, nor is it a rejection of theology as rational discourse. It is an affirmation that from a biblical perspective truth is always incarnate truth, truth embodied in action; by the same token, faith is always faith working itself out in love, and love is always engaged in the struggle for justice and peace in anticipation of God's kingdom.

Without in any way denying the important role of critical scholarship in determining the meaning of the biblical text, we always have to affirm—with both the Bible and liberation theology—that "knowing the truth" requires "doing it." Calvin was equally adamant. To know the truth of the Word was to do it. "If we are ready to obey God He will never fail to illuminate us by the light of His Spirit" (Calvin's comment on John 7:17).[93] And in his *Institutes* he writes: "Not only faith perfect and in every way complete, but all right knowledge of God is born of obedience."[94] For Calvin as for Augustine before him and Gutiérrez after him, what the Scots Confession calls "the rule of love" is the ultimate principle of biblical interpretation because it is the ultimate expression of our faith response to God's liberating grace. And, insofar as doing jus-

93. Calvin, *The Gospel according to St. John, 1-10,* p. 186.
94. Calvin, *Institutes,* 1.6.2.

tice is the way in which love engages social need and oppression, love working itself out in the struggle for justice becomes the crucial key to discerning God's liberating Word for the world today.

3. The Glory and Image of God

In his portrait of South African society, *Move Your Shadow*, the New York journalist Joseph Lelyveld reports a conversation between Steve Biko, the black consciousness leader in the seventies, and his close confidant and fellow worker, Malusi Mpumlwana, now an Anglican priest within the Order of Ethiopia. Mpumlwana had just been released from detention, and it was he who eventually related the account told to Lelyveld in these words:

> Only two brief weeks intervened between his release from detention in July 1977 and Steve Biko's last arrest. There was time for only one long and speculative conversation. Malusi tried to impart his sense of urgency about the need to consider the "role of God in this situation." Biko, a believer, was troubled by the theological problem of evil. Africa knew God, he felt, but God somehow overlooked Africa's suffering. The conversation reached no conclusion, and then Biko left on the trip from which he never returned. It would be hard to exaggerate this irony: two close friends—one who had just been tortured, the other about to be tortured to death on behalf of what is supposed to be Christian civilization in South Africa—and

92

in the little time left to them, they talk about the "role of God in this situation."[1]

If it were not for the fact that this conversation about God took place between two deeply committed black social activists, such God-talk could readily be dismissed as escapist piety. In other contexts it often is. But the God-talk in which Mpuml-wana and Biko engaged was not flight from reality. It was an urgent and intense attempt to discern meaning amid suffering, to understand both themselves and the ways of God in the affairs of humankind, to penetrate the mystery that lies at the heart of reality, and to determine their own responsibility in the struggle for social justice, liberation, and human dignity. The question raised about the "role of God in this situation," and therefore the character and will of God, remains *the* theological question, and the way in which we answer it has far-reaching ramifications for the life of the church and its involvement in society.

The "Battle of the Gods"

The question of God is fundamental to human existence, for it asks about that to which we give our ultimate loyalty. It is, therefore, not only a question about God, but also a question about ourselves. And not just ourselves understood as individuals, but ourselves in relation to others, to society, and to the environment as a whole. From the first edition of his *Institutes* in 1536 until the last edition thirty-three years later, Calvin begins by saying that "nearly the whole of sacred doctrine" (1536) or "nearly all the wisdom we possess" (1559) "consists of two parts: the knowledge of God and of ourselves."[2] There

1. Joseph Lelyveld, *Move Your Shadow: South Africa Black and White* (Johannesburg: Jonathan Ball, 1986), p. 297.
2. Calvin, *Institutes of the Christian Religion, 1536 Edition*, rev. ed.,

is good reason to regard this fundamental insight as one of the organizing principles of Calvin's theology, and therefore of considerable significance for Reformed theology as a whole. Without knowledge of ourselves we cannot know God; without knowledge of God we cannot know ourselves. "Knowledge of ourselves," Calvin writes, "not only arouses us to seek God, but also, as it were, leads us by the hand to find him."[3]

The word "god" is a symbol for what we worship, for what is ultimately important in our lives. What separates people from one another in this regard is not that some people believe in a "god" and others do not. What separates people is their understanding of who their "god" is, how their "god" relates to them, what moral values derive from their "god," and what all this means for them in their daily lives as individuals and as societies.

This remains true despite the radical critique of all theologies that has occurred since the Enlightenment. Paradoxically, the rise of secularism has not meant the demise of religion but the resurgence of human religiosity in a vast array of different and competing forms. Insofar as secular ideologies have replaced traditional religions they have exhibited the same claims of total allegiance and obedience, and have sought to provide explanatory worldviews that embrace the whole of reality. It is not surprising that in the process they have failed to meet human needs and expectations in a holistic and ultimately satisfying way, and that in recent years, as in past centuries, people have changed their ideological "gods" either for those trusted by their ancestors or for others less totalitarian in their claims and promises.

Some people, in fact, change their "gods" as their social and material circumstances change. Like Israel in the days of the eighth-century prophets, they might turn from the worship of Yahweh, who liberated them from slavery and led them

---

trans. Ford Lewis Battles (Grand Rapids: Eerdmans, 1986), p. 15; *Institutes* (1559 edition), 1.1.1.

3. *Institutes,* 1.1.1.

through the wilderness, to worship the Baalim and fertility gods of Canaan. The latter were apparently more appropriate for a settled, agricultural, and prosperous lifestyle. In a similar way Calvinism in Europe and North America changed in the eighteenth century from being a creed of social transformation to one of social preservation and control. This did not mean that its formal concept of God changed—it still adhered to traditional dogma in that regard. But "in actual fact God had become the safe guarantor of a specific time and place."[4] Similar changes have taken place in other Christian traditions as their adherents have moved up the social and class scale. By the same token, as God's perceived role in the situation changes, so those who believe in God understand their own role in different ways.

Insights such as these—which derive in large measure from social scientific research—were not readily available to Calvin, though his knowledge of human nature was such that he probably had a few good hunches that this was so. Thus Calvin remarks that it is idle speculation simply to ask, "What is God?" The important question is, "What is his nature?"[5] Indeed, we cannot know who God is in himself, but only who God is in his relationship to us and the world, and how we in turn relate to God. It is when we begin to explore this relationship that we discover that racism, injustice, or oppression, for example, are threats not only to humanity but also to the Christian understanding of God.

We are acutely aware today that we cannot talk about God any longer as if there had been no Jewish Holocaust or Hiroshima. We are also becoming more aware that we cannot talk about God seriously without relating our God-talk to human suffering, oppression, racism, sexism, and poverty. Who God is cannot be separated from what we know of ourselves and our world. Moreover, people who suffer, people who are poor and oppressed, blacks, and women have a different perception of God

4. Hans Mol, *Meaning and Place: An Introduction to the Social Scientific Study of Religion* (New York: Pilgrim Press, n.d.), p. 23.
5. *Institutes*, 1.2.2.

and God's role in their situation than those who are prosperous and powerful, white and male, even though they may call God by the same name. This is also why liberation theologians have found it necessary to speak of the God of the oppressed, or to coin the phrase "God is black," or to demand inclusive language for God-talk. All language for God is metaphorical, but metaphors convey what we know of ourselves. There is a world of difference between God as perceived by Job in his anguish and the orthodox belief of his companions, between the God of "state theology" and the God of "prophetic theology." We can legitimately ask, in fact, whether we are talking about the same God. Indeed, is not the hermeneutical struggle to which we referred in the last chapter really another way of describing a contemporary form of the "battle of the gods" in which Elijah the prophet was engaged on Mount Carmel?

For such reasons Barth wrote "that we cannot be content to make the word 'God' our final, or perhaps even our basic term."[6] We have to give content to the word "God"; we have to know what the name signifies, and what it means for us today. To put the task of theology in other terms, it is that of clarifying not only who God is in relation to us, but who God is not. This was fully understood by the early Greek church fathers for whom God could only be known through the stripping away of illusions, a task which remains essential for theology and which, in our time, has been so powerfully reinforced by the great "hermeneutists of suspicion," Ludwig Feuerbach, Friedrich Nietzsche, Karl Marx, and Sigmund Freud. In pursuing such a task we are also engaged in seeking to understand what is true humanity and what is not. For the two are inextricably bound together. Thus, theology is as much concerned to destroy idols or false gods and discern the true God as it is to combat dehumanization and enable the flourishing of life in all its fullness. The tasks are inseparable. In fact, we might say that the fundamental struggle facing Christian theology today is not between faith in God and secular atheism; it is the

6. Karl Barth, *Church Dogmatics*, III/4, p. 479.

struggle to distinguish between faith in the God who gives life and trust in those gods or idols which bring death. In this struggle genuine atheism, or what has been called "protest atheism,"[7] while inadequate in providing the world with meaning and hope, is itself an iconoclastic protest against false images of God and as such "is more true than are the many forms of idolatry which parade under Christian labels."[8]

It is our contention that Calvin and Reformed theology, on the one hand, and liberation theology, on the other, are allies in this "battle of the gods."[9] They find each other as allies not only in their common opposition to idolatry, but in their common affirmation that in Jesus Christ God affirms and restores our humanity and gives us life. For while the protest of atheism can strip away false images, and while its revolutionary forces may sometimes bring about political or psychological emancipation, it is unable to point us to the true image of God revealed in Jesus Christ the Mediator between God, ourselves, and nature. This means that it is powerless to liberate humanity fully from its bondage and give it life in its fullness, the restoration of God's image in ourselves and the world. To understand that restoration—or what St. Irenaeus, following Paul, called the "recapitulation" of all things in Christ[10]—we need to appreciate more fully the human predicament, and especially the enslavement of idolatry that keeps humankind in bondage.

A Perpetual Factory of Idols

Louis Bouyer, whose *The Spirit and Forms of Protestantism* was indicative of a more positive Catholic reassessment of the Prot-

---

7. See Jürgen Moltmann, *The Crucified God* (London: SCM, 1974), pp. 219-20.

8. Kenneth Leech, *Experiencing God: Theology as Spirituality* (San Francisco: Harper & Row, 1985), p. 194.

9. See Pablo Richard et al., *The Idols of Death and the God of Life* (New York: Orbis, 1983).

10. Irenaeus, *Adversus Haereses*, 5.20.2–21.2.

estant tradition a decade before Vatican II, mentions that one of the first things that strikes the reader of Calvin's *Institutes* is "Calvin's conviction that the fundamental error to be countered in medieval religion is idolatry."[11] The reason for this tragic error, Calvin rightly perceived, was a false understanding of God and what it means to be human. For the essence of idolatry traditionally understood is the denial of the transcendence or "otherness" of God and the concomitant false exaltation of the creature and the created order. This, in turn, means human bondage to the tyranny of human power acting as though it is divine.

Idolatry reveals the essence of sin—the desire to be like God, falsely understood, rather than to trust and love God truly understood. It expresses the human desire to control and manipulate the world, to dominate the destinies of others, to determine what is right and wrong in terms of self-interest and the will-to-power. Idolatry is the worship of the creature and created things rather than the worship of the Creator. Idolatry lies at the heart of the myth of the Fall. It separates God and humanity, defaces the image of God in men and women, and leads to the dehumanization of others and the destruction of the environment. Idolatry reveals the solidarity of human sinfulness, the hubris which leads groups, races, and nations to build their Towers of Babel and establish supremacy over the earth. Idolatry is fundamentally opposed to the true knowledge of God and ourselves; it prevents us from facing ourselves and reality. Indeed, from the perspective of liberation theology "the experience of idolatry, especially in situations of oppression, appears as a great historical obstacle to the revelation of God and faith in him."[12]

Humankind, for Calvin as well as liberation theology, finds its true humanity and freedom in the worship of God,

11. Louis Bouyer, *The Spirit and Forms of Protestantism* (London: Collins, 1963), p. 82. The original French edition was published in 1954.
12. Pablo Richard, "Biblical Theology of Confrontation with Idols," in *The Idols of Death and the God of Life*, p. 24.

correctly understood, and destroys itself in the worship of false gods. In the manner of more contemporary critics of religion, according to André Biéler, "the Reformers wanted to free mankind from all its servitudes and particularly from its religious mystifications."[13] Hence, it is of crucial importance today that in our attempt to develop a liberating Reformed theology we learn how to discriminate "between appropriate and inappropriate, 'alienating' and 'non-alienating,' objectifications of the mystery of the divine."[14]

Much of Calvin's discussion of idolatry focuses on the use of images in worship. In this respect Calvin was an uncompromising iconoclast,[15] though it must be noted that the destruction of religious works of art, often undertaken in the name of Calvinism, was deplored by Calvin himself.[16] His main argument against idolatry did not stem from a dislike of art; on the contrary, he acknowledged that "sculpture and painting are gifts of God."[17] Instead, he rejected idolatry—that is, the worship of images—on the grounds that it is expressly forbidden in Scripture and the early tradition of the church. But in doing so he continually reflects on the underlying reason for both idolatry and its rejection. "Man's nature," he remarks, "is a perpetual factory of idols." That is, human beings insist on "fashioning gods according to their pleasure."[18] An idol is something conceived inwardly; it has its origin in the mind and soul before it finds concrete expression. But once it is fashioned, then it is admired "as if something of divinity inhered there." This leads Calvin to what

13. André Biéler, *The Social Humanism of Calvin* (Richmond: John Knox Press, 1964), p. 69.

14. Nicholas Lash, *A Matter of Hope* (Notre Dame, Ind.: Notre Dame University Press, 1982), p. 181.

15. See Calvin, *Institutes*, 1.11; Calvin, "The Necessity of Reforming the Church," in *Calvin: Theological Treatises*, ed. J. K. S. Reid (Philadelphia: Westminster, 1984), pp. 184-85.

16. See *International Calvinism 1541-1715*, ed. Menna Prestwich (Oxford: Clarendon Press, 1985), p. 10.

17. *Institutes*, 1.11.12.

18. *Institutes*, 1.11.8.

might be regarded as his definition of the subject: "It is always idolatry when divine honours are bestowed upon an idol, under whatever pretext this is done."[19]

The biblical proscription of idols is thus the prescription that "nothing belonging to God's divinity is to be transferred to another."[20] This would imply that even, or especially, the metaphors or symbols we use to describe God must not become absolute. To fix God to a definite form, to an image we have created, is idolatry. This would apply equally to racist and sexist metaphors. Thus, as Elisabeth Schüssler Fiorenza insists, "Classical prophetic theology, often in abusive language, polemicized against the pagan idols and thus rejected goddess worship, but it did not do so in defence of a male God and a patriarchal idol." In fact, she continues further on, it "repudiated masculinity and femininity as ultimate, absolute principles."[21]

Calvin himself used many different metaphors to describe God, recognizing that God reveals himself to us in such metaphors because he accommodates himself to our capacity to grasp who he is.[22] Ford Lewis Battles refers to four in particular: father, teacher, physician, and judge.[23] In Calvin's day, not only the first but the last three as well were all masculine images. But it should also be kept in mind that Calvin does not hesitate to use specifically maternal images for God as well.[24] In a very revealing comparison of the idols of Babylon and the God of Israel in his commentary on Isaiah 46, Calvin not only says that

19. *Institutes*, 1.11.9.

20. *Institutes*, 1.12.1.

21. Fiorenza, *In Memory of Her* (New York: Crossroad, 1983), p. 133.

22. See Jane Dempsey Douglass, "Calvin's Use of Metaphorical Language for God: God as Enemy and God as Mother," in *Archiv für Reformationsgeschichte* (Gütersloh: Verlagshaus Gerd Mohn, 1986), pp. 126ff.

23. Ford Lewis Battles, "God Was Accommodating Himself to Human Capacity," *Interpretation* 31 (January 1977): 20.

24. See Jane Dempsey Douglass, "Calvin's Use of Metaphysical Language for God," and "Calvin's Teaching: What Still Remains Pertinent?" *Ecumenical Review* 39 (January 1987): 27.

the idols are impotent, that they are an inanimate burden to their devotees, and that they are themselves captives; he also says that in contrast Yahweh is like a mother who gives birth to her children, carries her people, bears their burdens, and empowers them. Indeed, Calvin does not hesitate to say that God as mother gave the Israelites new life and hope, and that in doing so throughout their historical experience God "has always manifested himself to be both their Father and their Mother."[25] It is surely remarkable that Calvin, who is so often regarded as a male chauvinist, could speak of God the liberator and giver of life in maternal terms. In anticipation of patriarchal objections he goes on to say:

> If it be objected that God is everywhere called "a Father," (Jeremiah xxxi.9; Mal. i.6,) and that this title is more appropriate to him, I reply, that no figures of speech can describe God's extraordinary affection towards us; for it is infinite and various; so that, if all that can be said or imagined about love were brought together into one, yet it would be surpassed by the greatness of the love of God.[26]

In attacking idolatry Calvin deals at length with the use of icons in the Eastern Orthodox Churches. While he hints at the possibility of allowing them to be used, as far as he is concerned they have no "value for teaching."[27] This indicates, of course, a failure to understand the real function of icons in the Orthodox tradition,[28] and Calvin's own didactic evaluation of aids to worship. Such didacticism has adversely affected Reformed worship and spirituality ever since, often reducing it to an arid intellectualism. It needs to be liberated from this

25. Calvin, *Commentary on the Book of the Prophet Isaiah*, vol. 3, trans. William Pringle (Grand Rapids: Eerdmans, 1948), pp. 434-35.

26. Ibid., p. 436.

27. *Institutes*, 1.11.12.

28. See Leonid Ouspensky, "The Meaning and Language of Ikons," in Leonid Ouspensky and Vladimir Lossky, *The Meaning of Ikons* (Crestwood, N.Y.: St. Vladimir's Seminary Press, 1989), pp. 23ff.

as much as from anything else, not least in contexts that are traditionally rich in symbol, where the cry for life is expressed in symbols of pain, and liberation is celebrated in symbols of joy. The alternative to the misuse of visible symbols is neither to reject them nor to consider them an end in themselves, but to use them properly as a means to worship.

Calvin's real attack on idolatry was more fundamentally aimed at the doctrine of transubstantiation associated with the Roman Mass.[29] Indeed, in an early writing Calvin goes so far as to liken participation in the Mass to fornication with idols![30] This was strong language, and Catholics might understandably react with an indignation as strong as Calvin's. But we need to get behind Calvin's acerbic statement in order to discover the real issue that concerned him and others. A Catholic Benedictine theologian, Kilian McDonnell, helps us to do so. "The judgment Calvin spoke over Roman Catholicism," he writes, "was a judgment concerning idolatry."[31] Rome

> was idolatrous not only in her use of statues, but in the proud assertion that she stood over against God, not as against an enemy, but as the self-divinized structure which bore God an adequate and proper witness. The highest expression of this presumption—or perhaps the lowest—was transubstantiation.[32]

Why, we may ask? Because, as McDonnell goes on to explain, this "objectified the divine person . . . through the localizing of the transcendent." "Men cling to the bread," Calvin writes, "as if to God, and worship it as God."[33] The church, in other words, claimed the power to bring God down to humanity, in fact, to control the process through the power of her priesthood. This

29. See Ganoczy, *The Young Calvin* (Philadelphia: Westminster Press, 1987), pp. 199-200.

30. Ibid., p. 201.

31. Kilian McDonnell, *John Calvin, the Church and the Eucharist* (Princeton: Princeton University Press, 1967), p. 160.

32. Ibid., p. 123.

33. Calvin, "The Necessity of Reforming the Church," p. 205.

was the focus of Calvin's iconoclasm. He did not go around overturning images, like some of his followers; "he looked for a more effective way of undermining the system that supported their existence."[34]

However we may evaluate Calvin's attack upon icons, statues, or transubstantiation today, his analysis of idolatry and his opposition to its root cause remain of fundamental importance, because, as Calvin perceived so clearly, the debate about idolatry cannot be confined within these obvious parameters. One of the dangers of the Reformed tradition is the illusion that having rid itself of statues, icons, and the doctrine of transubstantiation, it is beyond idolatry! Thus, in his commentary on the letter to the Romans (2:22), Calvin warns those who have got rid of external idols not to flatter themselves unless they have also sought "in the meantime to expel and eradicate the impiety which lies deep within" their hearts.[35] For if idolatry is something upon which we bestow divine honors, or, in Juan Luis Segundo's words, the "absolutization of what is false,"[36] then it applies to whatever we give our ultimate allegiance and which in turn shapes our values and lifestyle. Idolatry can therefore take on many different forms, as is already evident within Scripture itself.[37] Moreover, idols are never neutral; they are inevitably co-opted to legitimate the immoralities of their worshippers, and especially those that pertain to their material interests.

34. Carlos M. N. Eire, *War against the Idols: The Reformation of Worship from Erasmus to Calvin* (Cambridge: Cambridge University Press, 1986), p. 233. See also pp. 266-67.

35. Calvin, *The Epistles of Paul to the Romans and Thessalonians*, trans. R. Mackenzie, Calvin's New Testament Commentaries, vol. 8 (Grand Rapids: Eerdmans, 1961), p. 53.

36. Juan Luis Segundo, *Jesus of Nazareth, Yesterday and Today*, vol. 4: *The Christ of the Ignatian Exercises* (New York: Orbis, 1987), p. 39.

37. Richard, "Biblical Theology," p. 5.

The Idols of Material Interest

It is not difficult for us to identify the idols of our own time. Those with eyes to see are fully aware of the contemporary absolutizations of race, nation, the state, ideology, religion, and culture, as well as the worship of sex, technology, and militarism. Behind them all is the most potent idol of all, Mammon. Indeed, it is important to note that greed and money become the paradigms of idolatry in the teaching of Jesus and the New Testament. Paul, in writing to the Colossians, includes "sexual immorality, impurity, lust, evil desires, and greed" in his list of idols (3:5). The same emphasis upon the idolatry of greed or covetousness is found in the letter to the Ephesians (5:5), and Calvin's comment on it is significant:

> Covetousness . . . is the worship of idols . . . not that which is so often condemned in Scripture, but another sort. All covetous men must deny God, and put wealth in His place; such is the blind madness of their wretched cupidity.[38]

Calvin then goes on to ask why it is that greed is highlighted in this way—why not the other sins of human nature? "I answer," he writes, "that this disease is widely spread, and infects the minds of many like a contagion, but it is not reckoned a disease, but rather praised in the common estimation. Paul attacks it more harshly in order to tear from our hearts the false opinion." Thus, both in the New Testament and in Calvin idolatry is lifted out of the realm of the literal and of the sanctuary, placed firmly in the arena of our life in the world, and applied preeminently to human greed. Nothing could refute the popular notion, based on a misreading of Max Weber, that Calvin was responsible for capitalism, or that he would have approved the competitive nature of contemporary

---

38. Calvin, *The Epistles of Paul to the Galatians, Ephesians, Philippians and Colossians*, trans. T. H. L. Parker, Calvin's New Testament Commentaries, vol. 11 (Grand Rapids: Eerdmans, 1965), p. 198.

society.[39] Calvin spoke about the sanctification of human labor, but not the sanctification of the accumulation of wealth at the expense of others.[40]

If with Paul and Calvin we discern human greed as of the essence of idolatry we can understand why it is that Albert Nolan regards this as the essence of apartheid, for apartheid is at one level the absolutization of race, but at another, deeper level it is another word for greed.

> The system in South Africa has a momentum of its own, a driving force that keeps it going. It is the incentive of money or profit. Money has become an object of devotion that bewitches people and casts a spell upon them. Money has become the measure of all value. Reality is then turned upside down so that things, products, commodities, and possessions have value, while people as people have no value. Money, a mere thing, is divinised, while people are treated as mere things or objects. We can do without people but we cannot do without money. . . . It is our god and the pursuit of money is our religion.[41]

But greed for land, greed for privilege and power at the expense of others, greed for the controlling access to good housing, good education, and good health care, we must assert, is not confined to the advocates and beneficiaries of apartheid. Such greed is universal.

Several characteristics of idols are noteworthy with respect to what they tell us about ourselves and, in fact, what they do to us.[42] The first is that they reflect the values and

39. See Ronald S. Wallace, *Calvin, Geneva, and the Reformation* (Edinburgh: Scottish Academic Press, 1988), pp. 94, 96 n. 41.

40. See Henry Heller, *The Conquest of Poverty* (Leiden: E. J. Brill, 1986), p. 252.

41. Albert Nolan, *God in South Africa: The Challenge of the Gospel* (Grand Rapids: Eerdmans, 1988), p. 85.

42. See also *The Road to Damascus: Kairos and Conversion* (Johannesburg: Skotaville, 1989), pp. 10-11.

interests of those who create them and, in turn, begin to shape those values. In the words of the Psalmist:

> Those who make them will be like them,
> And so will all who trust in them. (115:8)

The second is that while idols, especially those of political or material interest, may not be referred to as divine, they function as divine, and the name of God is often used to legitimate them. The third is that instead of being creative, builders of community, and sources of inspiration, they are destructive and dehumanizing—they consume us. "If we idolize wealth," writes Thomas Cullinan, "then we create poverty; if we idolize success, we create the inadequate; if we idolize power, we create powerlessness."[43] By their very nature, the worship of the one inevitably results in the other. Fourth, they are a false source of security because they cannot possibly deliver what they promise; they entice misplaced confidence, and, by the same token, they block access to the sources of true security, liberation, faith, and redemption. In the telling words of the prophet Jonah:

> Those who cling to worthless idols
> Forfeit the grace that could be theirs. (2:8)

Fifth, idols have a propensity eventually to devour their creators, often quite literally in the modern world as much as in the ancient. In other words, idolatry is not only giving the glory due to God to idols; idolatry is the ultimate symbol of human bondage, the symbol of death in contrast to liberated life. Creating false images of God results in the destruction of the true image of God in women and men. In the words of the Psalmist:

> They worshipped their idols,
> which became a snare to them.

43. Thomas Cullinan, *The Roots of Social Injustice* (Catholic Housing Aid Society, 1973), p. 4, quoted by Kenneth Leech, *Experiencing God*, p. 412.

They sacrificed their sons
and their daughters to demons. (106:36-37)

The economy of South Africa has been built on gold, and whatever positive contribution gold has made to the economy and to philanthropy it has done at tremendous human cost. However important gold may be to the well-being of the economy, not least in a post-apartheid society (the African National Congress presently speaks of the nationalization, not the closure, of the mines), and whatever changes may now be occurring in labor practice, we cannot ignore or forget the innumerable victims of mining disaster, the very low wages paid, the migratory labor system and its breakup of family life, and the illnesses that result from working long hours underground. If apartheid has been the idol of Afrikaner nationalism, then material wealth—the discovery of diamonds and gold— was the motivation that led to the expansion of British imperialism in South Africa, the Anglo-Boer War with its senseless killing, suffering, and destruction of the land. That wealth has become the basis for the structuring of modern industrialized South Africa.

Gold is not only the basis of the South African economy but also the symbol of universal wealth. In the Bible, however, it is the symbol of domination. As such it provides a pertinent modern-day equivalent to the Hebrew prophetic depiction of the manufacturing and futility of idols. And the way in which it functions in our society provides a concrete example of the characteristics of idolatry, and especially the fact that "the life of an idol itself depends on the process of labour that produces it."[44]

One can imagine an eighth-century Hebrew prophet (see Isa. 44:9-20) scathingly highlighting the irony that once the precious metal has been brought to the surface and refined, traded, and hoarded, it is returned to the depths of the earth in tightly guarded vaults to ensure our economic well-being and security.

44. Richard, "Biblical Theology," p. 14.

We know, deep down, that it is no real security for the future, no guarantee that all will be well. It is a fickle god. Yet, in the same way as, according to Calvin, the medieval church indulged in vain pomp and ceremony in its worship of idols, so we worship gold with much pomp and splendor, building enormous empires and buildings in its service, and even seeking its justification in the name of the only true God, to whom we at least pay lip service. Gold has in fact replaced God; its influence is omnipresent and its goal is omnipotence. No wonder a shudder goes through the South African economy every time the price of gold falls—it is like the dethroning of a reigning monarch.

Calvin understood human nature very well. He knew the fatal attraction of wealth and its symbols. But this did not mean that he denied the reality of money or its importance for the well-being of the community. On the contrary, Calvin was fully aware of the need for a sound economic policy, and was, as a result, intimately involved in the shaping of Genevan economic policy—not, we should hasten to add, in the direction of a laissez-faire capitalism but in terms of the responsible use of money for the well-being of the community and especially the well-being of the poor.[45] Even gold he regarded as a gift of God and therefore not to be despised but correctly used, in ways which injure neither the user nor anyone else.[46] Calvin did not exalt poverty; neither does the Bible. Indeed, Calvin regarded it as a curse, a source of temptation, and thus not decreed by God.[47] Likewise, exponents of liberation theology do not deny the need for money, for money in itself is not an idol. It becomes Mammon only when we submit to its power, when it determines our lives and shapes our societies.[48] This implies that we

45. Calvin, *The Acts of the Apostles, 1-13,* trans. John W. Fraser and W. J. G. McDonald, Calvin's New Testament Commentaries, vol. 6 (Grand Rapids: Eerdmans, 1965), p. 129; see *Reformed Faith and Economics*, ed. Robert L. Stivers (New York: University Press of America, 1989), p. xiv.

46. *Institutes*, 3.19.9.

47. See John Leith, *John Calvin's Doctrine of the Christian Life* (Louisville: Westminster/John Knox Press, 1989), pp. 152-53.

48. See Richard, "Biblical Theology," p. 21.

ought, as Calvin himself sought, to "curb actively the aggressive power of money"[49] and use it responsibly on behalf of society and those in need. The generation of wealth is vital, but its just distribution is equally vital.

In a sentence, the final part of which reminds one of Karl Marx (though Calvin meant it in a different sense), Calvin wrote to Emperor Charles V: "It is certain that the *idolmania* with which the minds of men are now fascinated, cannot be cured otherwise than by removing the material cause of their infatuation."[50] For Calvin, opposition to the worship of relics and images and getting rid of idolatrous practices associated with the Mass had, as a result, far-reaching social consequences. A direct link has been drawn between Calvin's iconoclasm and later Calvinist revolutions.

> By calling on his followers to withdraw from the customs of their society and to abhor these practices with zeal, Calvin helped create an explosive situation, especially when one considers that "confession" became a special Calvinist trait. For Calvinists, "confession" was a socially oriented concern that transcended whatever personal fulfillment any individual might find in the *fides* that was at the heart of the Reformed message. To accept the Calvinist *credo*, body and soul, was to become an agent of change.[51]

But for Calvin, iconoclasm was only the negative side in the process, just as the ending of idolatrous and dehumanizing apartheid and economic injustice is but the negative side of the struggle for a new South Africa. This does not mean that the struggle against idolatry ever comes to an end. In Paul Ricouer's words, "we never reach an end of destroying idols in order to permit that the symbols speak."[52] The liberation and revitaliza-

49. Biéler, *The Social Humanism of Calvin*, p. 57.
50. Calvin, "The Necessity of Reforming the Church," p. 190.
51. Eire, *War Against the Idols*, p. 266.
52. Quoted by Laverne A. Rutschman, "Latin American Liberation

tion of the symbols of true faith in God, real humanity and just sociality, and their embodiment in the life of society and culture, require constant iconoclastic critique because it is a task that continually confronts new manifestations of idolatry. As an old social order decays or is overthrown and a new one is born, so new forms of old idols appear that must be challenged. This points us to the critical role theology is always called to play both in stripping away the illusions of idolatry and in its constructive task of pointing us towards a humanity and a world in which the true image of God is being restored. That is what Calvinists should mean when they affirm the glory of God alone, *soli Deo Gloria,* as the motivation for all they say and do.

To God Alone Be the Glory!

As we have noted before, it is ironic that both Calvin in his worse imperial moments and Calvinism on many occasions were responsible for dehumanization, sometimes in the very process of opposing idolatry and giving God all the glory. It is often felt that this derives from Calvin's awesome understanding of God, from the doctrine of the sovereignty of God attributed to him and the terrible decrees of double predestination in which some are elected to salvation and others to damnation.[53] But is not this understanding of God itself an idol that needs to be smashed in the service of human and social liberation? Is not the glorification of God at the expense of humanity a perverted form of religion? This was precisely the argument of Ludwig Feuerbach, for whom the exaltation of God meant the denigration of humanity, an argument upon which Karl Marx built his critique of religion as the opiate of the people. Thus, we have to ask ourselves whether or not the sovereignty

---

Theology and Radical Anabaptism," *Journal for Ecumenical Studies* 19 (Winter 1982): 48.

53. See, for example, Ernst Troeltsch, *The Social Teaching of the Christian Churches,* vol. 2 (London: George Allen & Unwin, 1956), p. 582.

of God and the doctrine of election, these symbols of what Troeltsch called "primitive Calvinism," are still serviceable. Are they worth retrieving or must they be ditched in the interests of affirming the truth of the gospel and its liberating power for today? But if we do ditch them, we then have to ask whether we have not ditched the Reformed tradition as well.

If the heart of Luther's theology was "justification by faith alone," then it is commonly assumed that the central focus of Calvin's theology was the "sovereignty of God" as this was articulated in Calvinism.[54] Certainly for Calvin, as we saw in the last chapter, the reign of God was fundamental to his theology. There can be little doubt that Calvin himself, in continuity with the Bible, perceived God as Lord of the universe as distinct from the idols of the nations. The problem is, however, that in Calvinism (unlike for Calvin), "the sovereignty of God" was understood and defined in terms more Aristotelian and speculative than biblical and trinitarian. Thus the reign of God became equated with the omnipotent, unmoved mover of the philosophers rather than the triune God of Christian faith.

The personal and political consequences of this unbiblical doctrine of divine sovereignty have been far-reaching and disastrous.[55] Karl Barth alluded to this in writing about Adolf Hitler's use of the term "the Almighty." "The Almighty," Barth reminds us, is not God, "and the man who calls 'the Almighty' God misses God in the most terrible way."[56] If God is defined primarily in terms of dominant will and power, as so often in Calvinism, does it not inevitably mean that human beings are understood in precisely the same way, so that they see their worldly vocation as one of domination and even manipulation, or conversely as dominated servitude and submission? Does this not also lead to that Calvinist otherworldly asceticism that is austere and rapacious at the same time? If God is sovereign

54. See *Institutes*, 1.13.1, editor's note 1, p. 121; François Wendel, *Calvin* (London: Collins, 1965), pp. 263-64.
55. See Jürgen Moltmann, *The Trinity and the Kingdom of God* (London: SCM, 1981), pp. 191ff.
56. Karl Barth, *Dogmatics in Outline* (London: SCM, 1955), p. 48.

111

does this not imply a relationship of human servitude and impotence? Does not such a God inevitably sanction similar social arrangements, legitimating unjust class structures, the domination of women by men, and even tyranny?[57] Does not such a God give to his adherents a status and authority over others, thus leading to the intolerance we sometimes find in Calvin and to what we have identified as imperial Calvinism? Is this not a fatal reduction of the gospel message that God has made us his daughters and sons—indeed, his friends? This is not the liberating God revealed in Jesus Christ, the God whom Calvin described as a mother who bears us up and gives us life and hope, but an idol from which we need to be liberated.

No one has formulated the critique of the sovereignty or monarchy of God more sharply in recent times than Sallie McFague in her *Models of God*. Speaking of the model of God as King and the consequent affirmation that Jesus is Lord, she writes:

> Think for a moment of the sense of triumph, joy, and power that surges through us when we join in singing the "Hallelujah Chorus" from Handel's *Messiah*. Probably we do not think about the implications of the images we sing, but we know they make us feel good about our God and about ourselves as his subjects: "King of Kings and Lord of Lords," "for the Lord God omnipotent reigneth." Our God is really God, the almighty Lord and King of the universe whom none can defeat, and by implication we are also undefeatable. It is a powerful imaginative picture and a very dangerous one.[58]

McFague argues that this image of God as monarch or sovereign is dangerous for three reasons: first, it removes God from the world and makes God distant from it. This, according

57. See the radical critique of a "dominating God" in Riane Eisler, *The Chalice and the Blade* (San Francisco: Harper & Row, 1987).

58. Sallie McFague, *Models of God: Theology for an Ecological, Nuclear Age* (Philadelphia: Fortress, 1987), pp. 63-64.

to McFague, means that God becomes "untouchable," remote, related only externally to the world. Second, it means that God relates only to the human world. It leaves out the rest of the cosmos—the world of nature; it is anthropocentric, and, moreover, dualistic and hierarchical, and thus it fuels many kinds of oppression. Third, such a God controls the world through domination and benevolence and thus inhibits human growth and responsibility. McFague is particularly concerned about the consequences of such an understanding of God for the world, and she sees a direct connection between it and the ecological disaster looming up on the world's horizon.

McFague accepts that her description of the classical doctrine of the sovereignty of God may be a caricature, but she is adamant in claiming nonetheless that her criticisms are "the direct implications of its imagery." And therefore, she argues, "if metaphors matter, then one must take them seriously at the level at which they function."[59] This is crucial to her argument. She is not in the first place criticizing the carefully articulated doctrine of God's sovereignty as this may be found in many theological treatises. McFague does not deny that God is "the agent, the self, whose intentions are expressed in the universe." What she proposes is that "the manner in which these intentions are expressed is internal and, by implication, providential—that is, reflective of a 'caring' relationship."[60] Her argument is that the image of God as king functions in a way that denies this caring relationship. God is removed from the world and acts from the outside rather than from within, with the world being "God's body," to use McFague's metaphor. Hence, "the sovereignty of God" is a destructive metaphor, destructive not only of human relations but also of the environment. It therefore needs to be changed.

Although McFague's critique was not aimed primarily at the Reformed tradition, it provides us with a useful foil in relation to which we can examine Reformed theology. In par-

59. Ibid., p. 65.
60. Ibid., p. 73.

ticular, we need to consider how the Reformed doctrine of God understands the relationship between God's sovereignty and our responsibility, between God's role and our own in the struggle for justice and liberation, between God's relationship to the world and our responsibility to sustain the earth and its resources. These and related themes will engage our attention not only in what follows in this chapter but also further on. But let us make a beginning here by focusing first of all on McFague's particular concern for the environment.

The connection between Calvinism, deism, and the rise of technology has often been commented on, particularly with reference to North America, most recently by the Canadian theologian Douglas Hall: "Incongruous as they may appear when considered in their original forms, Calvinism and Renaissance/Enlightenment humanism became co-partners in the formation of the North American spirit."[61] This spirit was, in essence, one of "human mastery over history and nature." This resulted in the development of the notion of "manifest destiny," a consciousness of being a special people, a chosen race. But it also led to the development of the most developed technocratic society, with its rampant consumerism and destruction of the environment. Once again, Calvinism, contrary to Calvin and more recent developments in the Reformed tradition,[62] allowed itself to be harnessed to a spirit alien to the gospel, both because of a congruence of interests and also, we wish to maintain, because of an inability to be self-critical in the light of its own theological foundations.

The sovereignty of God has never meant—for the Reformed tradition properly understood—a denial of human responsibility, but rather the ground for such responsibility. Certainly Calvin was more emphatic than most theologians on the responsibility of humankind and also in maintaining that being

61. Douglas John Hall, *Thinking the Faith: Christian Theology in a North American Context* (Minneapolis: Augsburg, 1989), p. 166.
62. See Calvin, *Institutes*, 2.2.15-16; Gordon and Jane Douglass, "Creation, Reformed Faith, and Sustainable Food Systems," in Stivers, *Reformed Faith and Economics*, pp. 138-39.

made "in the image of God" meant stewardship of the earth on God's behalf.[63] In fact, at the heart of the Reformed tradition is, in Gustafson's words, "an understanding of human life in relation to the powerful Other which requires that all human activity be ordered properly in relation to what can be discerned about the purposes of God."[64] Yet this responsibility has not, until very recent times, extended to the environment. If anything, the "cultural mandate" has been understood as an invitation to exploit rather than conserve the environment. This is precisely McFague's major concern, and, in relation to our concern, a major theme for us as well. You cannot have a Reformed theology of liberation committed to the liberation of the oppressed at the expense of the environment, nor the liberation of the environment at the expense of people. The caring for and sharing of the land and the earth's resources are fundamental to the liberation of people from poverty and deprivation. This is becoming increasingly apparent in South Africa, where apartheid has been a major contributor to land policies destructive of the environment.

When Calvin and his heirs have failed to recognize this interconnection, it has been due, in part, to a dualistic weakness in Calvin's and Calvinism's anthropology.[65] Calvin's anthropology, especially in his early theology, is clearly influenced by a residual Neoplatonism.[66] The spirit is exalted above the body in a way that is inimical to a wholistic understanding of human liberation. In fact, Calvin and much traditional Reformed thinking needs to be liberated from Neoplatonism in respect to both dualism and hierarchy if it is to become liberating and enable the flourishing of life in its fullness. Moreover, Reformed the-

63. See Leith, *John Calvin's Doctrine of the Christian Life*, p. 141; Douglas John Hall, *Imaging God: Dominion as Stewardship* (Grand Rapids: Eerdmans, 1986), pp. 103-4.

64. James M. Gustafson, *Theology and Ethics* (Chicago: University of Chicago Press, 1981), p. 164.

65. Suzanne Selinger, *Calvin against Himself*, pp. 109ff.

66. See *Institutes*, 3.9.4; Roy W. Battenhouse, "The Doctrine of Man in Calvin and in Renaissance Platonism," *Journal of the History of Ideas* 9 (January-October 1948): 468.

ology has to overcome the captivity to the Newtonian and Cartesian worldviews which played such a powerful role in shaping Calvinism in the seventeenth century, and which continue to bedevil attempts to think and act in wholistic ways.

Calvin's intention, however, was not to base his doctrine of God or his anthropology on philosophical speculation, but on the revelation of God as creator and redeemer in Jesus Christ according to the Scriptures. This does not deny that he sometimes fell into the trap of thinking of God by way of analogy and abstract rationalization to the glory of earthly kings and monarchs.[67] But Calvin's God, as distinct from the idols whom he opposed, is preeminently the living God who reveals his identity in what he does in creation and redemption, especially through the historical and personal mediation of Jesus Christ. This means that for Calvin, God is not remote from the world, as in deism, but directly involved in its life. Insofar as Calvinist scholasticism did, and still does, lead some to deism, then, of course, McFague's critique remains valid. But the distinctness which Reformed theology posits between God and the world, its emphasis on transcendent otherness, does not necessarily mean separation; it is rather intended to prevent confusion between the Creator and the created and thus avoid idolatry. This by no means places the world outside of God's active concern and care. On the contrary, it is precisely the property of idols that they are unable to care for the world, in contrast to the God of Israel, who like a mother gives life to the world.

Calvin's insistence on "the two-fold knowledge of God the Creator and God the Redeemer"[68] is, among other things, a strong affirmation of the interconnection between creation and redemption. If we take him seriously, it means that a liberating Reformed theology must, in principle, be as committed to the "liberation of nature" from human domination as it is to the liberation of the sinful and the oppressed. Contrary to the belief of some, there is evidence that the Reformed tradition

67. See Leith, *John Calvin's Doctrine of the Christian Life*, p. 42.
68. *Institutes*, 1.2.1; 1.14.20-21.

has both the commitment and the resources to make this connection.[69] The redemption of the human race and of the whole created order, disordered because of human sin, belong together.[70] Interestingly, while Calvin would not have spoken of the world as "God's body," he not only spoke of the world as the theater of God's glory,[71] but of God, "by other means invisible," clothing himself "with the image of the world."[72] Leith goes so far as to say that "Calvin's disavowal of all forms of deism brought him to the very brink of pantheism," and that Calvin "could agree with Zwingli's statement that nature is God when properly interpreted."[73] In like manner, in commenting on the Heidelberg Catechism, Barth refers to the world as "the theatre and instrument of" God's "righteous action, a mirror and echo of his living Word . . . the house of" the Father.[74] Even seventeenth-century Calvinists regarded the world, not only heaven, as the scene of God's glory and not just a vale of sin and sorrow.[75]

The primary reason why Calvin is able to avoid deism while stressing the sovereign reign of God is that his theology is essentially trinitarian, even though he does not care much for some of the traditional formulations of the doctrine. In his famous discussion on the "twofold nature of our knowledge of God," Calvin insists that God the Creator, whom we can discern in nature with the aid of Scripture, is God the Redeemer who encounters us in Jesus Christ.[76] This means that Calvin's doctrine of God cannot be understood properly if God as Almighty Cre-

---

69. Gordon and Jane Douglass, "Creation, Reformed Faith, and Sustainable Food Systems," p. 129.

70. Calvin, *The Epistles of Paul to the Romans and Thessalonians*, p. 174.

71. Calvin, *Commentaries on the First Book of Moses called Genesis*, vol. 1, trans. John King (Grand Rapids: Eerdmans, 1948), p. 64.

72. Ibid., p. 60.

73. Leith, *John Calvin's Doctrine of the Christian Life*, pp. 112, 110.

74. Karl Barth, *Learning Jesus Christ through the Heidelberg Catechism* (Grand Rapids: Eerdmans, 1964), p. 57.

75. See Jürgen Moltmann, *God in Creation: A New Theology of Creation and the Spirit of God* (New York: Harper & Row, 1985), pp. 80-81.

76. *Institutes*, 1.6.1.

ator is separated from God as Loving Redeemer in the crucified Jesus Christ who makes himself known through the Holy Spirit.

For Calvin, God's providential rule is to be understood not in terms of some overarching philosophy of history, even though God is supremely known through historical revelation. Calvin equally rejected the Epicurean espousal of chance and its rejection of purpose, the Stoical espousal of fate and its rejection of freedom,[77] and the Scotist notion of God as absolute, arbitrary power.[78] God's providence is known through his special care for people revealed in Jesus Christ; it is not the exercise of arbitrary will and power, but of justice and love. Jesus Christ is not only the mediator who reconciles us to God but also the mediator who enables us to know who God truly is. Without the trinitarian and christological qualifications which affirm that God's power is the power of grace and justice determined by his suffering love and overwhelming goodness in human history and experience, the monarchical concept of God as all-powerful is an idol. If Calvin sometimes failed to affirm this in practice and in some of his statements it was an aberration of his theology, at the center of which was the crucified mediator Jesus Christ.

The Crucified Mediator and Lord

In his commentary on Jeremiah (9:24), Calvin reminds us, in discussing the judgment and justice of God, that "the first thing to know about God is that he is kind and forbearing."[79] Commenting on Paul's description in Colossians that Christ is "the image of the invisible God," Calvin writes:

> The sum is, that God in Himself, that is, in His naked majesty, is invisible; and that not only to the physical eyes, but also to human understanding; and that He is revealed

77. See Charles Partee, *Calvin and Classical Philosophy* (Leiden: E. J. Brill, 1977), p. 95.

78. See *Institutes*, 3.23.2; Wendel, *Calvin*, pp. 127-28.

79. *Calvin: Commentaries*, trans. and ed. Joseph Haroutunian, Library of Christian Classics, vol. XXIII (Philadelphia: Westminster, 1958), p. 126.

to us in Christ alone, where we may behold Him as in a mirror. For in Christ He shows us His righteousness, goodness, wisdom, power, in short, His entire self. We must, therefore, take care not to seek Him elsewhere; for outside Christ, everything that claims to represent God will be an idol.[80]

Calvin continually reminds us that we can only truly know God through Christ. The corollary is that those "who conceive the naked majesty of God outside of Christ *(extra Christum)* have an idol instead of God."[81] Calvin does not say that God does not reveal himself elsewhere, for, as we have already seen, his glory is revealed in the earth and heavens. But that, as David Willis remarks, "is of secondary, because of abstract, importance to Calvin." Why? To quote Calvin:

> In this ruin of mankind no one now experiences God either as Father or as Author of salvation, or favourable in any way until Christ the Mediator comes forward to reconcile him to us.[82]

Only through the Mediator do we know God in creation and redemption.

Calvin strongly affirmed catholic Christology as expressed in the ancient creeds and the Chalcedonian formulae.[83] For him, the doctrine of Jesus Christ as "truly God and truly human," without confusion or separation, was fundamental to his theology as a whole. Jesus Christ was the true image of God; he was also the true image of restored humanity.[84] In Jesus

---

80. Calvin, *The Epistles of Paul to the Galatians, Ephesians, Philippians and Colossians,* p. 308.

81. E. David Willis, *Calvin's Catholic Christology: The Function of the So-called Extra Calvinisticum in Calvin's Theology* (Leiden: E. J. Brill, 1966), p. 105. See Calvin's commentary on 1 Peter 1:3, *The Epistle of Paul to the Hebrews and I and II Peter,* trans. W. B. Johnston, Calvin's New Testament Commentaries, vol. 12 (Grand Rapids: Eerdmans, 1963), p. 231.

82. *Institutes,* 1.2.1.

83. *Institutes,* 2.14.

84. *Institutes,* 2.12.1.

Christ, the gracious liberating Word, we truly know both God and ourselves.

This affirmation that Chalcedonian Christology protects and affirms the image of God in Jesus Christ relates well to Juan Luis Segundo's helpful insight that Chalcedonian Christology, far from being obsolete, has a richness and radicalness that is crucial for developing a liberating Christology today. At the heart of Segundo's argument is the claim that Chalcedon was not addressed to the question of atheism but to idolatry.[85] Chalcedon was not an apologetic for the existence of God but a confession of faith concerning who God truly is in relationship to the world in Jesus Christ. "In his limited human history Jesus, interpreted from the standpoint of a centuries-old tradition seeking the meaning of human existence, shows us the Absolute, the ultimate reality, the transcendent datum *par excellence.*" What is being countered is not lack of faith in God, but "any and every absolutization of values other than those manifested by Jesus in his human history. The target," Segundo declares, "is the absolutization of what is false: i.e., idolatry."[86] Paradoxically, the Incarnate Word, the embodiment and presence of God in human history, the infinite fully present in the finite, as Luther insisted, is the icon or image of the invisible God whose transcendent Otherness remains beyond human grasp and control—hence the Calvinist dictum *finitum capax infiniti.*

Formal faithfulness to Chalcedonian Christology does not necessarily mean, however, that either the Catholic, the Lutheran, or the Reformed dogmatic traditions remained faithful to the gospel. In fact, as Segundo argues, the Christ of Chalcedon became captive to Constantinian compromise and European culture in a way that seriously undermined the liberating power of the gospel. The transcendent image and glory of God in Christ was reduced to an idol. Segundo refers to several distortions in christological tradition which he traces back to the Constantinian captivity of the church.

---

85. Segundo, *The Christ of the Ignatian Exercises*, p. 39.
86. Ibid., pp. 39-40.

The first is that Jesus Christ became "the founder of the religion that grounds and justifies the established order of Western Europe."[87] This is a denial of who Jesus really was in history. He becomes the legitimator of political power, not the source of evangelical and prophetic ferment within history derived from his messianic mission. Consequently, Jesus becomes the one who holds the fabric of society together irrespective of its character, rather than the one who transforms society.

The second distortion is that, because Chalcedon is couched in Greek philosophical concepts, biblical thinking which stresses action over contemplation is subverted. What is now of primary importance is right belief rather than right praxis, contemplation rather than action. Hence, liberation theology's stress on orthopraxis is a necessary corrective.

The third distortion arose out of a genuine and deep devotion to the passion of Jesus Christ. But such a spirituality converted "the conflict-ridden project of Jesus into an atemporal demonstration of the values that God wanted to impress upon us through his Son's accomplishment of our redemption."[88] In other words, the focus of the passion becomes a set of moral values rather than the historical struggle that actually took place between Jesus and the principalities and powers of evil of his day.

The final distortion, which relates to the first, is that Jesus became the sponsor of "both defensive and offensive undertakings" in the protection and extension of Christendom. "People go to war in his name and kill in defense of his faith, just as they legislate, govern, reward, and punish for the same reason."[89] Jesus has in fact been co-opted by those in power to sanction both their position and their policies. He is no longer the liberating Word of God who comes to transform and redeem; like the Scriptures which bear witness to him, he has

87. Ibid., p. 106.
88. Ibid.
89. Ibid.

become captive to the dominant culture. The image of God which this Jesus portrays is not that of the gospel but that of an oppressive monarch. Instead of Chalcedon being a counter to idolatry, the Christ-symbol has been appropriated to justify an unbiblical idolatrous understanding of God. This is what happens when the sovereignty of God is separated from Jesus of Nazareth, the crucified Jewish Messiah who as Mediator enables us to know both God and ourselves as well as the glory of God in the world around us.

This brings us to the heart of the matter, for God's sovereign freedom for the world, God's gracious covenant with the world, and God's concern for justice and equity in the world find their normative historical expression not in the Chalcedonian formulae, but in the crucified Lord to which Chalcedon points. Louis Bouyer shows profound insight when he says that the essence of Calvin's doctrine of God's sovereignty is "that God reveals himself *precisely as a hidden God,*" an insight the Reformer discovered in Scripture but reached with the help of Luther's "theology of the cross."[90] Why is this profound? Precisely because it means that God's sovereignty is not thrust on the world in naked, patriarchal, paternalistic, and destructive power, the power displayed by the idols that devour and destroy, but in the obedient humiliation of the Son of God through whom God "accommodates" himself to our situation, need, and grasp.

The theology of the cross *(theologia crucis)* is normally associated with Luther rather than Calvin, who has in fact been accused of developing a triumphalist theology of glory *(theologia gloriae)* rather than one of the cross. But this is clearly a misunderstanding both of what Luther meant by a *theologia gloriae* and of Calvin's own theology. For Luther, theologies of glory are those which, like the theologies of the late medieval Schoolmen and some later Protestant scholastics, engage in metaphysical speculation about God but fail to discern God in

90. Bouyer, *The Spirit and Forms of Protestantism,* p. 83; see also Brian Gerrish, "To the Unknown God: Luther and Calvin on the Hiddenness of God," *Journal of Religion* 53 (1973).

the humiliation and shame of the cross.[91] Luther and Calvin agree that God is only truly and fully known in Christ crucified.[92] The difference between them is, in the first place, that "whereas Christ's humility and condescension are the preoccupation of Luther, Christ's obedience is determinative for Calvin."[93] But significantly, in the second place, "whereas Luther insists that we know God revealed in his hiddenness in the flesh, Calvin says this also but moves on quickly, perhaps too quickly, to say that God is revealed in Christ when he overtly displays the effects of his boundless power."[94]

Although Calvin starts with the obedient humiliation of Jesus that leads to the cross, this is always seen from the perspective of the resurrected and ascended Lordship of Christ which he exercises through the Spirit. The crucified One is the risen Lord, but equally, the risen Lord is the crucified Messiah. This means both that the nature of Lordship is radically qualified by the obedience of the cross and that the suffering and humiliation of the cross, its weakness, remains the power of God at work in the world through the Spirit. This is the heart of Calvin's trinitarian theology. It provides the basis for holding together both the evangelical message of the cross and the prophetic word of ideological critique and liberation without allowing the former to degenerate into pseudo-piety and the latter into Calvinist triumphalism. This enables us to see more clearly how

91. Martin Luther, *The Heidelberg Disputation* (1518), in *Luther's Works*, ed. Harold J. Grimm, vol. 31 (Philadelphia: Fortress, 1957), pp. 39-40.

92. Calvin, like Barth after him, is far more sympathetic than later Calvinists to the Catholic and Lutheran *communicatio idiomatum*, which means that "whatever is predicated of the divinity must be predicated also of the humanity and vice versa." Hence David Willis' critique of the label "extra-Calvinisticum" when applied to Calvin, and his stress on "Calvin's Catholic Christology." See Calvin's *Institutes*, 2.14.1; 2.16.11-12; 4.17.30; Willis, *Calvin's Catholic Christology*; R. V. Sellers, *The Council of Chalcedon* (London: SPCK, 1953), p. 240; I. D. K. Siggins, *Martin Luther's Doctrine of Christ* (New Haven: Yale University Press, 1970), pp. 227ff.; Barth, *Church Dogmatics*, IV/2, p. 78.

93. Willis, *Calvin's Catholic Christology*, p. 111.

94. Ibid., p. 112.

the message of the kingdom of God has to be understood not only eschatologically but also from the perspective of a trinitarian hermeneutics; otherwise it degenerates into individual subjectivity or fanatical ecclesial and political messianism.[95]

The proclamation of the reign of God, which was central to the ministry of Jesus and which embodied God's freedom, providential and covenantal care, and commitment to justice, was central to the apostolic preaching of the early Christian communities. In Pauline Christianity in particular it found its sharpest form in the confession that "Jesus is Lord," and in the doxologies of the Book of Revelation, which—as Sallie McFague reminds us, though critically—found such powerful expression in Handel's *Messiah*. It is true, as we have already said, that such confessions and doxological affirmations can be misappropriated so that they lead, as they often have, to a triumphalist faith, church, and missionary vision, to say nothing of the secular and political variations of the same theme. But let us recall the context within which they emerged.

Paul proclaimed that "Jesus is Lord" over against the idolatry of corrupt, absolute state power personalized in Caesar's claim to be god. The first Christians who made this confession did, of course, believe in the victory of Jesus over sin and death; they did believe in the ultimate triumph of God's kingdom, but the only power they had was that of the Spirit and their witness to the "weakness of the cross." Likewise, the doxologies of the Book of Revelation do portray the triumph of God and of his Christ, but it is their triumph over the idols of destruction, the apocalyptic beasts threatening to destroy not only humanity but the entire cosmos. There is undoubtedly a sense of sharing in the triumph of God, but it is the victory of "the Lamb that was slain," and the participants are the humble and meek of the earth who have known something of the suffering of the Son of Man and those witnesses or martyrs who have been washed in his blood. It is true that God is our friend, but in the confrontation with idols, with evil, with tyranny, with the

95. See Moltmann, *The Trinity and the Kingdom of God*, pp. 191ff.

"principalities and powers," the appropriate metaphor is surely not "friend," but "Lord and God." The doctrine of God's sovereignty puts limits on the human "will to power," the idolatrous desire to play God's role in human affairs. The doctrine of God's sovereignty read in the light of the theology of the cross is, in fact, the basis of ideological critique.

But there is another dimension to the doctrine that bridges the gap between ideological critique and the struggle for human liberation from oppression. On the one hand, the proclamation of the reign of God in the crucified Mediator is a check against arbitrary human power; but on the other it is a doctrine of empowering hope and encouragement for the oppressed. Indeed, it is only from this perspective—the perspective of suffering and struggle, the perspective of the cross—that we can begin to understand the sovereign reign of God in Jesus Christ and thus begin to appreciate the mystery of God's gracious election of a people through whom God's redemption becomes a historical reality. This is not the election of a people who are powerful, but of a people who, being rendered powerless by dominant society, have been empowered by God to be his witnesses for liberation and justice in the world. Through them God fulfills his redemptive purpose for all humankind and thus reveals his true glory in his redemptive acts in history.[96]

Election: God's Preferential Option

The doctrine of predestination or election, and especially the notorious Calvinist doctrine of the double decrees—whereby God elects some to salvation and consigns others to damnation—has long been a major problem for Reformed apologetics at the philosophical and theological level because it seems to deny any freedom to the human will. It has been faulted both

96. See Gustavo Gutiérrez, *The Power of the Poor in History* (London: SCM, 1983), pp. 75ff.

because of the image of God it portrays and for its human and social consequences. A God of such arbitrary power implies human beings devoid of any free will and responsibility. This, we recall, was a major criticism Sallie McFague levelled against the notion of God's sovereignty.

Moreover, the doctrine of election, we are told, is the root cause of the Calvinist sense of anxiety, the driving force behind the Protestant work ethic and capitalism, and, as Huddleston suggested, the theological basis for Afrikaner nationalism and apartheid. For when it is ripped from its theological context and placed in the service of colonial interest, the doctrine of election becomes the doctrine of manifest destiny and the idolatrous basis for the separation of white and black races as Christian and heathen, elect and damned. What kind of a God is it who wants to save some and damn others, who calls one group to a position of dominance and another to slavery? Is not belief in such a God idolatry?

Afrikaner Calvinism, like other nationalist ideologies of manifest destiny, has had a predilection for stressing the providential rule of God over history in a way that favors Afrikaner nationalism and white hegemony at the expense of other people. A classic example is found in the Preamble to the Constitution of the Republic of South Africa in 1961:

> In humble submission to Almighty God, who controls the destinies of nations and the history of peoples, who gathered our forbears together from many lands and who gave them this their own, who has guided them from generation to generation; who has wondrously delivered them from the dangers that beset them . . .

The problem with such a theology is not its sense of God's providential rule over history, something that would be affirmed both by the traditional Christian doctrine of God and by contemporary liberation theology. The problem is its implicit claim that God has exercised a special providence over the Afrikaner nation, or, more broadly, the white race in South

Africa. Nothing is said about the rights of the indigenous people who possessed the land before the advent of European colonialism. Rather, the claim is made that the white appropriation of land from indigenous peoples by the colonial settlers, often by force, then its legitimation through the Land Acts of 1913 and 1936, and finally its ideologization through the Bantustan policy and the notorious Group Areas Act, both cornerstones of apartheid, have the blessing of God—in fact, are part of God's plan. A further implication is that whatever the Afrikaner or white nation does is right and just, as long as it respects the sovereignty of God. In the 1984 amendment to the Constitution it was even suggested that capitalism itself is part of God's design for human society. Such an idea would not only have struck Calvin as bizarre but would have been equally strange to an older generation of Afrikaner Calvinists who were highly suspicious of capitalism and its agents.

Whatever faults we may find with Calvin's doctrine of election—and there are many thorny issues that are not easily resolved[97]—he cannot be faulted for ever confusing the elect people of God with a nation or racial group other than Israel or the church. God's providential rule over history certainly included shaping the destinies of nations, but that was not to be confused with his redemptive calling of a people, the church, to be the witnesses to his Word of justice, love, and mercy. Moreover, as Calvin's theology developed we find that his understanding of predestination focuses almost exclusively on the individual believer.[98] In any case, for Calvin God alone knows who the elect really are, so how could a nation or race make that claim?

The doctrine of election and predestination, we must remember, predates Calvin, and its roots are firmly imbedded in Scripture, especially in the writings of Paul. Then, in continuity with Paul, it is found in the writings of St. Augustine. Calvin

97. See Leith, *John Calvin's Doctrine of the Christian Life*, pp. 127, 132, 135, for a sympathetic but firm critique.
98. See Barth, *Church Dogmatics*, II/2, pp. 307-8.

was not introducing something new when he wrote about election, he was repeating traditional teaching. Not even his teaching on "double predestination" is original.[99] Calvin did not enjoy meditating on the logic of the "terrible decree" that if some are saved by God's decree others must likewise be damned, but he found it in Scripture. Hence, as he embarks on his exposition he utters many a warning about the dangers and difficulties ahead. For we are, he writes, "penetrating the sacred precincts of divine wisdom." Thus, "if anyone with carefree assurance breaks into this place, he will not succeed in satisfying his curiosity and he will enter a labyrinth from which he can find no exit."[100] In the same spirit, the Synod of Dort insisted that the doctrine had to be set forth with discretion so that "all inquisitive spying in the ways of the Most High" are ruled out.[101] As Heinrich Heppe points out, Reformed theology as a whole approached the doctrine of predestination "with quite unusual circumspection and care," insisting that while it should be taught because it was found in Scripture, it must nonetheless "be handled only within the limits which God has fixed in the revelation of this mystery."[102]

Despite these dangers, Calvin, like others before him and since, was firmly convinced that the doctrine was to be found in Holy Scripture. Therefore, as part of God's revealed will it had to be clearly and carefully expounded. What is noteworthy, however, is that in the course of his theological development Calvin not only increasingly placed the emphasis on the election of the individual believer rather than of the church, but he also separated his teaching on predestination from his doctrine of providence. In all the editions of his *Institutes* from 1539–1550 they are treated together. Then in the last edition, providence,

99. It is found, for example, in the teaching of Calvin's own teachers, especially John Major. See Lucien Joseph Richard, *The Spirituality of John Calvin* (Atlanta: John Knox Press, 1974), p. 169 n. 52.

100. *Institutes,* 3.21.1.

101. Canon 14, quoted in Heinrich Heppe, *Reformed Dogmatics,* rev. ed. (Grand Rapids: Baker Book House, 1978), p. 150.

102. Heppe, *Reformed Dogmatics,* p. 150.

God's sustaining presence in and rule over history, becomes part of Calvin's doctrine of creation (Book I) and predestination becomes part of his teaching on the doctrine of the Spirit and the Christian life (Book III).[103] This meant that Calvin wanted the emphasis to be placed on the assurance and comfort the doctrine gave to the individual believer; he did not want it to become a principle whereby human beings would seek to read God's mind in creation and history, and then, on that basis, erect sacralized ideologies of power and control. For Calvin, the heart of the doctrine was its affirmation of the mystery and the mercy of God's dealings with each person and especially God's loving redemption of believers in Christ. It was a doctrine not of arbitrary power but of unmerited grace. It was not a doctrine of Stoic fatalism, nor "a Scotist reduction to naked will, nor a metaphysical abstraction."[104] It was a practical doctrine, an exposition of God's saving grace.[105]

Later Calvinists, beginning with Calvin's own successor in Geneva, Theodore Beza, inverted the dogmatic order in Calvin's thought on the subject. Predestination was placed at the beginning of Christian dogmatics and so became the point of departure for understanding the nature of God, and not primarily one of assurance for the believer.[106] So began the identification of "primitive Calvinism" with predestination. While the focus here was also on the individual—those saved and those damned—it was difficult to keep predestination and providence apart in the doctrine of God. Once they were brought together it was but one step to the notion of elect nations who, in the providence of God, could claim a special divine calling, status, and role in history. This led eventually to the kind of confusion that we have noted in Afrikaner Calvinism whereby God's providence in history becomes conflated with his redemptive calling of a people to be a light to the nations. This inevitably conflates

103. See the editorial discussion on Calvin, *Institutes*, 3.21.1; Wendel, *Calvin*, pp. 263ff.
104. See McDonnell, *John Calvin, the Church and the Eucharist*, p. 163.
105. See Partee, *Calvin and Classical Philosophy*, pp. 20, 135ff., 145.
106. See its location in Heppe, *Reformed Dogmatics*, chap. 8.

nation and church, and it confuses the achievement of political goals with the arrival of the kingdom of God.

For many Reformed theologians today the traditional formulation of the doctrine of election no longer requires defense. Apart from those who remain tenaciously faithful to its traditional formulation, the most significant affirmation of the doctrine was by Karl Barth, who radically and christologically restated it.[107] Barth was of the opinion that if Calvin had only done the same, Geneva would not have been such a dismal place![108] All of creation and history finds its meaning in Jesus Christ, the beginning and end of God's redemptive purpose.[109] Moreover, the election of the individual, while central to God's redeeming grace and purpose, is now located firmly within the community of God's covenant—it is the goal of the election of the community.[110] In this way Barth is able to maintain the person as the object of God's grace without falling into the dangers of either individualism or collectivism.

In the process of restating the doctrine of election Barth sought to remain faithful to its original biblical intent, namely, to protect the mystery of God's counsel and assert God's unconditional grace as the ground of our salvation (cf. Rom. 11:33-34). But in the way Barth did this he affirmed that the freedom of God is a gracious, liberating freedom for humanity which seeks to give life to the whole world. In other words, God's freedom is the ground of human liberation. Human liberation is founded in God's liberating grace. To affirm God's freedom makes it clear that, unlike the idols, God is beyond human manipulation; to affirm God's freedom for humanity makes it clear that, unlike the idols, God is not only able but committed to save, redeem, and liberate humanity. God's freedom, in other words, is a covenanted freedom, not a capricious and arbitrary freedom. God's covenant with humanity and the whole created order, which was renewed in Jesus Christ, is a covenant of

107. Barth, *Church Dogmatics*, II/2, chaps. 32-35, esp. pp. 325-26.
108. Barth, *The Humanity of God* (London: Collins, 1961), p. 49.
109. Barth, *Church Dogmatics*, II/2, p. 104.
110. Ibid., p. 311.

liberation and therefore one in which both the community of faith and the believer discover freedom and life.

The question we now wish to pose is whether it is possible to discern an important link between this understanding of the doctrine of election and the claim of liberation theology that God has taken a "preferential option for the poor." Indeed, is it possible that in this controversial formula we may not only discern another important theological link between Reformed and liberation theology, but also be enabled to develop the doctrine in a way that is more profoundly biblical?[111] For while it is true that we must not confuse God's providence in creation and history with God's election of the community of faith and the believer, it is equally true that we cannot separate them if we understand God as both creator and redeemer in Christ. The Calvinists rightly saw the need to relate providence and predestination, to develop, as we shall note later in Kuyper, doctrines of "common" and "special" grace. But they failed to do so in a trinitarian way that prevented their distortion. Moreover, they dealt with them in a way that was ontological and static rather than eschatological and dynamic.

Without denying the evangelical truth that personal salvation is grounded in God's gracious and unmerited redemptive action in Jesus Christ, it must also be affirmed that the doctrine of election cannot be confined to individuals any more than it can be confused with doctrines of manifest destiny. From a biblical perspective, the elect in God's schema were a people, and not only a people, but slaves in Egypt. The foundation of the doctrine of God's redemption lies in the Exodus event in which God reveals himself as liberator. Hence, whatever the limitations and problems this Exodus motif may present— problems liberation theologians themselves have come to recognize, along with some of their critics—the Exodus remains fundamental to the Christian understanding of God. God is known by his liberating acts in history through which he calls

111. See Zwinglio M. Dias, "Calvinism and Ecumenism," in *Faith Born in the Struggle for Life*, ed. Dow Kirkpatrick (Grand Rapids: Eerdmans, 1988), p. 281.

a people into being who are to become his witnesses. This act of historical providence becomes an essential part of God's redemptive purpose, not least in the election of a people to be witnesses to his gracious liberation.

In the New Testament, election is likewise a matter not only of the individual believer but also of the community. It is related to the covenant which God established in Christ with his people. Like Israel, this people called the church exists in history and has a historical task of bearing witness to the gospel. That is its reason for existence. It is not an end in itself, nor is the elect people of God an ethnic group; it is a people gathered in Christ from every nation to serve the world. The coming of the Messiah and the birth of the church is not simply a religious event unrelated to sociopolitical history and therefore the destiny of nations and classes. God's election of humanity in Christ goes hand in hand with human liberation. Hence Mary's Magnificat, which heralds the coming of the Messiah to redeem the world, sees the significance of that event in relation to worldly reality.

> He has brought down rulers from their thrones
> but has lifted up the humble.
> He has filled the hungry with good things
> but has sent the rich away empty. (Luke 1:52-53)

It is not surprising to discover, then, that many of those who are called to be the church are, as Paul reminds the Corinthians, not powerful but powerless, not rich but poor, not dominating but the dominated (1 Cor. 1:26ff.).

Paul's comment is first of all sociological—the church at Corinth was made up of people from "the underside of history." Yet there is also a profoundly theological dimension. God's election is seen from the perspective of a *theologia crucis.* God's purposes in history as revealed in the weakness of the cross are discerned in his gracious favor to the poor and oppressed, and victims more generally, and thereby the rest of humanity is enabled to know the saving grace and power of God in Christ crucified, and to respond in faith, obedience, and love. This does not mean that only the poor or all the poor will be saved; nor does it mean that the poor are the church, which is sometimes implied or even claimed in liberation theology. It is to assert not only that we do not merit God's grace, but also that, like the slaves in Israel, the victims of society have a special place in the redemptive purposes as well as in the providence of God. They can become God's special witnesses to God's liberating grace and the promise of life in Jesus Christ crucified. Just as when we speak properly about the doctrine of election, in speaking about "God's preferential option for the poor" we are not talking about exclusivity but about the means whereby God actually works in history from the particular to the universal.[112] In language reminiscent of Barth and of other Reformed discussions of the mystery of election, Gutiérrez likewise speaks here of the fact that "we are standing point-blank before the mystery of God's revelation and the gratuitous gift of his kingdom of love and justice."[113]

What we are here affirming, then, is that without faith in a God who not only acts providentially in human history but also elects people to fulfill his redemptive purposes within that same history, it is impossible to understand the God of the Bible. For in "liberating slaves from oppression" and "taking a preferential option for the poor," this God acts not only providentially but also redemptively. This does not mean that the kingdom of God arrived when the slaves left Egypt and entered the Promised Land, but it does mean that without that act of political liberation God's redemptive purposes—and therefore the coming of the Messiah and the ultimate arrival of the kingdom—would not have been possible.

While we have by no means dealt with the doctrine of election in its totality, we have sought to affirm the reign of Christ over all reality in creation and redemption as its center. Some very thorny and difficult theological problems remain that require further reflection as we proceed to discuss in later chapters God's liberating grace in history and human responsibility, the church as Christ's community for and of the people, and the

112. See Gutiérrez, *The Power of the Poor in History*, p. 129.
113. Ibid., p. 141.

relationship between the church and politics. What we have sought to do at this stage is to insist that the problems are not solved either by conflating God's providential action in history with his redemptive work in Christ, or by separating history dualistically into profane and sacred or salvation history, as though Christ only reigned over the latter sphere. When we do the former, nations or groups or even the poor come to regard themselves as chosen and holy, as ends in themselves, specially elected to fulfill God's redemptive mission in the world. This is not only a danger we have identified in Afrikaner Calvinism but also a problem we encounter sometimes in liberation theologies.

The other side of the problem, however, is that if we rigidly separate creation and redemption, something Calvin himself refused to do, then we end up with a dualistic understanding of history in which the reign of Christ or the kingdom of God has nothing whatever to do with earthly reality and liberation from oppression into life. That, as both Reformed and liberation theologies insist, is equally unbiblical and unacceptable. What is required is an understanding of creation and redemption, providence and predestination, in which they are neither separated nor confused, but are understood, as in both Calvin and Barth, from a trinitarian perspective. God exercises his providential care *and* redemptive purposes in history through the *one* Mediator Jesus Christ in the power of the Spirit.

The doctrine of election is an expression of God's sovereign reign on behalf of humanity, and therefore for the sake of both personal and communal liberation. The significance of this in the struggle for liberation and justice was powerfully expressed in Archbishop Tutu's submission to the Eloff Commission of Enquiry into the South African Council of Churches in 1982. For Tutu, belief in the sovereignty of God did not mean abnegating on human responsibility in the struggle for justice; rather it provided the sure and certain basis for that struggle.

> God's purposes are certain. They [i.e., the government] may remove Tutu; they may remove the South African Council of Churches, but God's intention to establish his kingdom of justice, of love, of compassion, will not be

thwarted. We are not scared, certainly not of the government, or any other perpetrators of injustice or oppression, for victory is ours through him who loved us.[114]

The Glory of God Is Humanity Fully Alive

In this concluding section we return to Louis Bouyer's almost lyrical discussion of Calvin's doctrine of the sovereignty of God with which we began this chapter:

> We have only to re-read him without prejudice to banish the idea of a God, cold, aloof from feeling, that misguided followers and hasty opponents have agreed in regarding as the God of Calvin . . . his utterly uncompromising assertion of the sovereignty of God far from drying up the living stream of religion . . . has given it greater depth and purity. That God is the sole and absolute Lord of man and all things, that in all he does he acts ultimately for his own glory alone, signifies in Calvin's own explanation not the crushing down of man, but a liberation and expansion otherwise unattainable read in the light of the theology of the cross.[115]

In striking contrast to the false images and idols we create and which in turn dehumanize and devour us and our children, the Bible speaks of the image of God, which through Christ has been restored in humanity. The fall and restoration of God's image in humanity is the key to Calvin's anthropology, for it is in this doctrine that the dynamic (rather than ontological) relationship between God and humanity is expressed, a relationship of grace and gratitude, of faith and obedience to the Word of God.[116] But the *imago Dei* also has to do with human relationships. In fact, for Calvin it provides the basis for human

114. Desmond Tutu, *The Divine Intention* (Johannesburg: SACC Publication, 1982), p. 37.
115. Bouyer, *The Spirit and Forms of Protestantism*, p. 88.
116. See T. F. Torrance, *Calvin's Doctrine of Man* (Grand Rapids: Eerdmans, 1957), pp. 34ff.

relationships. In a powerful passage on what it means to love one's neighbor, Calvin bases all on the fact that we are made in the image of God:

> Say that he does not deserve even your least effort for his sake; but the image of God, which recommends him to you, is worthy of your giving yourself and all your possessions.

Calvin goes on:

> Assuredly there is but one way in which to achieve what is not merely difficult but utterly against human nature: to love those who hate us, to repay their evil deeds with benefits, to return blessings for reproaches (Matt. 5:44). It is that we remember not to consider men's evil intention but to look upon the image of God in them.[117]

The *imago Dei* is thus one of the key building blocks for Calvin's ethics, the doctrine which brings together not only our knowledge of God and of ourselves but also our relationship to others. We are to relate to other people on the basis of our all having been made in the "image of God."

While Calvin's emphasis on the glory of God often tended to obscure his insistence that humanity is made in God's image, this was certainly not his intention. "Calvin," Brian Gerrish reminds us, "builds his social ethics partly on the endurance of the divine image in fallen man. The sacredness and dignity of human life are guaranteed by the fact that man was made in the image and likeness of God, and that remnants of that image persist."[118] To discriminate against others because of their race, gender, or class is idolatry. "Our neighbor bears the image of God; to use him, abuse him, or misuse him is to do violence to the person of God who images himself in every human soul, the Fall notwithstanding."[119] The true icons of God

---

117. Calvin, *Institutes*, 3.7.6.

118. Brian A. Gerrish, *The Old Protestantism and the New* (Chicago: University of Chicago Press, 1982), p. 152.

119. A. L. Farris, "The Antecedents of a Theology of Liberation in the Calvinistic Heritage," *Reformed World* 33 (1974): 108.

are not those made with wood or silver, but human beings created out of the dust of the earth and redeemed through the blood of the cross. The true glory of God is not the denigration or dehumanization of men and women, but the reflection of God's glory in humanity restored to full life. It is, as Irenaeus, the second-century apologist and bishop of Lyons, proclaimed, "humanity fully alive" *(Gloria Dei vivens homo)*.[120]

What we are affirming is that just as humanity as a whole is in solidarity as a result of sin and idolatry—defacing the image of God by trying to be God or providing substitutes for God—so in Christ, the true image of God and humanity, humanity shares in the solidarity of redemption, in the restoration of God's image. And this solidarity means a common responsibility for each other. To worship God thus implies a commitment to humanity as a whole. "Not only do I despise my flesh when I wish to oppress someone, but I violate the image of God which is in me," declared Calvin.[121] This leads us further to Archbishop Oscar Romero's pertinent development of Irenaeus' evocative phrase. For Romero, as for liberation theology, the glory of God is not simply manifest in humanity come fully alive, but more especially in the liberation of the poor to full life *(Gloria Dei vivens pauper)*.[122] That is the touchstone for us today whereby we may evaluate whether or not we as Christians and the church are giving God all the glory or only part.

All of this ultimately implies a commitment to the renewal of the earth and the environment as a whole, for as we have already affirmed, the whole earth is the "theater of God's glory," and to be committed to the struggle for the liberation of humanity and the poor to the glory of God implies ultimately a concern for the liberation of creation so "that creation itself will be liberated from its bondage to decay and brought into the glorious freedom of the children of God" (Rom. 8:21).

120. Irenaeus, *Adversus Haereses*, 4.20.6.
121. Quoted by Leith, *John Calvin's Doctrine of the Christian Life*, p. 191.
122. Quoted in Jon Sobrino, *Spirituality of Liberation* (New York: Orbis, 1988), p. 52.

4. Set Free to Love and Obey

Adam Small, a "coloured" South African poet and playwright brought up within the Dutch Reformed Mission Church, some years ago explored his love-hate relationship with his Calvinist upbringing in a play entitled "The Orange Earth." As the following extract from the play shows, he can equate Calvinism with a generous, open spirit, and at the same time with legalistic bigotry. But it is the latter's self-righteous hypocrisy that really gets to him.

> You see this old man, there? He's been an open man . . . in his ordinary way. . . . Strict, yes. . . . Disciplined . . . Dutch Reformed . . . Nederduits Gereformeerd. . . . All that . . . Calvinistic. . . . Yes. . . . But never one of those sour-faced. . . . self-righteous people. . . . Those people of principle, who know what's right . . . exactly right . . . and only right . . . you know . . . who know the answers . . . all the answers . . . for everyone . . . who know what's good, for them, for everyone else. . . . And who enforce it . . . people of principle. . . . Dear God![1]

1. Quoted in Jo Dunstan, "A South African Dramatist's Critical Look at Calvinism: Adam Small's 'The Orange Earth,' " *Journal of Theology for Southern Africa*, June 1979, pp. 21-22.

In a similar but far more negative vein, the sceptical philosopher David Hume, who was brought up within the womb of strict eighteenth-century Scottish Calvinism, turned away from Christianity and described Calvinism as a form of idolatry whose deity was understood in terms of "wrath, fury, vengeance, and all the blackest vices."[2]

Calvin's own spirituality was in continuity with much of what was regarded as the best in medieval Christianity, being influenced in all probability by the likes of Bernard of Clairvaux and Thomas à Kempis. Some contemporary Roman Catholics have, indeed, discovered a lively spirituality in Calvin which they argue represents the best in the catholic tradition.[3] Those who know the tradition best will concur.[4] Moreover, if we fail to give attention to Calvin's spirituality we will fail to understand his theology.[5] Yet neither Calvin nor Calvinism are generally acknowledged for their contribution to Christian spirituality. Even those who may give Calvinism the benefit of the doubt would probably regard it as "awe-inspiring but bleak, covering the spiritual landscape with frost."[6] In the popular mind Calvinist piety does not suggest something loving, gracious, wholesome, and attractive, enabling growth towards personal and spiritual maturity, but something harsh, authoritarian, overly disciplined, anxiety-ridden, and joyless. Sobriety, legalism, and a this-worldly asceticism rather than celebration

2. David Hume, *The Natural History of Religion* (London: Freethough Pub. Co., 1889), p. 69.

3. See, for example, Lucien Joseph Richard, *The Spirituality of John Calvin* (Atlanta: John Knox Press, 1974).

4. See W. D. Jonker, "Die Eie-Aard van die Gereformeerde Spiritualiteit," *Nederduitse Geref. Teologiese Tydskrif* 30 (July 1989); John Leith, *An Introduction to the Reformed Tradition* (Atlanta: John Knox Press, 1978), chap. 3.

5. See Brian G. Armstrong, "*Duplex cogito Dei, Or?* The Problem and Relation of Structure, Form, and Purpose in Calvin's Theology," in *Probing the Reformed Tradition*, ed. Elsie Anne McKee and Brian G. Armstrong, (Philadelphia: Westminster/John Knox Press, 1989), p. 139.

6. Gordon S. Wakefield, "Calvinist Spirituality," in *The Westminster Dictionary of Christian Spirituality*, ed. Gordon S. Wakefield (Philadelphia: Westminster, 1983), p. 66.

seem to characterize its ethos from morality to liturgy, the kind of spirit that produces a relentless work ethic, or maybe political fanaticism.

Even if this may not be our experience of the Reformed ethos—indeed, even if our experience today is of something far more lax and, by Calvin's Genevan standards, even licentious, or perhaps guilt-ridden because of our failure to change the world—we still need to explore the reasons for the perversions which are so often attendant upon Calvinist piety and which may still lurk beneath the surface of our own. For if the Reformed tradition is to be a liberating tradition it has to enable people to discover the liberating power of the gospel and nurture them in mature faith, hope, and love. Only in this way can Reformed communities of faith become zones of liberation in the world. But first we must reflect a little on what might be called a pathology of Calvinist piety, what Calvin would have simply called "bad religion."

The Terror of Bad Religion

We start with a case study of an extreme example of Reformed piety become pathological. On May 25, 1989, a 23-year-old white Afrikaner, Barend Strydom, was found guilty of murdering eight black people and was sentenced to death by the Supreme Court in Pretoria. Strydom killed all but one of his victims one morning in downtown Pretoria, shooting them in cold blood. In testimony before the court he told how at an early age, under the influence of his father, he had been attracted to right-wing, racist views, and that he regarded his murders as an act of patriotic self-defense against a black political takeover in South Africa. He did not feel guilty, nor did he show any remorse for what he had done. On the contrary, he told the judge that, if released, he would do the same again. Prior to the passing of the death sentence, in pleas for mitigation, it was shown that while Strydom was bordering on psychological illness, he was responsible for his actions and not insane.

The horror of this event was multi-dimensional: the death of those killed, the agony of their families, the suffering of those maimed in the shootings, but also the tragedy of a young life emotionally maimed by an ideology of racist hatred learned from others, which set him on a path of destroying others. There was, however, a further dimension to his testimony that makes it a matter of special concern for those within the Reformed tradition and people of religious faith more generally.

Strydom's father, an elder in the Nederduitse Hervormde Kerk, testified that his son was a devout Christian who had been brought up a good member of the church, and Strydom himself told the court that before he went on his killing spree he had spent three days and nights alone meditating and praying to ensure that he was doing God's will. In his summing up, the judge mentioned that Strydom was well read in the Bible. In a letter to the *Weekly Mail,* a correspondent, C. J. de Villers of Krugersdorp, one of the citadels of conservative politics in South Africa, made this observation: "It is clear that Barend Strydom is not an aberration from our normal white South African: he is the logical manifestation of our militaristic and deeply racist society, driven by a bankrupt Calvinistic pseudo-Christianity."[7]

Stories similar to that of Strydom can be told about devout members of other Christian denominations who are citizens of other countries. The pathology of bad religion is not confined to South Africans who might have some Calvinist connection. Dutch Reformed Christians were as much horrified by Strydom's actions and claims as anyone else. A Gereformeerde congregation was so horrified that it specifically called for upholding the death penalty in the case of Strydom.[8] Yet the writer of the letter who regarded it as a sign of "bankrupt Calvinistic pseudo-Christianity" drew the connection between Calvinism and Strydom's actions in a way that probably would not have been done if Strydom belonged to some other mainline re-

7. *Weekly Mail,* May 26–June 1, 1989, p. 18.
8. *Cape Times,* July 13, 1989.

ligious group. The fact remains, Strydom was brought up within a Reformed church and his ideological views were somehow fused with his religious beliefs. Indeed, he believed, as he told the court, that he was doing the will of God when he shot and killed his victims. And, we must remember, he was found to be not insane but in his "right mind." Popular opinion could be forgiven for thinking that somehow, despite disclaimers to the contrary, Calvinism played some role in shaping Strydom's character and influencing his actions, just as, from Bishop Huddleston's perspective, it created the monster of apartheid.

We could mention other examples of bad Calvinist religion (such as the Salem witch-hunts) in other cultures and countries to show that it is not confined to South Africa. But why is it that Calvinism has sometimes led to these immoral consequences and gained this notorious image? There are several possible answers to the question, for the problem is clearly a complex historical and socio-psychological as well as theological one. But we suggest that Adam Small leads us to the heart of the problem when he refers to the self-righteous legalism that has too often characterized the Reformed tradition, even though it is not true of the vast majority of its adherents. This self-righteous legalism leads to the repression of instincts which, if not properly handled in the life of the church, can erupt in deeds that are evil, whether blatantly so or hidden in a more controlled, rational form. In this regard, there has sometimes been as much self-righteous legalism among those who have attacked Afrikaner Calvinism for its advocacy of apartheid as among those who defend it. Self-righteousness knows no cultural or confessional boundaries. But having said that, we still are faced with the reality of Calvinist legalism and the hypocrisy that has too often gone with it.

Calvin knew only too well about bad religion, its tyranny and terror. Early on in his *Institutes* he acknowledges the Epicurean argument, later to be used by Ludwig Feuerbach, Karl Marx, Sigmund Freud, and others, that "religion was invented by the subtlety and craft of a few to hold the simple folk in thrall by this device."[9] While refuting the argument as a reason for rejecting faith in God, Calvin was nonetheless most scathing in his attacks on the hypocrisy of those who used religion as a justification for their own purposes and will-to-power. Such cynical exploitation of piety for the sake of manipulating and dominating others, indeed, for striking the "common folk . . . with terror," was an abomination. Yet, as we know, Calvin himself was not altogether innocent of this, and within the Reformed tradition many have gone much further than he did—hence those literary portraits, grounded in reality, of elders, deacons, and dominees, as well as tyrannical fathers, who in the name of the sovereign God have ruled over congregations, communities, and households with a rod of iron, and in the name of religion have exercised dehumanizing power. No wonder that some of the products of such a legalistic and repressive upbringing treat others in the same way and project a pseudo-piety that is harsh, cold, censorious, and sometimes downright evil.

The psychiatrist Scott Peck, in his *People of the Lie*, comments on the ability of evil to disguise itself in people of principle, self-righteous people, religious people. "We see the smile that hides the hatred, the smooth and oily manner that masks the fury, the velvet glove that covers the fist." The tragedy is, as Peck points out, that "one of the places evil people are most likely to be found is within the church. What better way to conceal one's evil from oneself, as well as from others," he asks, "than to be a deacon or some other highly visible form of Christian within our culture?" Of course, such are a small minority, and the spuriousness of their religion does not imply that religious faith and conviction is spurious for the vast majority. But, to quote Peck again, "evil people tend to gravitate toward piety for the disguise and concealment it can offer."[10] This enables us to understand better what is commonly referred

---

9. See *Institutes*, 1.3.2; William J. Bouwsma, *John Calvin: A Sixteenth Century Portrait* (New York: Oxford University Press, 1988), p. 204.

10. M. Scott Peck, *People of the Lie: The Hope for Healing Human Evil* (New York: Simon & Schuster, 1983), pp. 76-77.

to as "false consciousness," a perception of reality based on illusion, self-deception, and self-justification that lies at the heart of idolatry, bad religion, and dehumanizing ideologies. Indeed, for Juan Luis Segundo, "the alienating sin of the world is ideology," understood as the means whereby people are controlled for the benefit of others.[11]

While it is true that much of the legalism found in Calvinism went beyond Calvin, there can be no doubt that it was also prevalent in Calvin's Geneva, that "perfect school of Christ" as John Knox called it, but which others, like Georgia Harkness, have considered somewhat less than perfect.[12] Part of Calvin's problem was not his own legalism, but his having to deal with legalistic and censorious Genevans. But there is no gainsaying the "shadow side" to Calvin's personality, exacerbated in later life by illness. This found its expression in Geneva in what we earlier referred to as "imperial Calvinism," with all its authoritarian rules and regulations for controlling the lives of the city's citizens. Indeed, Calvin's zealous defense of the truth and the glory of God as he understood it led him at times to harsh excess.

The most notorious instance of such excess was, of course, his celebrated complicity in the death of the unitarian Michael Servetus, though the burning of Servetus was exceptional and cannot be regarded as indicative of Calvin's daily attitudes. Indeed, the Inquisition had already condemned Servetus to death, and most Protestant leaders of the day approved Calvin's action in the interests of asserting their christological orthodoxy. Recent research into the Genevan Consistory records suggests that the condemnation of Servetus was a community process and a decision with which Calvin concurred, and not simply one he made on his own.[13] This does not mean that either Calvin or the

11. Juan Luis Segundo, *Evolution and Guilt* (Dublin: Gill & Macmillan, 1980), p. 54; see also Segundo, *Faith and Ideologies* (New York: Orbis, 1982), p. 97.

12. Georgia Harkness, *John Calvin: The Man and His Ethics* (Nashville: Abingdon, 1958).

13. I am indebted to Professor Elsie Anne McKee of Andover Newton Theological Seminary for information in this regard.

Genevans, or the Inquisition for that matter, can be exonerated for putting heretics to death, but it does enable us to place the event in perspective and to begin looking more deeply into Calvin's theology and piety for some clues in understanding such aberrations. What is required for our present project is not a chronicle, critique, or exoneration of Calvin's legalism in Geneva, but an understanding of what it was in Calvin's theology and especially in later Calvinism that led to such legalism.

A Will-to-Order for God's Glory

Calvin can neither be fully blamed nor fully exonerated for the legalism that has characterized many of his spiritual descendents.[14] Indeed, Calvin took great pains to show the difference between the liberating intention and integrity of the law as fulfilled in Jesus and the "leaven of the Pharisees."[15] Louis Bouyer argued that much Reformed spirituality was more influenced by Zwingli than by Calvin himself, and that Zwingli's understanding of "the 'evangelical' life" was "a thoroughly bourgeois humanism."[16] While this may be challenged, the Reformation in Zurich did secularize piety in the sense that it sought to engage the world, and this, when later allied to bourgeois culture and Enlightenment thought, inevitably led elements within the Reformed tradition to a denial of the mystery at the heart of true religion.[17] It was but a small step to Kant's religion within the limits of reason alone, and thus to privatized, moralized, and secularized piety. What began as an

14. John Leith, *John Calvin's Doctrine of the Christian Life* (Louisville: Westminster/John Knox Press, 1989), pp. 50-51.

15. *Institutes*, 2.8.7-8.

16. Louis Bouyer, *A History of Christian Spirituality*, vol. 3 (London: Burns & Oates, 1968), p. 86.

17. For an account of Zwingli's spirituality see Fritz Büsser, "The Spirituality of Zwingli and Bullinger in the Reformation in Zurich," in *Christian Spirituality II: High Middle Ages and Reformation*, ed. Jill Raitt (New York: Crossroads, 1989), pp. 300-301. See esp. p. 311.

145

intense form of personal and communal religion ended up as an individualism in which legalism, anxiety, and guilt were the dominant features.

The theological roots of Calvinist legalism are complex. The famous rationale put forward by Max Weber and Ernst Troeltsch was that it derived from the need to prove the efficacy of grace and election through good works. This certainly can be traced back to Calvin's "third use of the law" and his exhortations to demonstrate true religion through obedience to the commandments. Everything in personal and social life had to be brought into conformity with the will of God, which those who are called by God are privileged to know through the study of the Scriptures. Calvinism—following Calvin but going much further—pushed this "will-to-order" to extraordinary lengths. Troeltsch described it in the following way when comparing Lutheran and Reformed asceticism. The latter, he says, like

> Calvinism as a whole, active and aggressive, desires to re-shape the world to the glory of God, and make the reprobate bow submissively to the Divine law, and will with all diligence create and maintain a Christian commonwealth. To this end it rationalises and disciplines, in its ethical theory and Church-disciplinary instruction, the whole of action. . . . It scorns all mere emotion and sentiment as idle and frivolous, but is inspired by a profound sense of working for the honour of God and his Church. Thus there arises, in addition to an unresting activity and strict severity, a systematic completeness and a Christian-social trend in the spirit of Calvinistic ethics.[18]

By way of illustration, the Dutch Reformed Church in South Africa, like the Puritans of England, Scotland, and New England before it, has regularly emphasized the need for strict censorship of literature and the arts; it has sought to ensure

18. Ernst Troeltsch, *Protestantism and Progress: The Significance of Protestantism for the Rise of the Modern World* (Philadelphia: Fortress, 1986), pp. 50-51. First published in English in 1912.

that Sundays be controlled by sabbatarian legislation more in accord with strict Judaism than with the Christian celebration of the resurrection of Jesus and the teaching of Calvin himself; and it has downplayed human rights as a Christian mandate on the grounds that, due to sin, humans have only responsibilities, not rights.

A reasonable argument can be made on behalf of certain kinds of censorship—child pornography, for example; a concern for the sabbath could and should express a concern for labor practices and the renewing of the environment, as it does so often in the Old Testament; and an emphasis on human responsibilities rather than rights is not out of place in a world in which personal and social responsibility is seriously lacking. The problem is that this is not how such concerns have worked out in practice, not least in South Africa. Censorship has been used to suppress dissent and to repress sexuality in such a way that it actually reinforces rather than overcomes perverted forms of behavior. With regard to the sabbath, while concern for upholding it has been expressed in an outspoken manner, there has usually been a stunning silence on urgent issues of social justice. Undoubtedly behind this concern for doing what they perceive to be God's will is a concern for the well-being of people, perverted as it might have become, a will to order society for the common good. But how contrary to the gospel it has often turned out. In fact, how much it sometimes reminds us of those blind guides of whom Jesus spoke who strained out gnats but swallowed camels, being concerned about the minutiae of the law but neglecting the more important need for justice, mercy, and faithfulness (Matt. 23:23-24).

On a grander scale we can trace a clear line of connection between this will-to-order legalism, or what du Toit has called a "pathos for order,"[19] and the apartheid attempt to order society, to restructure it according to the perceived will of God

19. André du Toit, "Puritans in Africa? Afrikaner 'Calvinism' and Kuyperian Neo-Calvinism in Late Nineteenth Century South Africa," *Comparative Studies in Society and History* 27 (April 1985): 215.

for the nations. For Afrikaner Calvinism has insisted that even the perverted order of apartheid has had to be implemented through the proper channels of enabling legislation via the courts of the land, and enforced through the maintenance of "law and order." In the process, law and order, of vital importance in every society, has ended up subverting rather than serving the ends of justice and human rights, thus bringing the whole concept of law and personal and social responsibility into serious disrepute among those who have suffered as a result. In many respects, this Calvinist attempt at social engineering finds a counterpart in those socialist countries which likewise have sought to create the "new humanity" and new society through bringing everything into conformity to their utopian and often puritan vision. It is worth pondering the fact, however, that both Calvin and Marx were humanists, the one a believer and the other an atheist, whereas their followers have often been anything but humanist in their commitment to freedom and human rights.

Undoubtedly many Afrikaners, who are no better and no worse persons than anybody else, sincerely believed (as too many still do) that apartheid is right, moral, and Christian. This at least is better than those English-speaking South Africans who have espoused apartheid for purely pragmatic and selfish reasons. Afrikaner Calvinism, however, acted out of a sense of responsibility derived from what was perceived as a divine calling and mission to civilize and Christianize South Africa. It was not simply a concern to do what one willed, but to do what it was believed God willed, even though this so often masked material self-interest.

Within Afrikaner Calvinism, as in New England Puritanism before it and in much "manifest destiny" thinking since, there was the clear conviction that those whom God has chosen have a special knowledge of his will and a calling to ensure that that will is done, come what may. Dissent cannot be tolerated because it means challenging God. In an extreme form in which many other personal and socio-psychological factors are at work, this might well lead to the perverted ac-

148

tions of a Barend Strydom, for whom Christianity means the equation of the will of God with the will of the *volk*, and the special sense of calling which requires that that will be enforced, come what may.

The Calvinist will-to-order has, as we have intimated, complex though interconnected theological roots. Behind the effort to prove one's salvation by ordering life to the glory of God lies an Aristotelian understanding of God as primarily will and power rather than grace and love. Hence the need to bend one's will to the will of God, to obey the Kantian "ought" of the commandments, rather than to allow grace to transform sinful nature and bring it into harmony with the gratuitous purposes of God. Reflecting on Calvinist legalism, Bouyer argued that, despite what Calvin may have intended, "the rejection of all substantial sanctification of human doing and being in grace, carried right to the heart of the Calvinist doctrine of sanctification itself," cannot but lead to

> an activism in which we are forced to find, first in suggestions and then in external constraints, the driving power that we refuse to find any more in inner grace. Thus not only do we come back willy-nilly from grace to law, but from law to legalism, and finally to a fatalistic voluntarism, which, as Melanchthon rightly noted, can hardly be distinguished from ancient Stoicism.[20]

Calvin himself explicitly rejected what he called the Stoic "iron philosophy" condemned by both the word and example of Jesus, "who groaned and wept both over his own and others' misfortunes."[21] But there is profound truth in Bouyer's contention that the Calvinist doctrine of sanctification is problematic, not just because it tends towards legalism, but because of its implications when we begin to think in terms of the liberation of humanity in history and the liberation of creation as a whole.

Underlying Bouyer's critique is the Catholic under-

20. Bouyer, *A History of Christian Spirituality*, vol. 3, p. 89.
21. *Institutes*, 3.8.9.

standing that grace perfects nature rather than, as in classical Protestantism, having to re-create it due to the ravages of sin. This radical dichotomy between grace and nature, according to Catholic liberation theologians, undermines the liberating potential of the gospel. Thus, Leonardo Boff declares that a truly liberating theology and praxis calls "into question any schema that sets up an opposition between grace and nature, grace and human beings, or grace and creation."[22] This puts back on our theological agenda an issue which has divided Roman Catholics and Protestants from the time of the Reformation and which lies behind much of their theological divergence. Indeed, sooner or later the attempt to bring Reformed theology into creative dialogue with Latin American liberation theology must face this issue, for it affects so much else in theology, the life of the church, and its relationship to the world. But first we need to look more carefully at the way in which Calvin and the Reformed tradition have understood the doctrine of original sin, because the difference between Catholics and Calvinists on nature and grace derives from a different assessment of the extent of human fallenness, or what Luther in controversy with Erasmus called "the bondage of the will."

The Social Reality of Sin

In Kenneth Leech's excellent volume *Experiencing God*, in which he traces Christian spirituality through the centuries, it is noteworthy that there is only one reference to Calvin, and that has to do with total depravity![23] Calvin seldom if ever actually used the phrase "total depravity," and where he comes closest to doing so, he meant something different from what it generally conveys to us today. His pastoral letters, as distinct from some of his homiletic rhetoric, show a warm and profound under-

22. Boff, *Liberating Grace* (New York: Orbis, 1981), pp. 35-36.
23. Kenneth Leech, *Experiencing God* (San Francisco: Harper & Row, 1985), p. 342.

standing of human nature and need.[24] Of course, Calvin's rhetoric, which leads him in a sermon to describe humans as lower than "worms, lice, fleas and vermin,"[25] does not exactly suggest a positive view of humankind. There is also much else in Calvin's anatomy of human fallenness to supplement such sermonizing and thus give rise to Leech's conclusion, and to consequences which can eventually lead, paradoxically, to depraved behavior. But Calvin, his rhetoric notwithstanding, is seeking to be faithful to the Bible and especially St. Paul, particularly as mediated through Augustine. Calvin is at least an improvement on Augustine, for he does not confuse sin and sexuality.

What Calvin meant by human depravity is not that human beings are utterly bad, but that every part of human nature is affected by sin.[26] Sin extends to all parts, but it does not totally destroy the image of God in humans; on the contrary, remnants or relics of the image remain. This can be seen, argues Calvin, in the achievements of the great pagan philosophers, which, even if done for self-glory, indicate that some people are more gifted or virtuous than others. But it is also the reason why, for Calvin, the "image of God" continues to provide the basis for human relationships irrespective of whether people are in a right relationship to God or not.

What Calvin primarily meant by sin had to do with proudly rejecting God's Word, arrogating God's power for selfish and idolatrous interests, and, above all, being ungrateful for God's mercy, love, and grace in Jesus Christ. For Calvin, sin is far more than some moral failure—it is essentially human ingratitude, a rejection of God's grace and gift of life. Compare this with Gustavo Gutiérrez's definition of sin as the "rejection of friendship with God and, in consequence, with other human beings. It is a personal, free act by which we refuse to accept the gift of

24. Richard Stauffer, *The Humanness of John Calvin* (Nashville: Abingdon, 1971).

25. See Brian A. Gerrish, *The Old Protestantism and the New* (Chicago: University of Chicago Press, 1982), p. 151.

26. *Institutes*, 2.1.8-11; 2.2.12-17; 2.2.22, 24.

God's love."[27] In this proud refusal and ingratitude we find the origin of idolatry with all its dehumanizing consequences.

When rightly understood, Calvin's understanding of human depravity, shocking as this phrase may sound to our more enlightened ears, not only stands in continuity with the teaching of Paul and Augustine (as well as more recent theologians like Reinhold Niebuhr), but it is also true to human experience, especially when viewed from the perspective of the opening chapters of Genesis. Calvin's view of sin is derived from his reflection on the "history" of Adam in conjunction with his humanist knowledge of the history of human will-to-power in conflict with the will to order life according to the command of God. Experience corroborated the Genesis story, and both still provide profound insight into the human predicament just as they have through the ages. Calvin would fully agree with Gustavo Gutiérrez in saying that "only liberation from sin gets to the very source of social injustice and other forms of human oppression and reconciles us with God and our fellow human beings."[28] The doctrine of original sin is the only doctrine of the Christian faith that can be empirically demonstrated.

Sin, as Calvin saw it, lay behind everything that destroys human life and society. Thus, for the sake of human life it was necessary for the church to ensure godly discipline, both in its own life and in society. Given his Constantinian presuppositions, it was not only the church that was called to conform to the will of God, but also the world of Christendom. Calvin, the prophet called by God to do his bidding, not only believed he knew the will of God; he also believed he had a responsibility to ensure that it was done for the sake of God's glory and the restoration of God's image in the world.[29] Thus, part of the origin of the Calvinist "will-to-order" actually derived from the fact that the Genevan Reformer understood the restoration of

27. See Gutiérrez, *A Theology of Liberation*, rev. ed. (New York: Orbis, 1988), p. 226 n. 101.

28. Ibid., p. xxxviii.

29. See Ganoczy, *The Young Calvin* (Philadelphia: Westminster Press, 1987), pp. 293-94.

the "image of God" in the world in terms of restoring the order God gave to the world in creation. The re-creation of God's order, which had been so severely disrupted by sin, was the goal of redemption. Calvin's aim in affirming the law, if not always the effect, was the genuine freedom or liberation of women and men in which the glory of God would be mirrored. Hence, while human rights are God-given and therefore inalienable, they are inextricably bound up with human responsibilities towards God and the neighbor.

It should not surprise us that liberation theology has much in common with Calvin on the question of original sin, for liberation theology has its origin in a radically new perception of the radicality of evil in society as the cause of human bondage. If for Calvin sin affects every aspect of human life, the liberation theologians have had the resources to show how sin infects and operates at every level of human existence, whether personal, cultural, economic, or political. Sin—that is, human alienation from God, neighbor, work, and creation— permeates the very structures of society. When the Johannine writings in the New Testament speak of "the world" as something from which we must turn, they are referring to the "structures of sin."[30] In other words, human depravity, to use Calvin's terminology, not only extends to all aspects of individual human nature, but also extends to all corners of social existence. Sin is not only a personal but also a social reality; that is why it is handed on from one generation to the next.

Original sin, writes Enrique Dussel, "is constitutive of being from its origin, from our birth." He elaborates by saying that "our 'being' is more than our materiality, our corporeality, despite what some have thought. Our most radical *being* is our social being."[31] Original sin is not handed down by procreation,

30. See José Miranda, *Being and the Messiah: The Message of St. John* (New York: Orbis, 1973), pp. 100-101.
31. Enrique Dussel, *Ethics and Community* (New York: Orbis, 1988), p. 22; see also Juan Luis Segundo, *Grace and the Human Condition: A Theology for a New Humanity*, vol. 2 (Dublin: Gill and Macmillan, 1980), pp. 37-38.

as for Augustine, but is transmitted by our birth into and participation in human society, its structures and institutions. At this point theologians and sociologists concur, even though they may describe the ultimate cause of the social reality of sin differently and use a different vocabulary. In Gutiérrez's words:

> As seen in the light of faith, sin thus understood is the root of all social injustice, because sin, like every human act necessarily has a social dimension.[32]

Albert Nolan helps us to redefine the doctrine of "original sin" in the South African context, and in the process brings us back to its biblical roots:

> The system [i.e., apartheid] begins to affect us from the day we are born. As we grow up, it forms or at least tries to form our whole consciousness of reality. We are socialised into its false values of racism, individualism, selfishness, competition, possessiveness, and money as the measure of all value. From the beginning the system tries to cut us off from other human beings and to divide us against ourselves. We are socially conditioned into alienation. This is what the Christian tradition calls original sin.[33]

Barend Strydom's worldview and actions, which we reflected on earlier in this chapter, while undoubtedly deeply rooted in his own psyche, cannot be understood apart from the racism endemic to so much of white society in South Africa and elsewhere. He was guilty of pulling the trigger, but his actions reflect socially entrenched and communicated views. They were handed on to him through family, school, and church. They were deeply rooted in the corporate psyche of the race. Indeed, the structural and other forms of violence perpetrated in the name of ideology and for the sake of political power and material interest are no less evidence of the same solidarity in sin, even though they are "legalized." Torture in prisons and

32. Gutiérrez, *A Theology of Liberation*, p. 226 n. 101.
33. Nolan, *God in South Africa* (Grand Rapids: Eerdmans, 1988), p. 90.

the shooting of innocent victims, political opponents, or peaceful protesters in the name of "law and order" and security are not qualitatively different, though they may be protected by emergency and other regulations. In a real sense, moreover, all those who benefit from the system are implicated in its sinfulness.

At least two insights, common to Reformed and liberation theology, flow from this understanding of our solidarity in sin. The first is a critical attitude towards the exercise of power and domination in society. What some contemporary theorists call "the hermeneutics of suspicion" is, theologically speaking (which is not the conceptual framework of the theorists themselves), based on the conviction that all people are sinners. Therefore, their attitudes and actions derive at least partly from a self-interest contrary to God's purposes for humanity as a whole. Those with power are therefore particularly prone to corruption in the use of that power. There is a close connection between this "hermeneutics of suspicion" and what Luther referred to as the "second use of the law" (Calvin inverted the order and referred to this as the "first use")[34]—that is, its ability to destroy illusions, to drive us to despair so that we turn to Christ. The preaching of the Mosaic Law, as done by the eighth-century Hebrew prophets, reveals the extent of sin in society. It uncovers the way in which people hide from reality, misuse power—even God-given power—and turn to idols instead of facing God and the image of God in their neighbor. Like the "hermeneutics of suspicion," the prophetic preaching of the law seeks to uncover the hidden interests that lie behind ideas and actions.

The second insight is the need for repentance and conversion as fundamental to the process of personal and social transformation. This is not the simplistic notion that if individuals are converted then social structures will change for the better, though that may result. Rather, it is an awareness that psychological and spiritual liberation are inseparable

34. *Institutes*, 2.7.6-7.

from social and political liberation.[35] The evangelical liberation of those trapped in the bondage of racism, fear, legalism,
and every other kind of dehumanizing tyranny is bound up
with the liberation of society as a whole. Jesus' proclamation
of the reign of God as God's mandate for justice, and his
gracious offer of forgiveness, new life, and the invitation to
discipleship belong together and are fundamental to both liberation theology and Calvin. In a sermon preached in August
1977, Archbishop Oscar Romero made this remark:

> It's always the same. The prophet has to speak of society's
> sin and call to conversion, as the church is doing today
> in San Salvador: pointing out whatever would enthrone
> sin in El Salvador's history and calling sinners to be con-
> verted, just as Jeremiah did.[36]

Liberation by Grace Alone

There has been considerable debate about whether or not the
Protestant Reformers introduced a new doctrine into Christianity with their teaching on "justification by faith."[37] If they
did, then it could justly be said that they were departing from
the substance of catholic tradition and thus being heretical.
There can be little doubt, of course, that Luther made "justification by faith" the center of his theology in a new way. But it
is equally so that "within the flux of late medieval theology,
currents may easily be identified which demonstrate various
degrees of continuity with the emerging theologies of justification associated with the first phase of the Reformation.[38] The

35. Jürgen Moltmann, *The Crucified God* (London: SCM, 1974), pp.
291-92; Segundo, *Grace and the Human Condition*, pp. 37-38.
36. Oscar Romero, *The Violence of Love*, trans. and ed. James R. Brockman (London: Collins, 1989), p. 7.
37. For what follows see the important discussion in Alister E.
McGrath, *Iustitia Dei: A History of the Christian Doctrine of Justification*, vol.
1 (Cambridge: Cambridge University Press, 1986), pp. 180ff.
38. Ibid., p. 183.

continuity was, however, related to the mode of justification, not its nature. For medieval theology, justification was a process that included sanctification and regeneration; for the Protestant Reformers and especially their later followers, justification meant "the forensic declaration that the Christian is righteous, rather than the process by which he is made righteous."[39] In other words, it was a declaration of a change of status before God, extrinsic to the person, rather than an intrinsic process of personal transformation or regeneration. While justification and regeneration obviously cannot be separated (for they belong together within the doctrine of salvation), for the Reformers justification meant that the sinner had been pronounced righteous by God, while regeneration meant that the sinner had been made righteous by God. Thus the Reformers did not introduce a new doctrine, but a new understanding of what it means for human existence before God.

For Calvin, "justification by faith" remains what it was for Luther: "the principal article of the Christian religion."[40] Like Luther, Calvin also understood justification in forensic terms—through the death of Jesus Christ God has declared us to be righteous. But it is significant that Calvin discusses the doctrine of "justification by faith" only after his treatment of regeneration and sanctification. While he clearly makes a distinction between them, he equally clearly regards regeneration and sanctification as the goal of justification.

The separation of justification and regeneration or sanctification in both Luther and Calvin is novel, then, but it is also notional. Otherwise, both of them stand in continuity with Catholic teaching, except in its late medieval corrupted forms. What was central to both catholic tradition and evangelical doctrine was that we cannot save ourselves through any act of our own or our own merits. Our sinfulness is such that we can only be saved from our sins and set free to love and obey by God's grace in Jesus Christ alone. No matter how much we may seek

39. Ibid., p. 182.
40. *Institutes*, 3.11.1.

to justify ourselves before God, to conform to God's will, it is beyond our capacity to do so. This being so, it is not surprising to discover continuities between Calvin and contemporary Catholic teaching, not on the forensic nature of justification, but on its gratuitous character. Here the paths come together.

For Calvin, salvation is contingent upon God's gracious willingness to forgive our sins and set us free from them. In that act of forgiveness we are justified and restored to life in relationship to God. This has been made possible by the death and resurrection of the only Mediator, Jesus Christ, who has reconciled us to the Father and, through the Spirit, has given us the faith to respond. Faith is thus not an act of the will but a gift of God enabling us to acknowledge God's saving grace towards us in Jesus Christ. Such faith brings us to a true knowledge of God—what Calvin called *pietas*, or what we would now call spirituality, a reverence and love for God.[41] This is the heart of true theology—not simply an intellectual form of knowing, but existential knowledge, the knowledge of faith that results from hearing the gospel and responding to it in the power of the Holy Spirit.

Through the same Spirit who awakens faith and understanding we are also grafted into "union with Christ" and receive the gift of sanctification. For Calvin, "the Holy Spirit is the bond by which Christ effectually unites us to himself."[42] By this the Reformer means "that indwelling of Christ in our hearts," "that mystical union" whereby "Christ, having been made ours, makes us sharers with him in the gifts with which he has been endowed."[43] This "union with Christ" is not some kind of change in our essence, for we remain human, but it is a fundamental change in our historical existence. It is our regeneration or new birth. All of this is an intensely personal experience, because it is mediated neither through the church nor through sacraments, but through the Word and the Spirit directly.

41. See the *Institutes*, 1.2.1.
42. *Institutes*, 3.1.1.
43. *Institutes*, 3.11.10.

The gift of sanctification presupposes our justification, and we receive it along with our justification through faith in Christ. But whereas justification gives us life and restores our relationship with God once and for all, sanctification is the process whereby God's image in us is restored as we journey by faith through life, until it is fully restored beyond death in the image of Christ. We are, to quote St. Paul, "being transformed into his likeness with ever-increasing glory, through the power of the Lord who is the Spirit" (2 Cor. 3:18, REB). The ultimate cry for life is for that quality of life, eternal life, which transcends even the bondage and tyranny of death.

For Calvin our righteousness can never be self-righteousness, but the righteousness of Christ which we have received from him through the Holy Spirit.[44] To use the Pauline terms that both control Calvin's theology and lie at the heart of the evangelical spirituality of the Reformation, our justification, regeneration, and sanctification are all the work of Christ through the Spirit which we receive through faith and not through any merit of our own. In Calvin's words: "condemned, dead, and lost in ourselves, we should seek righteousness, liberation, life, and salvation in" Christ.[45]

Although we grow in our understanding of the mystery of our redemption, it is not something we can fully grasp with our minds; it is a matter of faith, indeed, something experiential. Calvin even speaks of it as something we feel.[46] Benjamin Warfield reminds us that Calvin was not merely seeking to secure "an intellectual assent to his teaching, but sought to move men's hearts. . . . All the arguments in the world, he [Calvin] insists, if unaccompanied by the work of the Holy Spirit on the heart, will fail to produce the faith which piety requires."[47] None of

44. *Institutes*, 3.9.23.
45. *Institutes*, 2.16.1.
46. Calvin, *The Epistles of Paul to the Galatians, Ephesians, Philippians and Colossians*, trans. T. H. L. Parker, Calvin's New Testament Commentaries, vol. 11 (Grand Rapids: Eerdmans, 1965), p. 210.
47. Benjamin B. Warfield, *Calvin and Augustine* (Philadelphia: Presbyterian and Reformed Publishing Company, 1956), p. 139; see Calvin, *Institutes*, 1.7.4.

this denies Calvin's stress on the objective work of grace mediated through Word and sacrament; it has to do, rather, with the
complementary subjective work of the Spirit whereby the means
of grace become existentially effective. For Calvin, salvation is
trinitarian, and in that act of God's grace the Holy Spirit fulfills
a crucial role. While we are saved by God's "grace alone"
through "Christ alone," salvation is effected through the "Spirit
alone" *(solo Spiritu)*.[48] Without doubt Calvin is a theologian of
the Holy Spirit, which may also be said for his fellow reformers
in Zurich: Zwingli and Bullinger.[49]

While this emphasis on the experiential work of the Spirit
suffered greatly at the hands of rationalist forms of Calvinism,
it has always been characteristic of important strands within
the Reformed tradition, notably those influenced by such Puritan divines as William Perkins, William Ames, and Richard
Baxter.[50] True piety for them, as for one of their distinguished
successors, Jonathan Edwards, has to do with "the religious
affections."[51] This is not a natural emotion but the work of the
Spirit. What could be more central to Christian spirituality than
the Calvinist piety expressed in Edwards' comment:

> The influence of the Spirit of God, thus communicating
> himself and making the creature a partaker of the divine
> nature, is what I mean by truly gracious affections arising
> from spiritual and divine influence.[52]

In Calvin as in Edwards, and in many other Puritan divines
and South African Reformed pietists like Andrew Murray, Jr.,
we are a long way from the image of cold, rational religion

48. Alexandré Ganoczy, "Observations on Calvin's Doctrine of
Grace," in McKee and Armstrong, *Probing the Reformed Tradition*, p. 98.
49. Büsser, "Spirituality of Zwingli," pp. 301-2.
50. See Basil Hall, "Calvin against the Calvinists," in *John Calvin*
(Appleford, UK: Sutton Courtenay Press, 1966), p. 29.
51. James M. Gustafson, *Theology and Ethics* (Chicago: University of
Chicago Press, 1981), p. 164.
52. Jonathan Edwards, *A Treatise on Religious Affections* (Grand
Rapids: Baker Book House, 1982), p. 138.

often associated with Calvinism. Yet whenever Calvinism denies or underplays this work of the "indwelling Spirit," its understanding of the gospel leads inevitably to biblicist legalism or theological positivism.[53] It is not surprising, then, that some Reformed Christians, in reaction to the legalism of their own upbringing, find release in more charismatic types of Christianity, nor that, in South Africa at any rate, the evangelical piety of Andrew Murray is more attractive to some than that of mainstream Reformed spirituality. But a proper understanding of Calvin's emphasis on the Spirit should equally prevent Christian obedience from degenerating into legalism and should also help us to discern more clearly the liberating power of the gospel.

Reformed theology is potentially liberating precisely because its center is the proclamation of the gospel of justification that sets people free from sin, gives new life, and leads to sanctification and righteousness not based on human merit, race, gender, or class. The gospel it proclaims is not the legalistic will-to-order to which all must conform, but the free gift of eternal life—that is, the life of the new age already experienced here and now. That is why Lekula Ntoane regards justification by faith as "the culmination point" of his study in search of an answer to his "cry for life."[54] That is why Moltmann speaks of faith in the risen Christ as that which transforms psychological and social systems, "so that instead of being oriented to death they are oriented to life."[55] Thus, too, Leonardo Boff, reflecting on Luther's teaching on justification by faith, declares that the Reformer thereby "introduces a radical liberation because the human being is free *from* all these demands [i.e., good works], and free *to* receive grace as a pure gift and free offering."[56]

53. Richard, *The Spirituality of John Calvin*, p. 180.

54. L. R. Lekula Ntoane, *A Cry for Life* (Kampen: J. H. Kok, 1983), pp. 186-87.

55. Moltmann, *The Crucified God*, p. 294.

56. Leonardo Boff, "Luther, the Reformation, and Liberation," in *Faith Born in the Struggle for Life*, ed. Dow Kirkpatrick (Grand Rapids: Eerdmans, 1988), pp. 202-3.

Indeed, many Roman Catholic theologians today agree that Luther's evangelical teaching on justification is not only biblical but also essential to the ongoing renewal of the church, and that its liberating significance for the world has to be retrieved.[57]

What we are dealing with in justification by faith is a radical break with the past and the entrance into the new order of God's reign. It is the very antithesis of bondage to the old order of death characterized by the dehumanizing power of self-made idolatry. For Calvin, human liberation is first and foremost redemption from the bondage of self-worship. All else derives from this act of God's undeserved grace. But through grace we are restored to our true nature as human beings made in the image of God, and therefore reconciled to God and to one another.

Such an understanding of true religion cuts at the very heart of any self-justification or self-righteousness, which lies at the center of bad religion. It is not surprising, then, that not only the proclamation of the law but also the gospel and the "renewal brought by Christ meets strong resistance in the very heart of humanity."[58] The proclamation of the gospel is not always heard and received gladly because it touches raw nerves, exposing our idols and revealing our hidden sins. Indeed, it produces conflict and evokes stubborn reaction. Sin was and is, after all, endemic to the human condition. People, societies, and interest groups do not by nature normally want to change. Yet just as refusal to hear the Word of God and respond in gratitude to God's gift of life in the gospel is the essence of sin, so redemption is accepting the gift of life in Jesus Christ with thankfulness. That is the turning point.

All of this has far-reaching implications for our under-

57. See Hans Küng, "Justification Today," a new introductory chapter to his earlier (1964) book, *Justification: The Doctrine of Karl Barth and a Catholic Reflection* (Philadelphia: Westminster Press, 1981), pp. ix-x; see also *The Condemnations of the Reformed Era*, ed. Karl Lehmann and Wolfhart Pannenberg (Minneapolis: Fortress, 1990), pp. 39-40.

58. Wilhelm Niesel, *The Theology of Calvin* (Philadelphia: Westminster Press, 1956), p. 22.

standing of ourselves, the church, and our role in society. For whereas in the first instance it means that our relationship to God is a gift of grace rather than something we earn, or something based on race, gender, or class, secondly and inseparably it means that we have been set free to live the life God intends us to live in gratitude, and that this is expressed in true worship, love of our fellow human beings, and obedient action. For, as Calvin insists, though we are not justified by works we are not justified without them.[59] Moreover, this did not imply the "relegation of faith to the private sphere." On the contrary, "Calvin, like liberation theologians in our time, envisioned an integration of holiness and virtue into the political order."[60]

Once again, here is a fundamental paradox in Calvin's theology expressed in the dialectic of justification and sanctification, which indicates not only a break with sin but a dynamic movement towards the renewal of life in its entirety. Reformed spirituality is not static; it is one of growth into wholeness. Repentance, conversion, or *metanoia* is, in Leith's words, "coextensive with the whole of life, that is, penetrating into every area of human existence and extending through all of life."[61] Conversion is the total transformation of life. Conversion, in Gutiérrez's words, sets us "free to love."[62] Or, to use Calvin's phrase which reveals the interconnection between grace and the genuine fulfillment of the law, God has set us free "for all the duties of love."[63] We have been graciously set free to love and obey God in loving our neighbor. For it is only once we have begun to understand and have gratefully received God's gift of justification and life that we are able to repent, be converted, and begin to express our gratitude in a life of genuine obedience. Faith precedes repentance just as grace precedes law, for without the gracious awakening of faith we are unable to see the awful reality of our sin and its personal and social

59. *Institutes*, 3.16.1.
60. Richard, *The Spirituality of John Calvin*, pp. 177, 179.
61. Leith, *John Calvin's Doctrine of the Christian Life*, p. 68.
62. Gustavo Gutiérrez, *We Drink from Our Own Wells* (New York: Orbis, 1985), pp. 91-92.
63. *Institutes*, 3.19.12.

consequences. In this way not only are justification and sanctification brought together as one action of the Spirit, but faith
and works, trust and obedience are inseparably linked.

We are now at the center of Calvin's theology. This is what
stamps it as thoroughly evangelical in the Reformation sense of
that much-abused word, but this is also what integrates it into
the prophetic tradition of social critique and transformation. We
are at the heart of the liberating potential of Reformed theology,
for the "ferment of the gospel" which begins with God's liberating action in our lives extends beyond our lives into the world.
We now begin, Calvin writes, "to be formed anew by the Spirit
after the image of God, in order that our entire renovation and
that of the whole world may afterwards follow in due time."[64]
Our liberation is a foretaste of the liberation of the whole of
creation. Our sanctification is a prelude to the sanctification of
the world. Grace alone makes the fulfillment of the law and its
demands of justice and equity not only necessary but also
possible.

In a very perceptive article provocatively entitled "Learning Reformed Theology from the Roman Catholics," Carol
Johnston has suggested how Protestants in general and Reformed Christians in particular need to learn again the liberating power of grace in relation to social action. For without this,
social action not only degenerates into self-righteous legalism
(the very antithesis of the doctrine of grace), but it also results
in a kind of guilt and anxiety that prevents genuine social
action. Reflecting on the pastoral letter of the U.S. Catholic
bishops on economic issues, Johnston writes:

> Roman Catholics have finally learned what we are forget-
> ting. In too many socially active Protestant churches I
> have heard people castigated and made to feel guilty for
> not doing enough for justice and peace. It is true: they are
> not doing enough, they are guilty, and they do participate
> in unjust social structures. But all the castigation and all

---

64. Quoted by Richard, *The Spirituality of John Calvin*, p. 175.

the rehearsal of grim statistics only leave people numb with guilt and paralyzed with hopelessness.[65]

The doctrine of justification by grace through faith alone must lead to participation in the struggle for justice, but the struggle for justice must not degenerate into a new form of "works righteousness" with its attendant guilt paralysis and despair. The "ferment of the gospel" refers to the integration of evangelical spirituality and prophetic ethics in social action which is both personally and politically transformative. At this point, once more, Reformed and Latin American liberation theology discover each other. Gutiérrez, reflecting on Matthew 25:31-46, expresses this in a way which must surely receive a Reformed "Amen!":

> We have also come to understand that a true and full encounter with our neighbor requires that we first experience the gratuitousness of God's love. . . . The other is our way for reaching God, but our relationship with God is a precondition for encounter and true communion with the other. It is not possible to separate these two movements, which are perhaps really only a single movement: Jesus Christ, who is God and man, is our way to the Father but he is also our way to the recognition of others as brothers and sisters.[66]

In dialogue with liberation theology, Reformed theology is able to make all the necessary connections between justification, sanctification, grace and nature, faith and obedience, the personal and the social, and thereby prepare the way for a new understanding of the church as the community of transformation in the world. In the words of Jürgen Moltmann:

65. Carol Johnston, "Learning Reformed Theology from the Roman Catholics: The U.S. Pastoral Letter on the Economy," in *Reformed Faith and Economics*, ed. Robert L. Stivers (New York: University Press of America, 1989), p. 207. See the pastoral letter by the National Conference of Catholic Bishops, *Economic Justice for All: Catholic Social Teaching and the U.S. Economy*, 1986.

66. Gutiérrez, *We Drink from Our Own Wells*, p. 112.

On the foundation of justification, without which there is no new beginning for the unrighteous, and on the basis of liberation, without which there is no new life, the meaning of the history of Christ is then unfolded in a new obedience (Rom. 6:8ff.), in the new fellowship (Rom. 12:3ff.), and in the manifestation of the Spirit in the charismatic powers of the new creation.[67]

Having laid this evangelical foundation for liberation, we turn to the struggle itself, the task of the liberated in the world. For it is here that the danger of self-righteous legalism and Calvinist imperialism is most evident, but it is also here that Reformed theology engages in its prophetic task in response to the liberating good news of Jesus Christ.

The Vocation of the Cross-Bearers

Recalling Luther's problems with the letter of James, it is fascinating to see how Calvin seeks to overcome what he rightly perceives as a false antithesis between Paul's teaching on justification by faith and James' stress on the need for works to justify our faith. He writes, "as Paul contends that we are justified apart from the help of works, so James does not allow those who lack good works to be reckoned righteous." Those "who by true faith are righteous" prove their faith by their actions, without which faith is but "a bare and imaginary mask."[68] This brings us to Calvin's very important and well-known "third use of the law."

While Luther did not speak of the "third use of the law," there are intimations of it in the *Loci Communes* of his close companion Philip Melanchthon.[69] But it is Calvin who really

67. Jürgen Moltmann, *The Church in the Power of the Spirit* (London: SCM, 1977), p. 31.

68. *Institutes*, 3.17.11-12.

69. Philip Melanchthon, *Loci Communes* (1555), chap. 7. See Clyde L. Manschreck, ed., *Melanchthon on Christian Doctrine* (Grand Rapids: Baker Book House, 1965), p. 127.

elaborates on it and uses it in such a way that it begins to distinguish Reformed and Lutheran theology as they later develop. Calvin's use of it ensured that in Reformed theology ethics was not to be regarded as an addendum to theology but of its essence. Here, paradoxically, where we see one of the reasons for Calvinist legalism, we also find a further fundamental building block for a liberating Reformed theological ethic.

For Luther, it will be recalled, the law has two uses, a civil and a spiritual. The second or civil use of the law is to restrain evil in society, but its first and proper use is to reveal human sin (hence its link, as we saw, with the "hermeneutics of suspicion") and our inability to be justified by our own works, thus leaving us inexcusable before God. This proper use of the law demonstrates the reality of our fallen humanity, and because it shows how incapable we are of achieving any righteousness, it has become, as Paul told the Galatians, a curse. Calvin shares both of these understandings of the law,[70] but he goes further and speaks of a third use, which is the reason the law was originally given—that is, as a guide to life in the world.[71] Christ, in fact, restored the law to its integrity so that now we can follow its precepts no longer as a burden but as a joy and delight.[72]

Thus we find, from the first edition of Calvin's *Institutes* published in 1536 to the last in 1559, an exposition of the Ten Commandments, not simply as a list of prohibitions but, following the teaching of Jesus, as God's claim upon our lives. Edward Dowey has rightly said that for Calvin "law in the new life under the Gospel is the structure of love."[73] Law, in this sense, enables life. The gospel, in other words, liberates us from the curse of the law and thereby sets us free to pattern our lives on the love of God and our neighbor. But this pattern is not vague in content; it is specific, contextual, and concrete. It does

70. *Institutes*, 2.7.6ff.; cf. 4.20.14-21.
71. *Institutes*, 2.7.12.
72. *Institutes*, 2.8.7.
73. Edward A. Dowey, "Law in Luther and Calvin," *Theology Today* 41 (July 1984): 152.

not simply tell us to love God and our neighbor; it seeks to help us understand what that means in the most concrete way possible in relation to our priorities, human relations, sexuality, work and labor, money, and material interests. This is what Calvin meant by the ordering of society, and, of course, here lies the danger of legalism, of the will-to-order. But it need not be so. Indeed, here also lies the counterbalance to much modern-day licence that can be as dehumanizing as any legalism.

Dietrich Bonhoeffer's distinction between "cheap" and "costly grace" goes to the heart of what Reformed theology is concerned about in stressing the "third use of the law."[74] This comes out most clearly in Bonhoeffer's *Ethics* where he discusses the need for the church to confess her guilt for what was happening in the Third Reich. If we examine what Bonhoeffer says in that regard, we discern the Ten Commandments interpreted both in terms of the gospel and in terms of the context in which the Confessing Church found itself in Nazi Germany. The church, Bonhoeffer argues, is not only guilty of idolatry; its loss of reverence for the sabbath is indicative of its complicity in the exploitation of labor. The church has become guilty for the collapse of parental authority, "of the breaking up of countless families, the betrayal of fathers by their children, the self-deification of youth." The church has failed to speak out on behalf of the victims of violence, oppression, murder; it has not raised its voice against sexual libertinism; it "has witnessed in silence the spoilation and exploitation of the poor and the enrichment and corruption of the strong"; indeed, the church is "guilty towards the countless victims of calumny, denunciation and defamation."[75] In other words, just as grace forgives, justifies, awakens faith, and gives new life, so the law enables the flourishing of life because it demands justice. If we consider what Bonhoeffer says in the light of his context as well as our

74. Dietrich Bonhoeffer, *The Cost of Discipleship* (London: SCM, 1959).
75. Dietrich Bonhoeffer, *Ethics* (New York: Macmillan, 1955), pp. 114-15.

own, we begin to discern the way in which the law understood in the light of the gospel is not a legalistic instrument of repression but a mandate for humanizing and liberating action; indeed, the law is the basis for the struggle for human rights.

At a more personal level, Jan Milič Lochman, in the preface to his exposition of the Ten Commandments, appropriately entitled *Signposts to Freedom*, gives testimony to the impact that the Ten Commandments have had on his life from his earliest days. The atmosphere of his Calvinist parents' and grandparents' home was, he writes, "of real down-to-earth delight— in the good gifts of creation, the solidarity of the human family, neighbours and church, and also, as the most natural thing in the world, in the good commandments of God. . . . Right from infancy," he continues, "I had learned to see the Ten Commandments themselves, and not just the 'glad tidings' of the New Testament, as a liberating message, as the 'other form of the Gospel.' "[76] How different was his experience from that of David Hume. Yet it was far closer to Calvin's intention than that of Scottish Calvinism in the depressed world of eighteenth-century Scotland.

Christian freedom for Calvin was the very antithesis of legalism, yet not an invitation to licence. It was freedom from the bondage of the law, but also freedom to obey the law joyfully.[77] Christian obedience is, in fact, the expression of thanksgiving for the gift of life and for the fact that we now belong to Jesus Christ. This sense of belonging to Jesus Christ out of gratitude for his saving death on the cross is fundamental to Reformed spirituality, as can be seen from the very first question in the Heidelberg Catechism and the second article of the Barmen Declaration. Precisely because Jesus Christ is "God's assurance of the forgiveness of all our sins," he "is also God's mighty claim upon our whole life." In passing, it might be noted that whereas the section on "man's redemption" in

76. Jan Milič Lochman, *Signposts to Freedom* (Minneapolis: Augsburg, 1982), p. 9.
77. *Institutes*, 3.19.1.

the Heidelberg Catechism includes only nine questions on sin and guilt, it has seventy-four on redemption, and twenty-six on thankfulness![78] And thankfulness or gratitude is the springboard for Christian ethics.

All this has its roots firmly in the following words of Calvin which have echoed down through the centuries, resonating with liberation theology in our own day. Gratitude to God for forgiveness and personal liberation is expressed in obedient love for others.[79] The importance of these paragraphs for Calvin can be seen in the fact that he shifted them from the end of the first edition of the *Institutes* to the center of his treatment of salvation in the final edition.

> We are not our own: let not our reason nor our will, therefore, sway our plans and deeds. We are not our own: let us therefore not set it as our goal to seek what is expedient for us according to the flesh. We are not our own: in so far as we can, let us therefore forget ourselves and all that is ours.
>
> Conversely, we are God's: let us therefore live for him and die for him. We are God's: let his wisdom and will therefore rule all our actions. We are God's: let all the parts of our life accordingly strive toward him as our only lawful goal. . . . For, as consulting our self-interest is the pestilence that most effectively leads to our destruction, so the sole haven of salvation is to be wise in nothing and to will nothing through ourselves but to follow the leading of the Lord alone.[80]

This leads Calvin to one of the most challenging and profoundly moving sections in his *Institutes*, that in which he

78. See Karl Barth, *Learning Jesus Christ through the Heidelberg Catechism* (Grand Rapids: Eerdmans, 1964), p. 47.

79. See Jon Sobrino, *Spirituality of Liberation* (New York: Orbis, 1988), pp. 61-62.

80. *Institutes*, 3.7.1. There is a striking similarity between these paragraphs in Calvin and the words of a concluding dedication in the Methodist Order for the annual Covenant Service in the *Book of Offices*, which suggests the influence of the Reformer.

speaks of "Bearing the Cross" as an integral part of self-denial.[81]

The cross of Christ is not, for Calvin, only an objective historical event whereby we are redeemed from beyond ourselves. It is, of course, such an event, but it is also an event that embraces us and the inevitable suffering which disciples of Jesus Christ have to bear. There are, Calvin tells us, "many reasons why we," like Jesus himself, "must pass our lives under a continual cross."[82] Not only is it entirely appropriate that the followers of the crucified Christ should suffer with him, but likewise the cross of discipleship brings us to a more profound trust in God. It helps us to experience God's faithfulness and gives hope for the future; it trains us in patience and obedience and nourishes and heals us. It is, indeed, a sign of God's love to us as his sons and daughters. But it is also an inevitable consequence of struggling for righteousness in the world. Poverty, exile, contempt, prison, disgrace, and death are all calamities, but they are transformed in the struggle for justice "into happiness for us." In this way, in fact, our lives are shaped by Christ and we imitate him not by withdrawal from the world, but by struggling to be faithful to the gospel within it.

Such suffering derives from the self-denial of discipleship. There is another form of self-denial that leads to a denigration of the body and of true self-esteem, and Calvin sometimes, and Calvinism often, tends in that direction. But Calvin at his best stresses not the self-denial of an unfeeling, fatalistic Stoic, nor the self-denial of a masochist, but the self-denial of gratitude and discipleship, self-denial as the antithesis of self-interest. It is doing the will of God, which requires that we put the interests of others before our own. After all, self-denial, as Calvin himself says, is not desiring "what makes men more miserable."[83] On

81. *Institutes*, 3.8; on the possible influence of Thomas à Kempis on Calvin at this point, see Ronald S. Wallace, *Calvin, Geneva, and the Reformation* (Edinburgh: Scottish Academic Press, 1988), p. 191.
82. *Institutes*, 3.8.2.
83. *Institutes*, 3.7.8.

the contrary, he tells us that the good things of life are to be enjoyed as gifts of God. Food, for example, is given by God not just "to provide for necessity, but also for delight and good cheer."[84] But once again, this is not a call to abuse of the good things of life, but a call to proper stewardship.

Calvin's doctrine of vocation, which has been the subject of much debate and much misunderstanding, lies at the heart of his ethics. Indeed, "the Lord's calling is in everything the beginning and foundation of well-doing."[85] It is a travesty of Calvin's critique of human ambition that this has often led his descendents to confuse their human achievements and successes with the will and calling of God. Calvin's doctrine of vocation did give labor and work a new dignity,[86] as St. Benedict had done centuries before in his famous Rule for the monastic life. But this sanctification of labor was not intended as a justification for achievements of the "self-made man" at the cost of others, especially at the cost of their alienation from the God-given dignity of work.

Likewise, Calvin's concern for equity among people does not allow him to confuse a person's class position in society with the will and calling of God. For Calvin, the essence of God's calling is that it is a vocation to service. This means that some might be called to be rulers and others to be servants, and both had better fulfill that calling to the best of their ability; but this is a functional, necessary arrangement for the well-being of society. Furthermore, it is not irreversible—in the providence of God the servants could become the rulers! However, the heart of the matter is not social relations but the Christian vocation to service. Servants as much as rulers, and no less than priests or monks, are called to regard their tasks as an integral part of their discipleship. All labor thus becomes sanctified, and the Christian is liberated by the gospel for service in the world as part of what it means to be a Christian.

84. *Institutes*, 3.10.2.
85. *Institutes*, 3.11.6.
86. See André Biéler, *The Social Humanism of Calvin* (Richmond: John Knox Press, 1964), pp. 47, 61.

That leads us, as Nicholas Wolterstorff rightly argues, to "the center of Calvinist social piety: obedience motivated by gratitude and expressed in vocation."[87]

This is of particular importance for a Reformed spirituality of liberation today. Many of the theologians of liberation in Latin America are members of religious orders committed by their vows to identification with poverty. While some of us who are heirs of the Reformation have grown to appreciate the importance of such religious orders, Calvin's protest against them in his own day was precisely that they were not only failing to fulfill their vocation, but they were also creating class distinctions in the life of the church. Some were called to full obedience to the gospel; the rest (the laity) need only obey the teaching of the church. Calvin did not simplistically reject monasticism; he sought to bring its vision into the life of the church as a whole. This is why important connections can be drawn between Calvin and Benedictine spirituality,[88] and why Lucien Richard can with good reason argue that the distinctive ideas in Calvin's spirituality, while originating in response to the challenges of the sixteenth century, "have a new and unmistakable validity today." He goes further and claims that "modern emphases have deepened Calvin's seminal concepts, giving his vision of the Christian life a new and broader dimension."[89] The circle has, indeed, come fully around in the formation of the Taizé community in France, where the best of monastic spirituality has combined with that of Calvin and the Reformed tradition and so has enabled lay people to discover what it means to be Christian in the world amid the struggle for justice and peace.

At this point, Catholic liberation and Reformed theology can find each other in a new way as they engage both theologically and practically in the struggle for justice arising out of a

87. Nicholas Wolterstorff, *Until Justice and Peace Embrace* (Grand Rapids: Eerdmans, 1983), p. 15.
88. See Barth, *Church Dogmatics*, IV/2, pp. 17-18; Jean-Marc Chappuis, "The Reformation and the Formation of the Person," *Ecumenical Review* 39 (January 1987): 4ff.
89. Richard, *The Spirituality of John Calvin*, p. 174.

renewed spirituality. But the moment we engage in serious theological reflection on the issues, we soon find ourselves up against the historic problem of nature and grace that has separated Roman Catholic and Protestant theology and practice since the time of the Reformation. This problem lay at the heart of Bouyer's critique of Calvin's doctrine of sanctification, and we have already encountered it in another form in the previous chapter's discussion on election.

The Nature-Grace Debate Revisited

The traditional debate about grace and nature between Catholics and Protestants has focused on the question whether grace perfects fallen nature (the Catholic view) or re-creates it (the Protestant view). Fundamental to that debate is the question concerning human choice and cooperation in the process of God's gratuitous salvation. Both sides agree that grace is prevenient—that is, it precedes human faith and endeavor—so that human salvation is always ultimately dependent upon God's redemptive love and action. But whereas Protestant orthodoxy has always stressed salvation by grace alone, which then issues in the good works of gratitude, Roman Catholic teaching since the Council of Trent has always insisted on the necessity of human cooperation, albeit preceded and aided by God's grace.

This traditional difference between Catholics and orthodox Protestants has had certain consequences, not only in understanding the human role in redemption, but also in understanding the nature and mission of the church, and therefore in determining the relationship of the church to culture in particular and more generally to the world as such. Whereas Catholic theology stresses the fundamental continuity between the divine and the human, between the church and the world, Protestant orthodoxy stresses the discontinuity caused by human sinfulness and therefore the need for a radical process of re-creation and transformation. In the latter scheme of things, any human initiative may become a challenge to God's pre-venient grace, any dependence for salvation on good works leads to self-righteousness and away from the righteousness of God through which alone we receive justification.

The terms of the debate between Catholics and Protes-tants about grace and nature were established by medieval scholastic theology building on the fourth-century legacy of St. Augustine, whose position in turn was the result of his heated controversy with the British monk Pelagius. Pelagius affirmed human free will despite sin, and he argued the need for human cooperation with grace in salvation; Augustine denied not the freedom of the will but fallen humanity's ability to choose the good, and he argued that salvation was only possible through the unmerited grace of God.

Without going into the details of the debate in the medi-eval church, with its many nuances and qualifications, we may say that while grace was generally understood by most scholas-tic theologians in an ontological or metaphysical way, there was no uniform Catholic position. Dominican theologians generally followed Thomas Aquinas's teaching on prevenient grace, while Franciscans, influenced by William of Ockham, taught that God's grace reached out to those who sincerely sought to do his will. Though all claimed to be in continuity with Augustine and therefore anti-Pelagian, there was considerable disagreement on what that meant.[90] Indeed, by the late medi-eval period on the eve of the Reformation, the situation was highly complex, and confusion abounded.

The central issue was precisely *how* God's prevenient "un-created" grace did relate to human nature. Luther formulated it by asking, "How can I find a gracious God?" By the time of the Reformation, the prevailing scholastic answer was that grace sacramentally infused nature and thus enabled human beings to believe in God and work out their salvation. This

90. See Karlfried Froehlich, "Justification Language and Grace: The Charge of Pelagianism in the Middle Ages," in McKee and Armstrong, *Probing the Reformed Tradition*, p. 24.

understanding of what was called "created grace" dominated the theological discussion on the subject. Grace was a virtue, an infused quality in humanity, by means of which sinful men and women could win the approval and thus the salvation of God.

The Protestant Reformation was, perhaps above all else, a reaction to this scholastic understanding of grace and a radical restatement of its biblical meaning as perceived by the Reformers. As far as the Reformers were concerned, medieval scholastic theology was not only semi-Pelagian at best, but its very confusion prevented people from knowing clearly and with certainty the good news of God's justifying and liberating grace in Jesus Christ. Precisely for this reason Luther and Calvin found it necessary to cut right through the sterile debates of the day and return directly to St. Paul's doctrine of justification by grace through faith, and they found St. Augustine a powerful ally in doing so.

In their return to the biblical sources and aspects of Augustinian theology for their understanding of the nature of God's grace, the Reformers restored its original personal and active sense against the current metaphysical and static meaning as it had worked itself out in the indulgence system of the Roman church. Grace was now understood as God's redemptive love, God's free gift of himself to women and men whereby he freely forgives sins and restores the relationship between himself and them. Salvation was not in any way dependent upon human effort aided by grace, but on grace alone. Good works which followed were signs of faithful obedience and gratitude. This view was not original to the Reformers—it even had its exponents within medieval theology. But for the Reformers it became the point of departure for everything else.

In the post-Reformation period the battlelines separating Catholics and Protestants were entrenched. The Council of Trent clarified the Catholic position against the Reformers, canonizing the Thomist position. Meanwhile, Protestant scholasticism gradually moved away from the dynamic and personalist categories of the Reformers, and, like their medieval counterparts, reduced them to metaphysical categories. Thus the debate, now between Catholics and Protestants, remained focused on the relationship between nature and grace as ontological entities. Calvinism in particular developed a whole set of concepts within which grace was defined and related to human experience and the world based on an Aristotelian understanding of God's being and relationship to the world as will and power.

One of the distinctions Calvinists made, derived from Calvin, was between "common grace" (Calvin called it "general grace"),[91] the grace present in the world restraining evil, and "special grace," the grace whereby we are saved. This eventually found expression in what Federal Calvinism and the Westminster Confession called the "covenant of works" and the "covenant of grace."[92] It also found expression in Kuyperian neo-Calvinism and in Afrikaner interpretations of it which have had serious social consequences. In this process, Calvin's own insistence on the priority of grace over law was subverted and the door was opened to a legalism of works, despite a confessional insistence on salvation by grace alone. Grace became a remedy for sin that enables men and women to fulfill their duty towards God as originally intended. The fulfillment of this duty thus became a sign of redemption, a proof of election. What was understood by Calvin as a response of gratitude expressed in loving obedience became a response of duty expressed in works—hence the legalism that has characterized Calvinism.

A further consequence of the scholastic understanding of grace, whether Catholic or Protestant, has been its privatization. The traditional Catholic understanding of the sacramental system as a means of grace focused on the individual in search of personal salvation. The sacraments became the means whereby grace was infused into the soul. The traditional orthodox Prot-

91. See the editorial notes on Calvin, *Institutes*, 2.2.17.
92. See Karl Barth, *Church Dogmatics*, IV/1, pp. 54ff.; Holmes Rolston III, *John Calvin versus the Westminster Confession* (Atlanta: John Knox, 1972).

estant view was that by grace the individual was made right with God and thus was regenerated, justified, and saved. The privatization of grace undermined not only its social and historical but also its personal character because it reduced the church as a community of persons in the world to an aggregate of individuals. This privatized, individualistic understanding of Christian faith has, more than anything else, undermined the Reformed tradition's commitment to the transformation of society. But it reflects a false, indeed, a fatal separation of nature and grace, of divine action and human responsibility.

Although differences remain between Catholic and Protestant theology on these issues, often exacerbated because of the use of different terminology, new ecumenical and historical possibilities have emerged in our time that have enabled theology to break through the inherited scholastic impasse and to lift the debate onto a new level.[93] Indeed, it can be argued that Calvin is closer to the Catholic tradition and even to Eastern Orthodoxy,[94] which largely escaped the nature-grace debate, than most of his descendents have appreciated. In Bouyer's opinion, Calvin's understanding of the gratuity of salvation and the transformation of the whole of life by grace is essentially the traditional Catholic position.[95] Moreover, despite a residue of Platonic dualism in his thought, Calvin's wholistic affirmations of God the creator and redeemer, of gospel and law, and of justification and sanctification, his insistence on the reign of Christ over all reality, and his teaching on vocation, prepare the way for an understanding of God's salvation that transcends privatized individualism and relates to the transformation of the world. In H. Richard Niebuhr's categories, Calvin's theology was not primarily one of "Christ against culture" but of "Christ transforming culture."[96]

93. See Lehmann and Pannenberg, *Condemnations of the Reformation Era*, pp. 36-37, 42-43; Segundo, *Grace and the Human Condition*, pp. 142-43.

94. See Barth, *Church Dogmatics*, IV/2, p. 233.

95. Bouyer, *A History of Christian Spirituality*, vol. 3, p. 86.

96. H. Richard Niebuhr, *Christ and Culture* (New York: Harper & Row, 1951), pp. 217-18.

Under the influence of Karl Barth and Karl Rahner, twentieth-century theology, both Reformed and Catholic, has rediscovered not only the priority of grace but also its interpersonal, dynamic character as God's love at work in Christ restoring our relationship with him in community. Both theologians clearly discerned the social significance of the doctrine of grace. Barth in particular saw an integral connection between the Reformation teaching on "grace alone" and the struggle of the church against Nazi ideology,[97] between justification by grace through faith alone and the struggle for social justice. In doing so he was following in the steps of Calvin, but he went one step further in relating justification and justice.[98] More recently, and on a more eschatological basis, this connection between grace and social justice within history has been powerfully argued by the Catholic theologian Johannes Baptist Metz and the Reformed theologian Jürgen Moltmann.[99] In doing so they have helped prepare the way for liberation theology, which has located the doctrine of grace firmly in the historical arena of the struggle for justice and liberation. The history of salvation and the history of human liberation and social transformation, while not to be confused, cannot be separated—they belong on the same continuum.

Grace in the Struggle for Liberation

Juan Luis Segundo has developed a theology of history in which God graciously sets people free for love and in a cumu-

97. See for example his famous controversy with Emil Brunner. Emil Brunner and Karl Barth, *Natural Theology* (London: Centenary, 1946).

98. See Barth's essays entitled "Rechtfertigung und Recht" ("Justification and Justice"), translated as "Church and State" in Barth, *Community, State, and Church* (New York: Doubleday, 1960). See especially Barth's comment on p. 148.

99. Johannes Baptist Metz, *Theology of the World* (London: Burns & Oates, 1969); Metz, *Faith in History and Society: Towards a Practical Fundamental Theology* (New York: Seabury, 1980); and Jürgen Moltmann, *A Theology of Hope* (London: SCM, 1967).

lative way transforms the world.[100] Likewise, Leonardo Boff can speak of grace as "the story of two loves written in the very arena of history,"[101] and of the need for theology "to discern the dimensions of grace and dis-grace in the reality of Latin America."[102] Grace thereby expresses God's purposes of salvation and liberation for the world as a whole in all its dimensions: for individual men and women in their personal struggles, their search for forgiveness, meaning, and eternal life, as well as in their corporate struggles for justice, reconciliation, and peace.

A close reading of Segundo and Boff will show that they remain Roman Catholic in their understanding of the relationship between nature and grace, and some elements in their thought may cause Reformed theologians to proceed with caution.[103] This is particularly so when the necessary distinction between salvation and liberation is in danger of being confused, thereby leading to unacceptable ecclesial and political consequences. Yet, having transcended the sterility of scholastic debate and rediscovered the biblical perspective on God's gracious activity in history and people, their central thrust resonates well with a truly Reformed theology. Both stress the priority of grace, both stress the character of grace as God's free gift in Jesus Christ, and both stress that grace liberates people for new relationships that have transforming significance for the world.

Liberation theology, however, has posed the question of the doctrine of grace—and therefore the question of human cooperation with God—in a new way by taking as its starting point the reality of social and structural oppression, or human

100. Segundo, *Grace and the Human Condition*, pp. 122-23.
101. Boff, *Liberating Grace*, p. 17.
102. Ibid., p. 81.
103. For an exploration of the issues see José Míguez Bonino, *Revolutionary Theology Comes of Age* (London: SPCK, 1975), pp. 132ff. It should also be kept in mind that there are differences between Roman Catholic liberation theologians on this issue, reflecting perhaps older debates between Thomists and the medieval Franciscan theologians.

dis-grace.[104] As we have already noted, sin is not only individualistic—it is social, embedded in the economic and political structures of which we are all a part. But, as Boff so perceptively writes, "since classical reflection on grace did not pay sufficient attention to the social aspect of sin, it did not discuss justification in social and structural terms." In fact, it did worse than that. Its reduction of justification to the private, individual sphere provided "ideological support for those in power and those responsible for oppression."[105]

> Now grace is being discussed in terms of the liberation of humanity from every sort of oppression. People are unmasking the situations embodying dis-grace and calling for the creation of situations where God's grace can be fleshed out in history in more fraternal and more just mediations.

Grace, as Boff understands it, is "God's free love and his liberating presence in the world."[106] Reflecting on this concern, Mark Kline Taylor has called for a more immanental understanding of grace within Reformed theology:

> The Reformed tradition's praiseworthy world-formative impulse has been guided by a theology that all too easily, perhaps unwittingly, accepts a world-repressive compromise with established orders. It does this, in spite of all its talk about doing good and practicing vocation, in part because its adherents think it possible to experience God's grace before, or apart from encountering radical

104. The use of the word "dis-grace" in this context could be misunderstood. From the perspective of a "theology of the cross," dis-grace could refer to the crucifixion of Jesus and to the witness of those who suffer rejection by others in their service of the gospel. But this is not what is intended here. Rather, "dis-grace" refers to those disgraceful actions in history which cause human suffering and oppression, not those actions of redemptive suffering which are its result.

105. Boff, *Liberating Grace*, p. 15. This relates well to the opening theme of Bonhoeffer's *Cost of Discipleship*, that is, "costly grace" as distinct from "cheap grace."

106. Boff, *Liberating Grace*, p. 40.

struggle in society and history. What is needed is an appropriation by us of those elements in our tradition which teach that God's presence and our receiving God's grace are immanent to social and historical struggle.

In the light of this Taylor proposes that we talk about "the pre-eminence of grace as the power of God that lures us to and meets us in social and historical struggle, above all in the cries of those suffering in our midst."[107] After all, if for Calvin God's activity is not confined to the soul but is manifest in history and the world as a whole, then it follows that we meet God in our historical context.

The fear that this undermines the prevenient nature of grace would be misplaced because God's grace still precedes our action and vocation. The choice is not between prevenient and preeminent grace, but between a Neoplatonic and an incarnational understanding of grace. The difference is that we as persons are encountered by grace in history rather than in the privatized realm of the soul. We encounter the grace or saving presence of God not in Word and sacrament isolated from, but, to adapt Luther's phrase, "in, with, and under" human suffering and the struggle for justice. This is precisely where God's grace was encountered by Israel and the early church according to the biblical record. The Word of grace addressed the people of God in their historical struggle and journey—indeed, the Word gave redemptive, liberating meaning to that history. We encounter the saving "Word become flesh" in history, and the proclamation and hearing of that good news, as well as the human response, continues within our own historical context.

If we seek to locate our understanding of grace within history and the saving power of the gospel as that which not only transforms individuals but remakes humanity, we are in fact in continuity with the Reformed understanding of sanctification as world-affirming and world-transforming rather than world-denying asceticism. In this regard, Wolterstorff sees a

107. Mark Kline Taylor, "Immanental and Prophetic: Shaping Reformed Theology for the Late Twentieth Century Struggle" (unpublished paper, Princeton Theological Seminary, 1983), p. 29.

connection between liberation and Reformed theologies, for they both

> consider the making of humanity in history to be intrinsic to the coming of the Kingdom of God—while at the same time both see the Kingdom in its fullness as a gift and not as an accomplishment; neither etherealizes human destiny.[108]

Rather than being an alternative above the history of the world, salvation history—the history of God's gracious election and redemption—is expressed within it, giving it meaning and direction. Thus, liberating moments in history which point to the ultimate coming of the kingdom as that has been made known to us in the crucified Mediator and Lord, while always penultimate and not to be confused with the kingdom, are integrally related to it. What this means for social and political involvement and action remains to be considered in the final chapter. But that the encounter with God's grace in history has implications for political praxis should now be beyond doubt.

Boff's reflections on grace thus help us consider the historical struggle for justice and liberation from a new perspective. He writes, "The reconversion of evil into good can serve as a criterion of historical interpretation of faith." One can feel the passion behind his words as he continues: "The age-old suffering of the Latin American people must have some meaning. It should be paving the way for a major turning point in history, for a more fraternal and humane type of human being."[109] In the same way, from the perspective of grace, we must believe that the suffering and struggle in many other situations of oppression are not without meaning. Is it possible to believe in God if the immense pain caused by racism, injustice, and oppression in South Africa has the last word?

Life is graced with meaning only if we can discern God's transforming significance in the historical process and through grace be enabled and equipped to participate in it. While the

108. Wolterstorff, *Until Justice and Peace Embrace*, p. 66.
109. Boff, *Liberating Grace*, p. 83.

kingdom of God remains a gift, human suffering, struggling, and hoping are thus in some real sense integrally related to the birth of a new humanity crucified and risen in Christ. That is the full substance of Christian hope, the anticipation of God's kingdom on "earth as in heaven."

Conversion in Its Social Context

Conversion is a cognate of repentance, or, to use the New Testament word, *metanoia*; it means a fundamental change of heart and mind, a radical reorientation of life and behavior. The gospel narratives include many illustrations of conversions that result from people encountering God's grace in Jesus Christ. While there are similar elements in the various conversions, they also vary a great deal depending on who the people are, their station in life, and their particular needs. Jesus' preaching of the kingdom of God, with its call to repentance and conversion, was very specific and concrete when related to the diverse people he met. If God's grace reaches out to us through the Word in relation to our daily life within a particular social and historical context, then our conversion to Jesus Christ will necessarily be related to that context and our life and place within it. Conversion is not something that takes place in the abstract or only in the hidden recesses of the heart. It also involves our social relations.

By the same token, what repentance and conversion to Jesus Christ and entry into the kingdom mean will vary from one person to another. What these mean for oppressors or rich people will differ from what they mean for social victims, the oppressed, and the poor, as they did in Jesus' own ministry. This understanding of conversion is fundamental to *The Road to Damascus*, which, as its subtitle indicates, relates our conversion to the "kairos" in which we live. It also reminds us that we all, whether oppressed or oppressors, "are in continuous need of conversion."[110] But precisely what that conversion means will vary from person to person.

110. *The Road to Damascus: Kairos and Conversion* (Johannesburg: Skotaville, 1989), p. 20.

There is no "universal person"; every person is located within a specific social context. This does not deny that all people share in the fallenness of human nature, or that there are no similarities or constants in the process of conversion. On the contrary, all Christian conversion is the result of God's gracious activity in Christ through the Spirit, whereby women and men come to trust in God and are set free to love and obey God in loving the neighbor as well as the enemy. But the conversion of people who are sinned against will undoubtedly be different from that of those who have sinned against them. The conversion of black people in South Africa will be different from that of whites, though this does not sanction stereotyping.

One of the problems with *The Kairos Document* is that it too rigidly and readily categorized people as oppressors and oppressed. This does not mean that such categories are inappropriate, but that in using them there is a danger that people are reduced to types and dealt with on that basis instead of as people with particular human and social needs. This does not downplay the fact that a struggle is going on in society in which some people oppress others, and therefore in which some are oppressors and others are their victims. Thus Leonardo Boff, like *The Kairos Document,* sees the need for theology to discern both grace and dis-grace, its sinful antithesis, in the historical process. The conflict in which we are engaged both within the church and within society can be expressed in these terms. For grace means God's liberation and dis-grace means human oppression and bondage. But Boff refuses to place people into any legalistic, ideologically structured straitjacket; oppressor and oppressed coexist and intermingle like tares and wheat:

> No historical situation is so bad that it is pure oppression and leaves no room for grace. No historical situation is so good that it contains no traces of sin and oppression. Thus a truly coherent theological reading of reality cannot divide human beings neatly into oppressors and oppressed, or nations into developed and underdeveloped.

Boff continues:

Faith transcends these limitations. It cannot exhaust itself within such neat divisions without losing its nature as faith. It must say that every human being is simultaneously oppressor and oppressed, graced and disgraced, however much this may offend political human beings and their desire to identify which is which.[111]

This leads Boff to the crucial point which relates so well to Luther's dictum that we are always and at the same time both sinners and saints *(simul iustus simul peccator)*. "No one," Boff writes, "is so completely an oppressor that he or she can evade liberative grace completely. No one is so completely graced that he or she does not harbour inner traces of sinfulness and oppression."[112] This is a crucial insight, for it means that our conversion is not ultimately dependent upon our social location but upon God's grace, and that while oppressors might have more to repent of, those engaged in the struggle for justice as well as the victims of injustice are not without the need for personal liberation from sin, whatever form that sin may take.

We began this chapter by considering some of the negative, even pathological results of bad religion in general and bad Calvinism in particular. Conversion to Christ means, in many instances, liberation from the tyranny of bad religion, as Luther and Calvin knew so well. It means liberation from personal and corporate self-justification, self-righteousness, and every kind of self-centeredness, for it is precisely such hubris that dehumanizes and destroys others. Within the South African context whites have to undergo such a conversion in order to come to terms with reality, to shed their racial and cultural prejudices, to overcome their fears for the future, and to participate with others in the process of building a new nation free from the bondage of injustice and oppression. But it may also mean, as Allan Boesak describes it from his own experience, saying farewell to an innocence that denigrates the self and

111. Boff, *Liberating Grace*, pp. 83-84.
112. Ibid., p. 84.

thus undergoing a radical change from self-hate to a recognition of God-given self-worth, from a slave mentality to an acceptance of one's status as a daughter or son of God, from resignation and hopelessness to a commitment to struggling for God-given rights against everything preventing a person from knowing and living the life God wishes to give us to the full.[113] Here we see the converse of self-interest as sinful, for the depreciation of self can also be sinful. God's liberating grace does not put powerless people down; it lifts them up as sons and daughters and empowers them in the struggle for what is right and just. Ultimately, conversion is about the gift of life, for it is to life that Jesus calls us and for life that he liberates us. Without this liberation, the liberation of society as a whole remains problematic and incomplete. The task of evangelism is to enable all people to participate in the history of grace rather than dis-grace. The promise of evangelism is that God's grace is able to liberate people from every kind of bondage.

This means that not only those on the "right wing" of the political spectrum can and need to be converted, but, as Boff pertinently points out, also those who "may be personally opposed to any and every sort of privilege," but whose class status places "them among the favored members of discriminatory society. Unwittingly, perhaps even against their will, they may be part of a structure that fosters structural injustice."[114] They have, in fact, inherited a history of dis-grace to which they may or may not have contributed, but by which they are held in bondage, that of "original sin" as we earlier redefined it. At the same time, however, it is possible through conversion to begin to inherit "a history of grace," the history that has been unfolding "through the life-style of the common people, their concrete values in history, and their yearnings for liberation and human betterment."[115]

113. Allan A. Boesak, *Farewell to Innocence: A Socio-Ethical Study in Black Theology and Black Power* (New York: Orbis, 1977).
114. Boff, *Liberating Grace*, p. 84.
115. Ibid., p. 85.

Dietrich Bonhoeffer spoke of *metanoia* as participation in the sufferings of God in the world,[116] and liberation theology speaks of conversion as a turning to the poor or other victims of society in order to be in solidarity with them.[117] All of this points to the fact that conversion—the process of transformation from sin to righteousness through repentance, faith, and obedience—is not to be conceived of in the ahistorical and static way of privatized piety, but as a new praxis. Conversion or *metanoia* is a new way of life. While it is in the first instance facing reality, perceiving its injustice and our role in it and turning away from it, it is also beginning to participate in the process of its transformation.

> When Christians take cognizance of the link between the personal and the structural levels, they can no longer rest content with a conversion of the heart and personal holiness on the individual level. They realize that if they are to be graced personally, they must also fight to change the societal structure and open it up to God's grace.[118]

Conversion remains an intensely personal process or event, an ongoing *metanoia* through which we begin to identify, and then identify more fully, with God's liberating grace at work in the world. In the process we are ourselves transformed by grace and become partakers of the new humanity. "Evangelical conversion," writes Gutiérrez, "is indeed the touchstone of all spirituality. Conversion means a radical transformation of ourselves; it means thinking, feeling, and living as Christ-present in exploited and alienated persons."[119] Such transformation is the common denominator which should bind together the spirituality of both Catholic liberation theology and a truly liberated Reformed tradition, enabling both to witness to the transforming ferment created by the gospel.

116. Bonhoeffer, *Letters and Papers from Prison* (London: SCM, 1971), pp. 361-62.
117. Sobrino, *Spirituality of Liberation*, p. 63.
118. Ibid., p. 85.
119. Gutiérrez, *A Theology of Liberation*, p. 118.

5. *The Church Always Reforming*

In 1981 the Dutch Reformed Mission Church (NG Sendingkerk) in South Africa celebrated the centenary of its founding. In normal circumstances such an event would have been a joyous, uniting occasion. But in this instance that was not to be, for many members and ministers of the Sendingkerk regarded its original inception as wrong and heretical, a testimony to the power of racism rather than the reconciling gospel of Jesus Christ. For them the centenary was an occasion for protest against the policy of the white Dutch Reformed Church that had resulted in the creation of apartheid-churches, of which theirs was the first.

A year later, in 1982, at the Assembly of the World Alliance of Reformed Churches in Ottawa, Canada, eleven South African delegates from the NG Sendingkerk, as well as Presbyterians and Congregationalists, refused to participate in the service of Holy Communion with which the Assembly began. The decision created considerable controversy because it seemed to go against the very meaning of the sacrament as a sign of Christian love, reconciliation, and unity. But it was precisely for this reason that the eleven refused. They believed it would be hypocritical to share in the Lord's Supper with members of the white Dutch Reformed Church who were present on the grounds that the Dutch Reformed family of churches in South Africa was racially segregated. It was not possible to celebrate the sacrament of unity and fellowship in Canada when it was impossible to do so back home as one body in Christ. The church had become a "sign of disgrace," and therefore a "site of struggle" within the broader struggle for a nonracial and just South Africa.

The process of ecclesial segregation began at the synod of the Dutch Reformed Church in the Cape in 1829, when calls for segregation at Holy Communion were heard but were rejected as contrary to the Word of God and the Reformed Confessions. Gradually, however, segregation became a common practice at the Lord's Table. Despite opposition at several synods on the ground of incompatibility with the teaching of Scripture, by 1857 the Synod finally gave way to racial prejudice. The resolution adopted did not retract the church's understanding of biblical teaching, but it allowed the dictates of white racism and missionary pragmatism to override Scripture:

> The Synod considers it desirable and according to Holy Scripture that our heathen members be accepted and initiated into our congregations wherever it is possible; but where this measure, as a result of the weakness of some, would stand in the way of promoting the work of Christ among the heathen people, then congregations set up among the heathen, or still to be set up, should enjoy their Christian privileges in a separate building or institution.[1]

By 1881 this allowance for exceptions had become the rule, and the Sendingkerk for people of mixed race ("coloured") was founded, the first of several racially based Dutch Reformed Churches in South Africa. This later provided the ecclesiological basis and theological justification for what was to be called "apartheid," and it is precisely for this reason that it has been

---

1. See Chris Loff, "The History of a Heresy," in John W. de Gruchy and Charles Villa-Vicencio, *Apartheid Is a Heresy* (Grand Rapids: Eerdmans, 1983), p. 19. Loff's essay outlines the historical development of the NG Sendingkerk in detail.

rejected as "nothing but a heresy."[2] Instead of the church and the sacraments being signs of God's liberating grace, they became a means of social and political disgrace. Such disgrace is by no means confined to the Dutch Reformed Church in South Africa, for much the same is true for other churches in the country and similar arguments for segregated churches were used in the United States and elsewhere. But wherever it is found it is contrary to the teaching of Scripture, as well as that of Calvin and the confessions of the Reformed tradition.

Restoration of the Ancient Church

The Reformation proclamation of the gospel as justification by faith alone created ferment in the medieval church because it set people free from ecclesiastical tyranny and enabled them to live life on the basis of personal faith and responsibility. But this did not mean that the church or sacraments were no longer important for the Reformers. On the contrary, for Calvin the church was "the mother of all Christians,"[3] for it was only through the church's faithful ministry of the Word and sacraments that the gospel could be heard, that faith could be sustained, and, especially for the Genevan Reformer, that the world could be transformed to the glory of God. Calvin's concern was by no means to replace the Catholic church with an association of individuals drawn together by their evangelical piety. His concern was the reformation of the church so that it could fulfill its mission.

Calvin was a "second generation" reformer, building on and consolidating the work of others. Whereas Luther resisted far-reaching structural reforms, Calvin saw them as a fundamental necessity. Thus François Wendel concludes his study of Calvin by observing that the Genevan Reformer has left the imprint of his personality on history not through the formula-

2. See David Bosch, "Nothing but a Heresy," in de Gruchy and Villa-Vicencio, *Apartheid Is a Heresy*, pp. 24-25.
3. *Institutes*, 4.1.4.

tion of any new doctrine but because "he was the founder of a powerfully organized Church and at the same time the author of a body of doctrine which was able to rally round it an intellectual elite as well as the mass of the faithful."[4] Wendel is correct, but two qualifications are necessary.

The first is that while Calvin's legacy was a carefully balanced account of Reformed doctrine and ecclesiology, it was really his successor in Geneva, Theodore Beza, along with John Knox in Scotland and the Puritans in England, who consolidated Calvinism into an ecclesiastical and political force. Calvin, for example, was "not a doctrinaire Presbyterian";[5] it was Beza who claimed that form of church government as the only biblical form, and it was Beza who made discipline a mark of the true church.

The second qualification is that while Calvin eventually sought to turn Protestantism into a unitive force, he originally had no intention of starting a new church or founding a new tradition. He saw himself as part of a reform movement within the Catholic church and regarded his primary task as rescuing it from the "tyranny of tradition" which destroyed its catholicity and prevented it from hearing the liberating Word of the gospel. Indeed, Calvin categorically rejects the possibility that there can "be two or three churches unless Christ be torn asunder—which cannot happen!"[6] From beginning to end Calvin confesses one holy and catholic church. As Troeltsch observes, it was only "the resistance of German Lutheranism, and the independence of Anglicanism, which forced Calvinism to become an independent Protestant Church."[7]

The Reformers discovered, of course, that you cannot restore the ancient church in the sixteenth century as it was in the first centuries any more than you can in the twentieth, for history has moved on. What is possible, and what was impera-

4. François Wendel, *Calvin* (London: Collins, 1965), p. 360.
5. Basil Hall, "Calvin against the Calvinists," in *John Calvin* (Appleford, UK: Sutton Courtenay Press, 1966), p. 26.
6. *Institutes*, 4.1.2.
7. Ernst Troeltsch, *The Social Teaching of the Christian Churches*, vol. 2 (London: George Allen & Unwin, 1956), p. 579.

tive for them, is that the church be reformed and renewed through Word and Spirit in correspondence with the ancient church and the reality of a new historical context. But this is not founding a new church, and that was never the intention of the Reformers. Their struggle was always a struggle to renew the old church, to restore its worship and its structure, to rediscover the true preaching of the Word and the right administration of the sacraments as its focus and form. The Second Helvetic Confession (1566), for example, clearly sets out to show that the Reformed believers are in unity with the old true church and therefore are not sectarian or heterodox.[8] In other words, the Reformers saw their task as enabling the church to get back on track in its task of bearing witness to God's saving and sanctifying purposes for the world.

Calvin would have been horrified by the many schisms that have taken place within the Reformed movement and would have found denominationalism incomprehensible. He would have been even more horrified by the fact that many divisions and schisms have been for personal, social, and political reasons contrary to the gospel. This largely explains why Calvin was more harsh in his attitudes towards the Anabaptists and others, like Michael Servetus, whom he regarded as heretics and schismatics, than he was towards Rome. Georgia Harkness is correct in her assessment that "in Calvin's eyes apostasy was worse than papistry; the virus of Protestant heresy a more deadly poison than that of Roman error."[9]

In the same passage in which he speaks of the "tyranny of human tradition," Calvin makes it very clear: "For we do not scorn the church (as our adversaries, to heap spite upon us, unjustly and falsely assert); but we give the church the praise of obedience, than which it knows no greater."[10] And in his debate with Cardinal Sadoleto he claims:

8. Second Helvetic Confession, for example, chaps. 13 and 17.
9. Harkness, *John Calvin: The Man and His Ethics* (Nashville: Abingdon, 1958), p. 97.
10. *Institutes,* 4.10.18.

All that we have attempted has been to renew that ancient form of the Church, which, at first was sullied and distorted by illiterate men of indifferent character, and was afterward flatigiously mangled and almost destroyed by the Roman pontiff and his faction.[11]

Several years later, in 1543, in his address to Emperor Charles V in which Calvin set out at length and with great style his rationale for "The Necessity of Reforming the Church," Calvin reiterates a constant theme that the Reformers "had no other end in view than to ameliorate in some degree the miserable condition of the Church."[12] Moreover, he goes on to speak of the Reformers as those who have "done no small service to the Church in stirring up the world as from the deep darkness of ignorance to read the Scriptures." Clearly, even at this stage, when the break with Rome was complete and his work at Geneva in full swing, Calvin understood his work as reforming the Church, not creating a new one. With reference to auricular confession, but with wider significance, Calvin concludes, "we have no controversy in this matter with the ancient Church; we only wish, as we ought, to loose a modern tyranny of recent date from the necks of believers."[13]

Luther had perceived early on that the Reformation was a struggle between the true and false church, between the church that sought to be faithful to the gospel and the church that was in bondage to the law of human tradition, epitomized by the papacy. Calvin inherited this view, and his work as a reformer confirmed the fact that the reformation of the church was a continuous struggle—not only against the papacy but also against radical schismatics and civil authorities. For Calvin, as for contemporary liberation theologians, the church was

11. John Calvin and Jacopo Sadoleto, *A Reformation Debate*, ed. John C. Olin (Grand Rapids: Eerdmans, 1976), p. 62.

12. Calvin, "The Necessity of Reforming the Church," in *Calvin: Theological Treatises*, ed. J. K. S. Reid (Philadelphia: Westminster, 1984), p. 186.

13. Ibid., p. 216.

and is a "site of struggle" against tyranny, and any attempt to reform it inevitably meant conflict within it.

The focus of Calvin's attack was the triumphalist and absolutist claim of Rome, the claim to be the kingdom of God on earth with control of the keys to the kingdom of God in heaven. This, as we have seen, lay at the heart of Calvin's critique of the idolatry of Rome. Over against these claims, Calvin insisted that the kingdom of God is God's reign in Christ over the church, and that therefore the church is called to be obedient to the Word of God. Furthermore, the true Church is known only to God—it is the church of God's elect, and therefore no one can control or manipulate it. On the contrary, its unity does not lie in allegiance to Rome but is a gift of God's grace in Jesus Christ. Kilian McDonnell puts Calvin's position in a nutshell: "The lordship of Christ is effective in her only on condition of her unconditional poverty. The lordship of Christ stands over against all human presumptions, all self-redemption, all ritual exhibitionism, and all ecclesiasticism."[14]

The undeniable fact that Calvin and the other Reformers were no longer within the Roman church was attributed by Calvin, on the one hand, to their having been "expelled with anathemas and curses,"[15] and, on the other, to the necessary act of separating themselves from falsehood.[16] But as Calvin understood this, it was not separation from the Catholic church but separation from the papal control of the church so that Christ alone should reign. Calvin, unlike Luther, was even reticent to speak of the "false church" precisely because there was only one church. The struggle was rather within the one church between truth and falsehood.[17] It was not that there were no true Christians within the Roman Catholic church, for even there the Word of God could be rightly proclaimed, heard,

14. Kilian McDonnell, *John Calvin, the Church and the Eucharist* (Princeton: Princeton University Press, 1967), p. 172.

15. *Institutes*, 4.2.6.

16. *Institutes*, 4.2.10.

17. Alexandré Ganoczy, *The Young Calvin* (Philadelphia: Westminster Press, 1987), p. 282.

and obeyed.[18] But the papacy, curia, and their supportive theologians had placed the church in bondage to their unbiblical teaching, teaching that was also at variance with the ancient traditions of the Catholic church itself. Hence, according to Calvin, the unity of the universal church is preserved not by allegiance to Rome but by allegiance to the Word of Christ.[19]

Calvin and his descendents pursued the task of reforming the church according to the Word of God with considerable vigor and thoroughness. "Reformed teaching," writes Jaroslav Pelikan, "put at the head of its agenda the task of carrying 'reform in accordance with the Word of God' to its necessary consequences, with a consistency and a rigor that went considerably beyond Luther."[20] But it did not go as far as the Anabaptists; indeed, as we have already intimated, Calvin's criticism of Rome is often far less harsh than his rejection of the more radical Reformers of his day. The reason for this was largely Calvin's own commitment to Christendom—that is, to the Christianization of civilization and the maintenance of its unity, a concern Catholics and Calvinists shared alike. Unlike Luther, for Calvin the church was far more than an instrument of salvation; it was a means of grace for the sanctification of society and every dimension of life within it.[21]

Reform within Christendom

In seeking to reform the Catholic church, then, Calvin did not see any need to break with Constantinian Christendom. His appeal to the Fathers of the first three centuries (that is, prior to the Constantinian settlement) and his critique of the temporal claims of the Roman see that derived from that settlement did not lead him to reject Constantinianism or connect it with the tyranny he so strongly opposed. On the contrary, Calvin

18. *Institutes*, 4.2.12.
19. *Institutes*, 4.1.9.
20. Jaroslav Pelikan, *The Christian Tradition*, vol. 4: *Reformation of Church and Dogma* (Chicago: University of Chicago Press, 1984), p. 186.
21. See Troeltsch, *The Social Teaching of the Christian Churches*, p. 591.

was, in George Williams' terminology, a "magisterial re-former."[22] He did not hesitate to use the instruments of the state to further the interests of the church. In other words, Calvin not only refused to follow the Anabaptists' rejection of Christendom, but he used the established position of the church to persecute its more radical reformers even while he attempted to restore the church to its pre-Constantinian glory. This cling-ing to the prerogatives of Christendom lay behind Calvinist imperialism, and it remains a source of tension and contradic-tion in Reformed as well as Catholic ecclesiology even today. This is particularly true in places like Latin America and South Africa, where Constantinianism has been cultivated by the state in the service of its own legitimation, and where the church has cooperated in the process.

One of the legacies of Constantinianism endemic to the medieval church was, in Segundo's words, "that new members no longer entered Christianity through personal conversion but rather through the simple process of birth."[23] This meant that the growth of the church became vegetative rather than trans-formative, a church of the unevangelized. This phenomenon, as Segundo notes, had disastrous consequences in Latin Amer-ica as well as in many other places where Christianity has been by law, custom, or dominance the established religion. Segun-do's comment reveals, however, the very dilemma in which the Reformed tradition has found itself ever since Calvin struggled to maintain the tension between a church of committed mem-bers and a church established in society, a church seeking to be faithful to Scripture, yet trapped by the prejudices and weak-nesses of its members, their cultural norms, and the protective cocoon of Christendom.

An illustration of this struggle on two fronts, the one Roman and the other Anabaptist,[24] is seen in Calvin's somewhat

22. George Williams, *The Radical Reformation* (Philadelphia: West-minster, 1962), p. xxiv.
23. Juan Luis Segundo, *The Community Called Church* (Dublin: Gill & Macmillan, 1980), p. 45.
24. See Willem Balke, *Calvin and the Anabaptist Radicals* (Grand Rapids: Eerdmans, 1981), p. 45.

laborious and tortuous defense of infant baptism.[25] What is of interest to us here is not whether infant baptism can be defended, or Calvin's lapse from exegetical integrity, but the motivation for his argument. His defense of infant baptism is an affirmation of continuity with the Catholic church, an affirmation of the church as a covenant community in which grace precedes individual faith, and an insistence on the need for the church to remain an institution at the center of the public arena in order to Christianize it. Calvin was well acquainted with Anabaptist thought and practice, but because he desperately wanted to distance himself and the Reformation from Anabaptist radicalism he tended to react very strongly and negatively. For Calvin as for Luther, Anabaptism meant social revolution.[26] But he was also fearful of its sectarianism and scornful of its claims to be "pure and undefiled," even though he himself believed that the church should endeavor to be holy and blameless.[27]

Calvin was seeking to resolve one of the crucial problems left unresolved by medieval ecclesiology and later Christian humanism, and one that remains with us. The corruption of the late medieval church was such that many who ardently desired reformation fell back upon Augustine's teaching on the "invisible church." Augustine clearly did not deny the importance of the visible church, its structure and witness in the world. But he recognized that the visible church included many nominal members and had many blemishes. It was not the pure "bride of Christ" it was meant to be, nor was it possible, as the Donatists argued, for it to be pure in this world. But this was no excuse for not striving after holiness; it was not an excuse for the visible church to be a sign of disgrace rather than a means of grace.

The way in which Calvin sought to resolve the tension between the purity of the church and the inevitability of nominal membership was, theologically, through the doctrine of election, and practically, through the preaching of the Word and

25. *Institutes*, 4.15-16.
26. Balke, *Calvin and the Anabaptist Radicals*, pp. 41, 43, 48.
27. Ibid., pp. 50-51.

the exercising of discipline. Both of these became central tenets of Calvinist faith and practice and were fundamental to the legalistic ethos that emerged within the Reformed tradition.[28] Yet, despite the need to create a disciplined church, Calvin argued that the true church is known only to God, that it even existed within the corrupt Roman church, and that while every effort must be made for the church to be pure the Anabaptists were wrong in believing that such a state could be achieved in this world. Thus Calvin rejected any absolutist claims by the church to be the only true church on the grounds of its historic structures and hierarchy or because of its sectarian exclusiveness. There was a qualitative distinction between Christ, the head and Lord of the church, and the empirical church; the kingdom of God and the church were not coterminous. The true church, the elect, were ultimately known to God alone. Thus the doctrine of election, rather than providing a basis for what became "imperial Calvinism," was protection from absolutist claims and triumphalist pretensions. It was central to Calvin's ideological critique of what he perceived to be the idolatrous claims of Rome.

What Calvin sought to avoid, however, was not only the absolutizing of the church but also the development of a doctrine of "two churches," the one "invisible," the other "visible."[29] "The church," Calvin wrote in the first edition of his *Institutes*, "can exist without any visible appearance."[30] Yet for him the "invisible" church was not an alternative church, but a critical means to challenge and reform the "visible" church. There is, in fact, "only one church which is distinguished from

28. See Troeltsch, *The Social Teaching of the Christian Churches*, pp. 590ff.

29. The term "invisible church" *(ecclesia invisibilis)* occurs only once in the final edition of the *Institutes*, 4.1.7. See Wilhelm Neuser, "Calvin's Teaching on the *notae fidelium:* An Unnoticed Part of the *Institutio* 4.1.8," in *Probing the Reformed Tradition*, ed. Elsie Anne McKee and Brian G. Armstrong (Louisville: Westminster/John Knox Press, 1989), p. 83.

30. Calvin, *Institutes of the Christian Religion, 1536 Edition*, rev. ed., trans. Ford Lewis Battles (Grand Rapids: Eerdmans, 1986), p. 9.

the spurious church by the fact that it exists to serve Jesus Christ."[31] In Niesel's words, Calvin "does not intend his description 'visible' church to be taken as a cloak behind which human weakness and sin, and the deliberate disavowal of the Lordship of Christ, may undisturbedly work themselves out."[32] Hence, Calvin's "humble exhortation" to Emperor Charles V on "The Necessity of Reforming the Church" was written, as Calvin put it, on behalf "of all those who wish Christ to reign." Indeed, for Calvin, as McDonnell perceptively notes, "where the lordship of Christ is actualized there is the church."[33] This was the basis for the later development of the Free Church tradition in England for which the "crown rights of the Redeemer" required the disestablishment of the church from the control of the state. There we find, as P. T. Forsyth so rightly discerned, a creative blending of Calvinism and Anabaptism, a blending of the "gathered church" of believers and the "public church" engaged in its mission to the nation.[34] This relates well to the ecclesiology that has emerged among Latin American Catholic liberation theologians for whom the church is essentially a minority community of committed disciples, yet not one that withdraws from the world; for them the church is engaged in a universal mission to "fashion human history" according to the gospel.[35]

Protestantism has often been criticized as a religion of individualism. That it should have become so would have been inconceivable to John Calvin, but it is nonetheless a critique with good foundation.[36] The origin of Protestant individualism is complex both theologically and sociologically. Theologically, it is rooted in pre-Reformation piety, in Luther's emphasis on

31. Ibid., p. 192.
32. Wilhelm Niesel, *The Theology of Calvin* (Philadelphia: Westminster Press, 1956), p. 191.
33. McDonnell, *Calvin, the Church and the Eucharist*, p. 173.
34. P. T. Forsyth, *Faith, Freedom and the Future* (London: Independent Press, 1955).
35. Segundo, *The Community Called Church*, p. 79.
36. See Troeltsch, *The Social Teaching of the Christian Churches*, p. 587.

personal faith and conversion, the priesthood of all believers, and the right of each person to interpret Scripture under the inspiration of the Holy Spirit. Within Calvinism more specifically, the way in which the doctrine of election was interpreted tended to reinforce such individualism. The real church was the invisible church known only to God, those individuals whom God had called and chosen from the foundation of the world.

Sociologically, Protestant individualism is related to the collapse of feudalism, the rise of capitalist trade, and the growth of towns during the Reformation period. An ideological link between Luther's personalism and the emergence of a Protestant bourgeoisie was the individualism that emanated from the Enlightenment with its stress on human rights and freedoms. In other words, the break with Constantinian Christendom that began to occur in the aftermath of the Enlightenment—and especially after the French Revolution—gradually, in Leonardo Boff's words, tied Protestantism "to the historic liberal subject."[37] Thus, despite the fact that "the communal character of human existence is found in all" of Calvin's writings[38] ("humanity was formed to be a social animal," Calvin writes in his commentary on Genesis 2:18)[39] the Reformed tradition has been strongly influenced by the individualism that has pervaded European society since the Enlightenment. This has been especially true of the Reformed tradition within the Swiss, Anglo-Saxon, and Dutch worlds, where theology, sociology, and politics combined to shape a character of personal initiative and responsibility, human rights and democratic freedoms, and the liberty of conscience. The importance of this liberalizing development for the liberation of the Reformed tradition must not be underestimated, but it must also be recognized that it was not without its cost.

37. Leonardo Boff, "Luther, the Reformation, and Liberation," in *Faith Born in the Struggle for Life: A Rereading of Protestant Faith in Latin America Today*, ed. Dow Kirkpatrick (Grand Rapids: Eerdmans, 1988), p. 199.

38. See John Leith, *John Calvin's Doctrine of the Christian Life* (Louisville: Westminster/John Knox Press, 1989), p. 166.

39. John Calvin, *Commentaries on the First Book of Moses Called Genesis*, vol. 1, trans. John King (Grand Rapids: Eerdmans, 1948), p. 128.

Just as the Reformed tradition in the modern period has been tied to the liberal subject, so by extension it has also been tied to liberal political programs of reform rather than the restructuring of society on a collective or communal basis. This can be seen, for example, in the way in which many churches in the Reformed family in the West, and in English-speaking churches such as the Presbyterians and Congregationalists in South Africa, have been in the forefront of liberal causes but have been far more reserved in their support for radical social change. By way of contrast, Afrikaner Calvinism, in its legitimation of apartheid, rejected liberal reformism and supported the radical restructuring of society on a collective basis founded on cultural, ethnic, and national identity. Aligned to this has been an understanding of the church which, in its visible manifestation, is defined and structured by Afrikaner Calvinism according to race and nationality rather than individual piety.

At various moments in its history, then, Reformed ecclesiology has not escaped from falling prey to rampant individualism and the pietism that goes with it or ecclesiastical triumphalism and its attendant legalism. Yet its twofold character, its attempt to combine "the ideals of a free church with those of an establishment," which has rendered it "at once so prone to divide," has also enabled it to make a significant contribution to the rediscovery of the ecumenical church in our time.[40] It was this understanding of the church, for example, that was to play such a vital role in the shaping of church-and-state relations in the United States. It has also kept alive the notion that the "separation of church and state" does not lessen the public responsibility of the church but rather makes it even more needed, though in ways that are no longer Constantinian.

What is often forgotten, however, and yet what is crucial in Reformed ecclesiology for determining the freedom of the church to be the church, is not its formal relationship to the

---

40. G. S. M. Walker, "Calvin and the Church," in *Readings in Calvin's Theology*, ed. Donald K. McKim (Grand Rapids: Baker Book House, 1984), p. 223.

state but its freedom to confess Jesus Christ as Lord over all realms of life, not least its own.[41] This freedom implied that the church could never settle down on the assumption that its institutional form guarantees faithfulness. That was the Roman heresy, and it inevitably leads to triumphalism, whether Catholic or Reformed. For Calvin, the church under the Word and Spirit only existed in the process of reformation—hence the slogan *ecclesia semper reformanda*. The church is only the church when it is reforming according to its confession of Jesus Christ as Lord. Its structure is determined by its confession.

The Confessing Structure of the Church

The problem this presented for the Reformed tradition was that of ecclesial continuity. For the Roman Catholic Church, continuity was guaranteed by the doctrine of apostolic succession, the cornerstone of the institution. The Spirit had been given to the church and Christ reigned through those appointed to the episcopate. For the Reformers, the Spirit had likewise been given to the church and Christ reigned, but through the Word, not the hierarchy. Continuity thus became dependent upon divine grace and confessional faithfulness in fulfilling its task in the world. In the case of Luther this was more than sufficient and therefore the inherited church structures could be maintained, though under new evangelical management. For Calvin, however, the maintenance of evangelical faith required a church order consonant with Scriptural teaching and therefore an order that enabled the true and faithful ministry of the Word and sacraments, as well as the exercise of a godly discipline. For the Reformers the church was thus not hierarchically structured, for all its members were priests; it was structured functionally according to the charisms of the Spirit, and especially

41. See de Gruchy, "The Freedom of the Church and the Liberation of Society: Bonhoeffer on the Free Church, and the 'Confessing Church' in South Africa," in *Dietrich Bonhoeffer's Ethics: Old Europe and New Frontiers,* ed. Guy Christopher Carter et al. (Grand Rapids: Eerdmans, 1991).

the gift of preaching and teaching, in order that this priesthood might flourish and fulfill its role both in the church and in the world.

Calvin's decisive break with Roman ecclesiasticism and the stress on the need for the church to be always reforming did not mean, however, a lack of church order. Indeed, church order became an essential element within the Reformed tradition, sometimes to an exaggerated and unevangelical degree. But this concern for church order was based on the conviction that even though the true church could not be equated with its visible structure, its visible structure was part of its witness. The marks of the true church are visible.[42]

What Calvin saw so clearly was not only that individuals should be converted by the preaching of the gospel and should bear witness to Christ, but that the church itself needed to be reformed on an evangelical basis and to become a witness to the gospel. He saw, like any good Catholic ecclesiologist, that if the church was to be the mother of believers—nurturing them in the grace of Christ—and a sign of God's kingdom in the world, then it could not be relegated to an invisible role; it had to be structurally transformed so that it could truly fulfill its divinely given function. If Calvin had had recourse to sociological theory he would have argued that "the structure of the church has an effect on the consciousness of its members."[43]

Calvin allowed for disagreement on matters of secondary importance and on matters of indifference (*adiaphora*), and he affirmed the right of individual conscience in this regard.[44] But the true church lived by proclaiming the gospel and thus confessing Christ "according to the Scriptures." Anything that undermined this witness was to be opposed. Thus, once the church had been restructured according to the Word of God Calvin expressed reluctance about further change, and on his deathbed he even charged the Genevan pastors to resist change

42. See Neuser, "Calvin's Teaching on the *notae fidelium*," pp. 86f.
43. Gregory Baum, *Religion and Alienation* (New York: Paulist Press, 1975), p. 249.
44. *Institutes*, 3.19.7; 4.1.12.

as dangerous and harmful.[45] Yet he accepted the fact that restructuring the church according to the Word of God could lead to different forms of church government, including episcopacy, as long as they enabled the true preaching of the Word and administration of the sacraments.

Calvin, within limits, was flexible. This has not prevented churches within the Reformed tradition from an ecclesiasticism giving some kind of absolute status to particular forms of government, as though the Spirit was bound to Presbyterianism, Congregationalism, or Episcopalianism. But such ecclesiastical fundamentalism, like confessionalism, must be rejected as contrary to the liberating message of the gospel and contrary to Calvin's own protest against Rome.

The Reformed concern to ensure that everything is done "decently and in order," a commendable virtue, can become a damnable vice when it prevents the kind of transformation the gospel required at the time of the Reformation and still requires in our own time. In South Africa, Reformed church order and ecclesiastical legalism often have prevented the Dutch Reformed and other Reformed churches from being able to move responsibly against injustice, and, by the same token, they have enabled the churches to still the voice of the church's prophets. One such prophet was Beyers Naudé, a former moderator of the Dutch Reformed Church in the Transvaal, to whom we referred earlier.

Naudé's career as a "prophet without honor" in his own Afrikaner community was launched after the Sharpeville massacre of black protesters in 1960.[46] Sharpeville led to the convening of the Cottesloe Consultation of South African member churches of the World Council of Churches, a grouping that at that time included the Cape and Transvaal Synods of the Dutch Reformed Church, as well as the smaller, more politically con-

45. See Walker, "Calvin and the Church," p. 213; B. J. Kidd, *Documents Illustrative of the Continental Reformation* (Oxford: Clarendon Press, 1967), p. 650.
46. See Peter Randall, ed., *Not without Honour: Tribute to Beyers Naudé* (Johannesburg: Ravan, 1981).

servative Nederduitsch Hervormde Kerk. Although the Dutch Reformed participants at Cottesloe agreed to the decisions adopted at Cottesloe, which gave support to a process of racial reform, the Synods, under the powerful pressure of Prime Minister Verwoerd, rejected them and forced their participants to toe the line. Naudé refused and in 1963 founded the Christian Institute, the first attempt at creating an ecumenical confessing church in South Africa in relation to apartheid, thus laying the foundations for many of the confessing and prophetic initiatives taken by Christians since then.[47]

In the process, however, Naudé was, step by synodical step, excluded from the ministry of his own church, and, in 1977, together with the Christian Institute, Naudé was banned and silenced for seven years by the state. It is not for nothing that Douglas Bax rhetorically asked, when the Christian Institute was initially condemned by the church: "Has the Dutch Reformed Church become Roman Catholic?"[48] Ironically, the Catholic archbishop of Durban, Denis Hurley, was later to praise Naudé as a "Calvinist and Catholic," likening Naudé to Catholic liberation theologians in Latin America, and using "catholic" in its broader and more inclusive sense.[49] A further sign of Naudé's stature and commitment to the cause of justice and liberation was his inclusion in the African National Congress's delegation to their historic talks with the South African government in May 1990.

While aspects of church order may be, as Calvin maintained, matters of indifference, it is not an indifferent matter for the church always to be reforming according to the Word of God as this is heard, obeyed, and confessed in new historical contexts. This does not mean an indefinite or haphazard form, as Karl

47. See John W. de Gruchy, "A Short History of the Christian Institute," in *Resistance and Hope*, ed. Charles Villa-Vicencio and John W. de Gruchy (Grand Rapids: Eerdmans, 1985), pp. 14ff.

48. Douglas Bax, "Has the Dutch Reformed Church Become Roman Catholic?" *Pro Veritate* 5 (October 1966).

49. Denis Hurley, "Beyers Naudé—Calvinist and Catholic," in Randall, *Not without Honour*, pp. 70-71.

Barth stressed,[50] a continual tinkering with structures, or a restless introduction of novelty. It means a form that "arises from a hearing of the voice of Jesus Christ." It is neither enslavement to church law nor lawlessness, but "confessing" law, law derived from obedience to Christ.[51] Therefore, the church is always "ready for fresh obedience and prepared for the discovery and establishment of a new order on the basis of new and better instruction."[52] In this, as in other respects, the essence of Reformed ecclesiology is faithfulness to the gospel, for this not only determines its structure but also enables it to be the community of Christ in the world, truly united in its faith and praxis. Thus, the ecclesiological watchword *ecclesia semper reformanda*

> does not mean always to go with the time, to let the current spirit of the age be the judge of what is true and false, but in every age, and in controversy with the spirit of the age, to ask concerning the form and doctrine and order and ministry which is in accordance with the unalterable essence of the Church. . . . It means never to grow tired of returning not to the origin in time but to the origin in substance of the community. The Church is catholic when it is engaged in this *semper reformari*, so that catholicism has nothing to do with conservatism either.[53]

The characteristic order of elders (or presbyters) and deacons and, for Calvin, doctors of theology—which in varying combinations found embodiment in Reformed, Presbyterian, and Congregational churches—has been regarded by the tradition as being faithful to Scripture and to the substance of the gospel. Elders govern the church, deacons serve the community, and doctors of theology provide teaching and instruction in the Word of God.

Of particular significance was Calvin's work in restoring and redesigning the diaconate, for it not only demonstrates

50. Karl Barth, *Church Dogmatics*, IV/2, p. 676.
51. Ibid., p. 682.
52. Ibid., p. 717.
53. Barth, *Church Dogmatics*, IV/1, p. 705.

how a fresh understanding of the gospel led to a change in church order, but in the process the diaconate was rescued from being a stepping-stone to priestly orders and became the means whereby the church related its liturgical life—the service of Word and sacrament—to its service of the needs of the world. By making the diaconate an essential part of the life of the church and not just a stepping-stone to ordination or a stopgap until the secular authorities took over such responsibilities, Calvin ensured that the service of the world remained a central focus of the life and worship of church. This has led Elsie McKee to comment that "the Calvinist Reformed understanding of the church's diaconal ministry seems to offer one of the best patterns for relating corporate ethics to corporate worship in the religiously plural global village of the modern world."[54]

For the Reformed tradition, then, the faith confessed and ecclesiology are inseparable; the message of the church cannot be separated from its order. Indeed, its structured existence in the world is an integral part of its message. A church divided by race or gender or class, a church captive to political ideologies, or a church in bondage to a particular culture, irrespective of the purity of its message or confession, is in danger of becoming a false church. For while the Reformed churches, no less than others, sometimes become captive to culture, it is fundamental to the tradition that the structure of the church, its existence in the world, must reflect the gospel. "There is no area of the church," wrote Bonhoeffer, "which is not wholly and exclusively subject to Christ."[55] The being of the church is part of its mission, or, to put it differently, its existence is hermeneutical; it interprets the gospel in the world.

Thus, the Barmen Declaration of the Confessing Church in the German Third Reich not only rejected the ideology of

54. Elsie Anne McKee, *Diakonia in the Classical Reformed Tradition and Today* (Grand Rapids: Eerdmans, 1989), p. 46; see also William Innes, *Social Concern in Calvin's Geneva* (Allison Park, Pa.: Pickwick Publications, 1983), pp. 103ff.

55. Bonhoeffer, *The Way to Freedom*, ed. E. H. Robertson (London: Collins, 1966), p. 178.

Nazism but in its third article also rejected a church order that denied the sole Lordship of Jesus Christ, the "One Word of God." It refused to be restructured on principles alien to evangelical faith because through its order it testified to Jesus Christ.

> The Christian Church is the congregation of the brethren in which Jesus Christ acts presently as the Lord in Word and sacraments through the Holy Spirit. As the Church of pardoned sinners, it has to testify in the midst of a sinful world, with its faith as with its obedience, with its message as with its order, that it is solely his property, and that it lives and wants to live solely from his comfort and from his direction in the expectation of his appearance.[56]

It went on to say: "We reject the false doctrine, as though the Church were permitted to abandon the form of its message and order to its own pleasure or to changes in prevailing ideological and political convictions." It is precisely for this reason, too, that many Christians engaged in the struggle against apartheid in South Africa have begun to see the connection between that struggle and the unity of the church. For while it always remains true that the unity of the church is given to it in Jesus Christ, the way in which unity is appropriated and expressed in the life and structure of the church is related to the faithfulness of its witness and confession.

Church Order and Ethical Heresy

In 1925, in an address given to the World Alliance of Reformed Churches meeting in Cardiff, Wales, Karl Barth addressed the question of "The Desirability and Possibility of a Universal Reformed Creed." For Barth, such a creed was neither desirable nor possible for several reasons, one of which was that there was no consensus on what concrete situation was forcing the church to

56. The Barmen Declaration, art. 3.

confess its faith anew. "The Church must have something to say, some pronouncement to make which concerns the concrete life of men." Almost as though he were contradicting himself, Barth then went on to speak of one such concrete situation by way of illustration. "The Church must have the courage to speak today (I mention only one specific problem) upon the fascist, racialist *nationalism* which since the war is appearing in similar forms in all countries."[57] But Barth doubted whether the church really wanted to say anything on such burning and dangerous questions. If it did not want to address them while they were still hot, then it was preferable to say nothing at all.

The situation changed dramatically within a few years with the advent of Nazism and the Third Reich. In discussion by correspondence with Dietrich Bonhoeffer in September 1933, Barth and his younger colleague came to the conclusion that a *status confessionis* had arrived, the first since the time of the Reformation in the sixteenth century.[58] By this they meant that a situation had arisen within the German Evangelical Church requiring the church to confess its faith anew against an ideology that was subverting the gospel and its proclamation. Suddenly matters which under other circumstances might have been indifferent or of secondary importance in the life of the church, such as its form and structure in the world, became fundamental to its life and witness. The church was forced to take a stand for the truth if it wanted to remain the church of Jesus Christ. Its unity became contingent upon its confession—hence the importance of the Barmen Declaration and the decisions made at the Dahlem Synod about church order.[59] The confessing of Christ had redrawn the boundaries of the church, separating the true church from the false within the German Evangelical Church itself.[60] It was no longer a

57. Karl Barth, *Theology and Church* (London: SCM, 1962), pp. 132-33.
58. See the correspondence in Dietrich Bonhoeffer, *No Rusty Swords*, ed. E. H. Robertson (London: Collins, 1970), pp. 226-27.
59. See Barth, *Church Dogmatics*, II/1, p. 175; Bonhoeffer, "The Question of the Boundaries of the Church and Church Union," in *The Way to Freedom*, p. 87.
60. Bonhoeffer, *The Way to Freedom*, p. 79.

conflict between the Reformation churches and Rome, but a struggle for the very life of the Evangelical church.

Since the Second World War many different attempts have been made by churches within the Reformed tradition to restate and confess their faith anew. There has also been considerable ecumenical discussion in recent years as to whether or not the church is faced with a *status confessionis* in a variety of contexts.[61] Barth himself believed that the possibility of nuclear war created a new *status confessionis*. This was not a self-evident doctrinal matter, at least traditionally conceived, but it affected the very life and destiny of the world as a whole. But that, for Barth, was precisely at the heart of a *status confessionis;* it was a moment in which the crisis facing society impinged directly upon the life and testimony of the church. As Barth told the World Alliance in Cardiff in 1925, the "old Reformed Creed" was "wholly ethical," and was always addressed to the public sphere. This was especially true of Heinrich Bullinger, Zwingli's successor in Zurich and author of the Second Helvetic Confession in 1566. Bullinger stressed not only the importance of doctrine and ministry for the continuity of the church but faithfulness in its life and witness to the gospel.[62] Thus, when Visser 't Hooft, the general secretary of the World Council of Churches, spoke about "ethical heresy" at the 1967 Assembly of the WCC in Uppsala, he was standing firmly in line with early Reformed tradition.[63]

Yet it was only with the Presbyterian Confession of 1967 in the United States, as Edward Dowey points out, that "a strong social-ethical hermeneutic of faithful obedience is introduced into a Reformed confessional document."[64] This was not true of the Barmen Declaration, for though it addressed the heresy of

61. Eugene TeSelle, "How Do We Recognize a *Status Confessionis?*" *Theology Today* 55 (April 1988): 71-72.

62. A. C. Cochrane, "The Mystery of the Continuity of the Church," *Journal of Ecumenical Studies* 2 (Winter 1965): 83-84.

63. W. A. Visser 't Hooft, "The Mandate of the Ecumenical Movement," in *The Uppsala 68 Report* (Geneva: World Council of Churches, 1968), app. 5.

64. Edward J. Dowey, Jr., "Confessional Documents as Reformed Hermeneutic," in *Journal of Presbyterian History* 61 (Spring 1983): 94.

Nazi ideology it did not deal concretely and specifically with anti-Semitism and other evils in society. The Confession of 1967 is strikingly different. Reflecting the burning, critical issues of that time, and in many respects ours, we now find within a Reformed confession reference to the fact that God's revelation in Jesus Christ requires that the church must work for the abolition of racial discrimination, engage in the struggle for justice and peace in society, work to end poverty, and promote a genuinely Christian understanding of human sexuality.[65]

Alongside this strong socioethical dimension there is also another very important innovation. Instead of anathemas against others there is a confession of guilt regarding the church's own failure in the past, indeed, its complicity in the very sins which the gospel calls it to oppose. Without pronouncing any anathemas as such, the Confession of 1967 makes it clear that faithfulness to the ethical demands of the gospel is the mark of a true church, while disobedience marks a false church. While the Confession of 1967 today is in some respects already dated, and while its treatment of reconciliation may reflect what *The Kairos Document* calls "church theology," its intention is clearly prophetic and liberatory. In fact, while it predates liberation theology it already anticipates something of its challenge.[66]

Of particular significance for our discussion is the declaration, made by the Lutheran World Federation meeting in Dar-es-Salaam in 1977,[67] that a *status confessionis* existed in South Africa. And then, of great importance for the Reformed tradition, came the Ottawa meeting of the World Alliance of Reformed Churches in 1982. In the words of Allan Boesak, the WARC recognized "that apartheid is a heresy, contrary to the

65. The Confession of 1967, arts. 9.43-47. *The Book of Confessions* (United Presbyterian Church in the U.S.A., 2d ed., 1970).

66. See Daniel J. Migliore, "Jesus Christ, the Reconciling Liberator: The Confession of 1967 and Theologies of Liberation," *Journal of Presbyterian History* 61 (Spring 1983): 38-39.

67. See "Southern Africa: Confessional Integrity," in de Gruchy and Villa-Vicencio, *Apartheid Is a Heresy*, pp. 160-61.

Gospel and inconsistent with the Reformed tradition."[68] The World Alliance had come a long way since Barth addressed it at Cardiff in 1925. But in a very real sense it had got back to the Reformation struggle for the true church as against the false, to the church as "a site of struggle," and to the problem with which we began this chapter—the segregation of the Reformed church in South Africa even though segregation went against both Scripture and the confessions.

Many have found it difficult to refer to apartheid as a heresy, not because they approve of apartheid—quite the contrary—but because they find the category of heresy inappropriate. For some it is, in fact, too medieval, too reminiscent of the Inquisition, witch hunts, and the like. For others it is inappropriate because apartheid is seen as a political rather than an ecclesiastical issue. In response to the first objection it should be said that while the word *heresy* conjures up much that we would prefer to relegate to the dark pages of ecclesiastical history, it is a word the church needs in order to state categorically that a false choice has been made. For that is literally what a heresy means. If the church is committed to the truth of the gospel, it must likewise be willing to identify and reject falsehood.

In response to the second objection it should be pointed out that the slogan "apartheid is a heresy" refers specifically to its theological justification within the life of the church and its embodiment in the structures of the church. Apartheid as a political ideology is, from a Christian point of view, evil and sinful. However, its theological justification and ecclesiastical embodiment is heresy.[69] Heresy is a category that only makes sense within the life of the church, for it has to do with the struggle between the true and false church. But we must go further. A truly Reformed confession of faith is not "a hole-in-the-corner affair," but a public event irrespective of whether or

68. Quoted in de Gruchy and Villa-Vicencio, *Apartheid Is a Heresy*, p. 88. See also the foreword by Allan Boesak.
69. See the essays by Simon Maimela, Charles Villa-Vicencio, and John W. de Gruchy in de Gruchy and Villa-Vicencio, *Apartheid Is a Heresy*.

not the public recognizes its significance. It is public because it arises out of a particular social and historical context. Thus, the struggle for truth against heresy within the church relates to social realities and struggles beyond the church. In a profound sense, the church struggle in South Africa epitomizes the struggle for South Africa.

Following on from Ottawa, several member churches of the WARC in South Africa affirmed its decision and declared apartheid a heresy. The Nederduitse Hervormde Kerk, which together with the Dutch Reformed Church had been suspended by the WARC, resigned its membership. The Dutch Reformed Church (NGK) itself sought to find ways out of the dilemma in which it was now placed. But of particular importance, the Dutch Reformed Mission Church drafted a new confession, the Belhar Confession of Faith, adopted by that church in 1986, which brought its century-long history round full circle and contradicted the very reason for its formation and existence.

Belhar: Connecting Reformed and Liberation Theology

The adoption of the Belhar Confession by the Dutch Reformed Mission Church was a historic event because it was the first time in the history of the Dutch Reformed family of churches since the seventeenth century that a new confession had been adopted by one of its member churches as an authoritative standard of faith and practice.[70] Thus it has become not only a confession whose acceptance is necessary for ordination, but one that is determinative in the discussions pertaining to the uniting of black and white Dutch Reformed churches. Its significance can only be truly appreciated, however, when it is related to the segregationist origins of the church in the nineteenth century and its formation in 1881. For the Belhar Confession categorically rejects the synodical decision of 1857

70. On the background to the Belhar Confession and the issues which it raises, see *A Moment of Truth: The Confession of the Dutch Reformed Mission Church*, ed. G. D. Cloete and D. J. Smit (Grand Rapids: Eerdmans, 1984).

to allow segregation in the church, it equally rejects apartheid as a heresy, and it affirms the true nature of the church's unity and mission: a confession of Jesus as Lord and a commitment to the struggle for God's justice in the world.

But the Belhar Confession is also significant for another reason. It reinterprets the confession of Jesus Christ from the liberatory perspective of a commitment to the poor. In this we see a creative Reformed response to the challenge of liberation theology. Faithfulness to Jesus Christ made known through Word and Spirit has to relate not only to the struggle against apartheid; the God who has revealed himself in Christ is "in a special way the God of the destitute, the poor, and the wronged" and "calls his Church to follow him in this." This means "that the Church must therefore

> stand by people in any form of suffering and need, which implies, among other things, that the Church must witness against and strive against any form of injustice. . . .
>
> that the Church as the possession of God must stand where he stands, namely against injustice and with the wronged; that in following Christ the Church must witness against all the powerful and privileged who selfishly seek their own interests and thus control and harm others.
>
> *Therefore, we reject any ideology which would legitimate forms of injustice and any doctrine which is unwilling to resist such an ideology in the name of the gospel.*[71]

In the light of this we are able to discern why the unity of the church is contingent upon its faithful confessing of Christ not only in relation to racism, but also in relation to poverty and other forms of social injustice. Here we see in unambiguous terms how the faith and the structure of the church are inseparable, and why the racial separation of the churches and its theological legitimation is a heresy. Here, too, we see the extent to which church order and unity in turn impinge upon the social and political situation in South Africa. For if black and

71. The Belhar Confession, art. 4.

white are baptized into the same Christ they are part of the same church, privileged to share in the same Eucharist, and this means that there can no longer be any theological grounds for segregation in society.

Baptism, which has become such a private ecclesiastical affair, rightly becomes once again a public event, a confessing event, with far-reaching social implications. Already at the Synod of Dort in 1619 Calvinist divines had decided that the baptism of a slave necessitated that slave being set free.[72] Thus the early Dutch settlers at the Cape knew that if you baptized slaves it would require their liberty; if you baptized black persons, it would not only mean their entry into the "body of Christ," but it would also require their acceptance into the body politic. Hence their reluctance to engage in evangelism! A true understanding of baptism not only undermines apartheid in the church; it should also undermine apartheid in society, and all other forms of oppression as Paul indicates in Galatians 3:27-28. For baptism is a sign of human solidarity redeemed in Christ.

The celebration of the Lord's Supper, which should be the sacrament of Christian community transcending all human barriers, was likewise reduced to an individualistic rite engaged in by members of the same ethnic group. A means of grace was turned into an instrument of disgrace. Hendrikus Berkhof sees a common eucharistic thread binding the conflict between Jews and Christians in the New Testament with the Confessing Church in Germany and with the struggle against apartheid in South Africa:

> From the struggle of the Confessing Church under the Nazis we remember how the open admission of Christian Jews to the Lord's Supper became the first test in the clash of spirits. In our day the meal serves a similar disclosing function in the *apartheid* problematic in South Africa.[73]

72. See Richard Elphick and Hermann Giliomee, eds., *The Shaping of South African Society, 1652-1820* (Cape Town: Longman, 1982), p. 120.

73. Hendrikus Berkhof, *Christian Faith: An Introduction to the Study of the Faith* (Grand Rapids: Eerdmans, 1979), p. 364.

No wonder that at the Ottawa Conference of the World Alliance of Reformed Churches in 1982 the catalyst for the debate on the heresy of apartheid was the Eucharist. There could be no genuine communion without community in the truth of the gospel and therefore solidarity in the struggle against the heresy of apartheid.

The unity of the white and black Dutch Reformed Churches has been one of considerable controversy over the past fifteen years. It has now become not simply a matter of union but also a matter of a confession that explicitly rejects the Dutch Reformed Church's historic ties with apartheid. Whereas previously the various churches were bound by the same historic confessions, the Belhar Confession has made church union dependent upon the white church rejecting apartheid totally. That is not simply an ecclesiastical or theological issue but also a highly politicized one. There are, however, some ironic twists in the whole matter. The first irony is the fact that the NG Sendingkerk and the other Dutch Reformed black mission churches have now become recognized within the World Alliance as *the* authentic representatives of that tradition in South Africa. The second irony is that the dividing issues are no longer simply those separating black from white. On both sides, they divide whites as well as blacks, and they also unite whites and blacks. In other words, the issue can no longer be reduced to racism; it also has to do with other forms of oppression. Thus, an Occasional Bulletin of the *Belydende Kring* points out that while apartheid is the first major obstacle to church unity, the matter goes much deeper.

> The theology of the Confession of Belhar is now struggling to gain dominance over what the Kairos Document called "church theology." It is the traditional pietism, fundamentalism, biblicism and individualistic moralism which the white missionaries bequeathed to black Christians, and which black Christians took over uncritically. Black preachers preach this old-style faith ad nauseum, thinking that it is the equivalent to "sola Scriptura" reformed theology. The spirit of the Belhar Confession, that God struggles on the side of all those who struggle against

apartheid, is still foreign to the very church which produced the Confession.[74]

It would be wrong to conclude that the conflict between the unity and the faithful confession of the church is confined to the Dutch Reformed family of churches. It reaches into other Reformed churches in South Africa and beyond. By way of example we may refer to the fact that the proposed union between the majority white Presbyterian Church of Southern Africa and the majority black United Congregational Church of Southern Africa ground to a halt in 1986 for reasons not unlike those that split the white and black Dutch Reformed churches apart. It was never officially stated that race or politics was the issue, but there were clear indications that many white Presbyterians feared being dominated by a black majority in the united church, despite the fact that over the years the Presbyterian Church has taken some important resolutions in opposition to apartheid. An important moment of truth and opportunity was squandered. Even if the so-called English-speaking churches (and that includes both the Presbyterian and Congregational churches) are not guilty of condoning the heresy of apartheid, they have to confess their guilt in the struggle to overcome the hypocrisy of confessing "Lord, Lord!" but not doing what the Lord of the church requires.

The Belhar Confession is the confession of a particular denomination, but it has important ecumenical significance and potential. As a confessional document it could become the basis for a united Reformed Church in South Africa, and in that respect it is different from *The Kairos Document*. It is also different for another reason. While it is part of the theological continuum that leads from Cottesloe to *The Kairos Document*, and while it parallels the development of the crisis brought about by apartheid, resistance, and repression, and symbolized by Sharpeville, Soweto, and the State of Emergency, it stops short of the more radical conclusions to which *The Kairos Document* finally comes. Yet it provides a vital link between the Reformed

74. *Belydende Kring Occasional Bulletin*, 1. nd.

tradition and liberation theology in South Africa. It has, in fact, opened up fresh possibilities for the emergence not only of a united Reformed church but also of an ecumenical confessing church that transcends traditional confessional boundaries. But, by the same token, it recognizes other boundaries of division and conflict in the same way as the Barmen Declaration did. Whether or not the Belhar Confession actually achieves its potential is another matter, of course, one that has to do with whether or not the opportunity it offers is grasped.

Ulrich Duchrow rightly perceives that "the apartheid system in southern Africa is only the microcosm of the world system."[75] By this he means that racism and economic exploitation in South Africa are linked to the worldwide oppression of people, and that if apartheid is the reason for a *status confessionis* in South Africa, then it implicates the church universal. But it implicates the church universal not simply because of its connection with the church in South Africa and its concern for the situation, but because of the possibility of a *status confessionis* in its own backyard. The critical task of theology in the life of the church is to enable the church to discern precisely and concretely "when a situation becomes a clear case for confession *(casus confessionis),* a situation calling for the *status confessionis.*"[76] This is when the struggle within the church reaches a new moment of intensity and clarity, the point, indeed, where the tension between maintaining the unity of the church and its confession of the truth and solidarity in the struggle for justice is put to its most serious test.

Judgment Begins with the Church

Throughout this chapter we have stressed that both Luther and Calvin were aware of the conflictual character of the church. For them the Reformation was a struggle between the true and false church within the one Church of Jesus Christ. While they

75. Ulrich Duchrow, *Conflict over the Ecumenical Movement* (Geneva: World Council of Churches, 1981), p. 342.
76. Ibid., p. 19.

may have hoped that once the Reformation was complete conflict would subside, the very fact that they proclaimed the necessity for the church to be always reforming suggests that they saw this struggle as part of the very nature of the church, though the immediate cause for the conflict may vary greatly.

In recent times it has become commonplace to speak of the church as a "site of struggle," a phrase we have already used several times. This means that the struggle for liberation, justice, and truth in the world is not simply a struggle between the church and the powers of the world beyond its boundaries, but a struggle within the life of the church itself—a struggle for the soul of the church that relates to the social struggles of the world. This is not clearly recognized in times of relative harmony and peace, though the struggle may then reach new and subtle depths; but in times of social and political crisis it becomes intensely apparent. The church struggles in Germany, South Africa, and Latin America have shown that the conflict with the state is a conflict within the church as well. This becomes clear the moment the church begins to identify with the struggle for justice in society, as Christians throughout the world have discovered anew in recent years.

The Kairos Document did not create the conflict in the church in South Africa, contrary to some of its critics. It recognized and gave expression to it. "What the present crisis shows up, although many of us have known it all along, is that *the Church is divided.*"[77] By this is not meant the disunity of different denominations, but rather division within the life of the churches brought about by different social interests and different understandings of the gospel. A historic process is repeating itself because present denominational and confessional differences, however rooted they may be in matters of doctrine, were also the products of social forces in their period of historical formation.[78] Present battle lines are no longer coterminous with these confessional boundaries of the past. They are products of

77. *The Kairos Document*, p. 1.
78. See H. Richard Niebuhr, *The Social Sources of Denominationalism* (New York: Meridian, 1960).

fresh understandings of the gospel arising within a new historical context, understandings shaped by different social perceptions, political commitments, material interests, and praxis.

For *The Kairos Document* the crisis has shown that the church is divided against itself in terms of the way in which it perceives and responds to the critical public and political questions of the day. These have become the confessional issues because they have to do with what it means to confess Jesus Christ as Lord concretely and in context. In particular, *The Kairos Document* focuses on the church's relationship to the struggle against racial and other forms of oppression. It is no longer simply apartheid as an ideology that is the *status confessionis,* but the praxis of the church in response to the oppression apartheid has created. "Church theology," as *The Kairos Document* rightly points out, also condemns apartheid, but its praxis undermines its confession and prevents it from actually helping to get rid of apartheid.[79]

The division within the church was most starkly put when *The Kairos Document* declared that both the oppressed and the oppressor claim loyalty to the same church:

> They are both baptized in the same baptism and participate together in the breaking of the same bread, the same body and blood of Christ. There we sit in the same church while outside Christian policemen and soldiers are beating up and killing Christian children or torturing Christian prisoners to death while yet other Christians stand by and weakly plead for peace.[80]

Nothing could put the issues more sharply. What does it mean for the church to confess Christ concretely, and to be "one body in Christ" in such a situation? This question has always arisen when the church has attempted to be a faithful community of committed disciples confessing Christ against the tyranny of church and state within a Constantinian context, where both

---

79. See Sheila Briggs' contribution to *The Kairos Covenant,* ed. Willis H. Logan (New York: Meyer-Stone Books, 1988), pp. 80ff.

80. *The Kairos Document,* pp. 1-2.

persecuted and persecutors claim allegiance to the church. In their struggle against "the tyranny" of Rome both Luther and Calvin knew the reality of this question. Yet they failed in turn to appreciate their own contribution to the problem as experienced in the immense suffering of the Anabaptists. This presents a major challenge to the Reformed tradition today, a challenge presented to it by all forms of liberation theology that seek to address the oppression of both the church's and society's victims, whether they be poor, blacks, women, or other persecuted minorities.

The nature of the present conflict in the church is complex. Yet it is possible to distinguish between those who regard the gospel as socially liberating and transformative, those who link faith and the struggle for justice, and those who do not. Among the latter are the advocates of a right-wing form of Christianity for whom the watchwords are uncritical patriotism, uncritical anti-communism, anti-ecumenism, and an authoritarian fundamentalism. This brand of Christianity is particularly virulent in Latin America and South Africa at present, having been imported in large doses from the United States during the last decade.[81]

There is, as *The Kairos Document* recognized, another large group of Christians who might reject oppression and racism in principle, but who seek to be neutral in their political commitments and uninvolved in the struggle for liberation and justice. Many Christians take the position that the church should work for justice and reconciliation, but not by taking sides that would undermine and destroy the unity of the church. We have yet to consider the role of the church within the political arena as such. Yet, as Albert Nolan has rightly observed, "If the Church, or part of the Church, were to begin to relate its preaching and its sacraments directly to the concrete realities of life in South Africa today in a way that is honest, bold and consistent, the

81. See Paul Gifford, *The Religious Right in Southern Africa* (Harrare: University of Zimbabwe Publications, 1988); *Journal of Theology for Southern Africa* 69 (December 1989).

immediate result would be division and dissension." The dilemma of church leaders is to seek to speak prophetically and, at the same time, to maintain the sometimes fragile unity of the church. Nolan recognizes the dilemma but sees no easy way out of it if the church is to remain faithful to the gospel.

> That the Church should become a site of struggle is regrettable, but the fact of the matter is that we are not all on the same side and we do not all believe in the same gospel. What we have in common is a longing to be faithful to Jesus Christ and perhaps a loyalty to the same Church tradition, such as Catholicism or the Reformed tradition. For the rest, we are divided and we shall have to confront one another and struggle against all the forms of "worldliness" and blindness that have crept into the Church because of the system.[82]

Conflict in the life of the church is part of its historic identity—or better, it is how its identity was and continues to be shaped.[83] Speaking theologically, we may say that the judgment or crisis experienced by the world is or should always be experienced first within the life of the church. It is the *kairos* moment that arises during times of crisis (*krisis* = judgment), the moment of truth that requires decisive response in word and deed, by which the church is to be judged by God as true or false. It is, in fact, the *status confessionis* of the Reformation that impels the church to be continually reforming according to the Word of God. For the church is called to be the pioneer of the new age. Commenting on 1 Peter 4:17: "For it is time for judgment to begin with the family of God," Calvin writes "that the beginning of the reformation should be in the church." This being so, God "deals more strictly with his own people under the discipline of the Cross."[84] Such judgment is the necessary pre-

82. Nolan, *God in South Africa* (Grand Rapids: Eerdmans, 1988), pp. 214-15.
83. See Jon Sobrino, *Spirituality of Liberation* (New York: Orbis, 1988), chap. 9, where he deals with "Conflict in the Church."
84. Calvin, *The Epistle of Paul to the Hebrews and I and II Peter*, trans.

lude to redemption, the means whereby the church becomes an instrument for the salvation of the world.

Whatever the historical or sociopolitical reasons for conflict in the life of the church, theologically speaking it may be accounted for by the reality of sin and by the prophetic preaching of God's law of righteousness revealed in the crucified Christ. Sin identifies the problem as rooted in selfish human nature, both individual and corporate. The proclamation of the gospel of the crucified Messiah brings alienation to the surface, thus highlighting the division and making repentance a necessary step towards reconciliation. But by the same token, the prophetic Word of the cross and the call to justice and righteousness that creates crisis and conflict within the church is also the means whereby it contributes to the transformation of the world into the new humanity. The sanctification of the world cannot bypass the judgment of the cross and the justification and repentance—the confession of guilt—of the sinful. But the church acts, as Bonhoeffer saw so clearly, as the vicarious representative of the world in this process.[85]

The historical purpose of God's reconciling action in Jesus Christ was, and remains, the creation of a new humanity out of people and nations divided by ethnicity, culture, gender, and material interests. But this does not imply that these sources of alienation are sanctified; they must surrender their absolute status and claims. It therefore requires the conversion of people in relation to their historical and social location and interests. The reconciliation in Christ that lies at the heart of the unity of the church is not Platonic, nor invisible, nor based on neutrality with regard to the issues and conflicts within the world. Reconciliation, God's gift of grace, becomes an ecclesiological reality through repentance, conversion, and engagement in the struggle for justice.

W. B. Johnston, Calvin's New Testament Commentaries, vol. 12 (Grand Rapids: Eerdmans, 1963), p. 311.

85. The concept *Stellvertretung* ("representative" or "deputyship") is one of the key christological concepts in Bonhoeffer's theology which describes Christian and church responsibility on behalf of the world.

In order for the church to fulfill its vocation as the sign of God's reconciliation and sanctification of the world, it therefore can neither remain neutral to the issues of oppression and injustice nor remain within some ethnic or class ghetto. It must reach out and embrace all of humanity in such a way that dividing and dehumanizing powers are not only transcended but also defeated. Yet it is called to do so not from the side of the powerful—that is, not as a Constantinian church—but as a church of the victims of society, a church that is truly for the people. In doing so, however, the church draws into its very life the factions and interests that divide sinful humanity; it embodies the conflict, as it were, as God's representative, in order that the whole of humanity might be transformed by the gospel and brought under the reign of God.

Church of the Word, Church of the People

The contemporary struggle for liberation and justice in Latin America and elsewhere and the participation of Reformed as well as other Christians in that struggle in South Africa has helped to rediscover the meaning of human solidarity. One of the commonest sayings among those involved in the mass democratic movement in South Africa is this: "an injury to one is an injury to all." Nothing could be more biblical. To share with others in the struggle, in suffering, pain, and even death, to participate in vigils of prayer for those in detention and in the funerals of those who have died in the struggle for justice, and to celebrate moments of victory and hope together, have been transforming experiences for many, but especially for individualized white South Africans. They have also made it necessary to redefine the church as a church of and for the people.

If black Christians have helped white Christians in no other way, they have enabled them to discover what it means to belong to the "body of Christ." In Africa, despite the inherent individualism of Protestant evangelism, privatized faith has always been an anomaly. To believe implies belonging. To be human means to participate in community and to belong to the very environment within which human existence is sustained. One reason why the African Indigenous Churches and the Roman Catholic Church have experienced the greatest growth of all churches in recent years in South Africa is because their focus has not been individualistic but communal. The needs of persons are met in community.

Fundamental to the ecclesiology of *The Kairos Document* and liberation theology is that the church must not only take the "preferential option for the poor," but it must also become the church of the poor. To take that one step further, it must become a church of the common people, those who are struggling against oppression of various kinds, "a people's church." This is precisely what is meant by basic Christian communities in Latin America. But there are equivalents in other contexts—indeed, wherever there exist Christian communities which seek to embody an alternative lifestyle and witness to that of the dominant ecclesial culture, and to do so from within the struggle for justice and liberation.[86]

Without surrendering their Roman Catholic identity, it is remarkable how the base communities in Latin America reflect a Reformed understanding of the church as a local gathered church of committed believers. Such an understanding of the church is a central theme in Leonardo Boff's *Ecclesio-genesis*.[87] The local community of faith, gathered as a eucharistic fellowship around the Word in order to serve the world in their own specific context, was precisely what Calvin had in mind, however much that vision may have been distorted in practice and history. Indeed, the Vatican's major problem with Boff's ecclesiology is not unlike its concern at the time of the Reformation—namely, that a church of the people, as a national or a Popular Church, means a church in parallel or even in opposition to the institutional church under the authority of the

86. See, for example, Rosemary Radford Ruether, *Women-Church: Theology and Practice* (New York: Harper & Row, 1988).
87. Leonardo Boff, *Ecclesio-genesis: The Base Communities Reinvent the Church* (London: Collins, 1986).

pope.[88] In fact, Boff has been accused of congregationalism! Yet it was none other than Karl Rahner who argued that the Catholic church should now "grow quite differently from the past, from below, from groups of those who have come to believe as a result of their own free, personal decision."[89]

In considering the controversy between Cardinal Ratzinger and Boff it soon becomes apparent that for Ratzinger the reforms of Vatican II should not lead to any fundamental restructuring of the life of the church, whereas for the liberation theologians this is essential to both Vatican II and the renewal it sought.[90] It is essential not just for the sake of the future life of the church, but also for the world. The liberation of the church and the liberation of society are bound up together. Clodovius Boff sums this up when he writes:

> A church of liberation must also be liberated within: a church which seeks to fight for a juster society, for a society in which there is a sharing in the economy, in culture and in power, must have within it a structure of communion and participation in which the voice of the least is heard and participation is shared.[91]

Several issues both resonate with and confront the Reformed tradition from this perspective of the church identifying with a particular group of people and their struggle for justice and liberation and then seeking to develop structures to express that commitment. Indeed, when Bax asked whether the Dutch Reformed Church had become Roman Catholic in its treatment

88. Instruction on Certain Aspects of Liberation Theology, *Libertatis Nuntius* (Vatican City, 1984).

89. Karl Rahner, *The Shape of the Church to Come* (New York: Crossroads, 1983), p. 121.

90. V. Messori, *The Ratzinger Report* (Hertfordshire: Fowler Wright, 1985); Ronaldo Munoz, "The Historical Vocation of the Church," in Rosino Gibellini, *Frontiers of Theology in Latin America* (London: SCM, 1980), pp. 15-16; see also Harvey Cox, *The Silencing of Leonardo Boff* (London: Collins, 1988).

91. Clodovius Boff in R. Gibellini, ed., *The Liberation Theology Debate* (London: SCM, 1987), p. 92.

of Beyers Naudé and the Christian Institute, he was suggesting that the Reformed church was reacting to liberation within its own structures in precisely the same way as Rome responded to Luther and Calvin, and as the Vatican has more recently responded to Boff. Yet this runs counter to the best in both traditions and is certainly contrary to the fundamental Reformation impulse that the church must always be reforming according to the Word of God. But let us reflect on the issues raised by liberation theology's commitment to the Popular Church, or the church of the people.

The notion of a church of the people raises fundamental questions about the identity of the church. Can the church be identified with a particular group and their sectional interests? Is it not the responsibility of the church to exist for all people irrespective of their race, gender, class, and location on the oppressor-oppressed scale? Moreover, can the people of God ever be equated with the "people" as such, whether they are understood in Afrikaner Calvinism as the *volk* or in liberation theology as the "oppressed"? Indeed, in equating the church with a particular group—the "oppressed"—is not liberation theology making the same false move as Afrikaner Calvinism made when it identified with the oppressed Afrikaner and laid the foundation for apartheid in church and society? How does a church that is largely middle class in orientation, even within the black community, become a "church of the poor"? Can this be anything other than rhetoric that cannot be embodied in reality? Indeed, do "the people," the poor and the oppressed, really want to be part of a church that is only *for* them, but not *of* them?

The problem becomes more acute when it is recognized that commitment to the struggle against oppression unites some Christians with groups outside the church who are likewise engaged in the struggle. In other words, believers are divided from each other, but some are united with people who are not necessarily Christians by commitment. Is that not a strange state of affairs, that some Christians have more in common with nonbelievers than with their fellow church members? This was the position Dietrich Bonhoeffer found himself in during the Third Reich, especially at the time when, becoming disillusioned with the Confessing Church, he became part of the conspiracy against Hitler. At that time he reflected on the words of Jesus, "He that is not against us is for us," and the paradoxical statement, "he who is not for us is against us."[92] The crucial phrase binding these two statements together is "for us." But it is not primarily an ad hominem statement; it refers to the messianic project upon which Jesus and his disciples were engaged. Those who shared in that project were for him; those who did not were against him. In other words, if people outside the church are committed to the struggle for justice and liberation they are in solidarity with us and we with them.

To be brief, let it be said that a church for and of the people is not to be confused with a *volkskerk* when that is understood in an exclusively nationalistic or ethnic sense. Thus, we are not talking about the same thing when we speak of a "church of the people" as we find it in Afrikaner Calvinism. Nor are we saying that the church is to come under the control of what in South Africa we refer to as the "mass democratic movement." The church remains the church of Jesus Christ called to serve the kingdom of God. From a Reformed perspective, the church must always be under the Word; even Congregational polity, with its emphasis on the participation of all church members in the government of the congregation, insists that it is not the people who govern, but Christ through his Word and Spirit. But this does not make it any less a church of the people. What Latin American liberation theology is speaking of when it talks about a "church of the people" is not simply a coming together of poor people, but "a church that will be marked by the faithful response of the poor to the call of Jesus Christ."[93] The true church of Jesus Christ is that community in which the poor and other social victims not only find a home but also shape its life and existence in the world.

Thus we must rework the Reformation doctrine of the church by saying that the true church only exists where the

92. Bonhoeffer, *Ethics* (New York: Macmillan, 1976), p. 57.
93. Gustavo Gutiérrez, *The Power of the Poor in History* (London: SCM, 1983), p. 21.

Word is rightly proclaimed as the liberating Word and the sacraments are duly administered as signs of God's transforming grace in society as in each person who believes. It is precisely this commitment and character of the church under the liberating Word in Jesus Christ which opens up not only the possibility but also the necessity for the church to be for and of the people. José Míguez Bonino has expressed this well:

> The greater the church's identification with Jesus Christ, the more the church will be driven to an identification with the common people; the more the church is identified with the people, the more it will be in a position to reflect the identity of its Lord. Identity pushes towards identification, and identification is the matrix of authentic identity.

He continues:

> It will not try to absorb the people into it, nor will it proclaim itself to be the "leader" of the people. Instead it will structure itself as a community of faith and incarnate itself in the very midst of the people, giving impetus to the quest of the Kingdom from there.[94]

A liberating Reformed ecclesiology is one in which obedience to Jesus Christ through the Word and Spirit and solidarity in the struggle for justice and liberation come together in critical coherence. The more the Reformed churches take God's "preferential option" for particular groups who are disadvantaged and oppressed in a given historical context, the more they identify with Christ and open up the possibility that they will become churches not only for but also of the people. That means that even a bourgeois Reformed church, without seeking to dominate "the poor" or oppressed, should take definite steps to be in solidarity with them and to begin to celebrate with them the hope of God's liberation.

94. José Míguez Bonino, "Fundamental Questions in Ecclesiology," in *The Challenge of Basic Christian Communities*, ed. Sergio Torres and John Eagleson (New York: Orbis, 1982), pp. 147-48.

The Celebration of Hope in Solidarity

We began this chapter by recounting the occasion in 1982 when, at the Assembly of the World Alliance of Reformed Churches in Ottawa, eleven South Africans refused to participate in Holy Communion. The reason they gave was that the Eucharist, instead of being a sign of unity in Christ and therefore solidarity in the struggle against apartheid, had itself become a reason for racial division and a sign of disgrace. Some may well argue that the Eucharist should not be abused for the sake of protest, and that all come to the Table of the Lord as sinners in need of forgiveness and grace. Yet those in the Reformed tradition would do well to reflect on the fact that the medieval Mass was precisely the focus for Calvin's protest against idolatry. In the same way, R. Avila, a Catholic Latin American liberation theologian, speaks of the celebration of the Eucharist as "a loud cry of alarm and of protest," indeed, "one that is extremely dangerous for every inhuman and oppressive system."[95] Why? Because it brings us face to face with the reality of the cross, a reality that calls into question everything dehumanizing people and destroying community. It demonstrates the basic contradictions in a society that claims to be Christian but which is unable to celebrate its solidarity in Christ's death and resurrection in the eucharistic meal.

Much of our attention in this chapter has been focused on the struggle for the church in terms of faithfulness to Jesus Christ as Lord, a faithfulness expressed in a true confession and prophetic praxis. This may unfortunately give the impression that the church is a matter of words and deeds rather than a community of worship and spiritual empowerment. But nothing would be further from the vision that Calvin had for the church, or from the ecclesiology recently emerging in Latin American liberation theology.

The evangelical confession and prophetic proclamation of the church, in both word and deed, arises out of the worship and communal life of the church, and, in turn, they inform that

95. R. Avila, *Worship and Politics* (New York: Orbis, 1981), p. 84.

231

worship and common life. For Calvin worship and mission belonged together, eucharistic celebration and ethics could not be separated,[96] the struggle against dehumanizing idols and the worship of the true God belonged together.[97] Unfortunately this is too often not the case in the Reformed tradition.

Jürgen Moltmann has rightly pointed to the fact that a Reformed theology of the Word continually needs to be balanced by Eastern Orthodoxy's theology of the Spirit. "Reformed theology cannot get along without Orthodox theology's perception of the breadth of the Spirit's gifts; just as Orthodox theology is seemingly thrown back on the Reformed perception of the depths of the cross of Christ and the realistic justification of the unrighteous."[98] It is not that Reformed theology has no doctrine of the Spirit. But in practice the emphasis has always been so strongly on the Word, on doctrine and order, that the Spirit and the charismatic gifts, doxology and sacramental life in the Spirit have been seriously neglected to the impoverishment of the life and witness of Reformed Christians and the church.

A great deal of Calvin's work as a reformer had to do with the renewal of worship, and in this regard as in other aspects of the Reformation he sought to return to the liturgical forms of the ancient church in a way that expressed the fresh insights of the Reformation and the local needs of the church.[99] Of particular importance for him was the need for the Eucharist to become a public rather than a private occasion, a communal rather than an individualistic event, a means of inward transformation that led to obedience rather than a matter of outward show and ritual, an act that included the

96. See Elsie Anne McKee, *John Calvin on the Diaconate and Liturgical Almsgiving* (Geneva: Droz, 1984); see also McKee, *Diakonia in the Classical Reformed Tradition and Today*, pp. 27-28.

97. Carlos M. N. Eire, *War against the Idols* (Cambridge: Cambridge University Press, 1986), pp. 195ff.

98. Jürgen Moltmann, *The Church in the Power of the Spirit* (London: SCM, 1977), p. 37.

99. William D. Maxwell, *An Outline of Christian Worship* (London: Oxford University Press, 1952), pp. 112-13.

participation of the whole people of God and a means of grace in which all shared.[100]

For Calvin, the Eucharist meant both the proclamation of the Word and the celebration of the sacrament of Holy Communion. But if Calvin insisted that the Word always be proclaimed at the sacrament, he also believed that Holy Communion should be celebrated each Sunday, and that infrequent communion was of the devil.[101] As is well known, he was unable to introduce this in Geneva because of opposition from the city fathers who, ironically, as Catholics had only been used to participation in the Mass on the high festivals of the church. Nevertheless, the proclamation of the Word and the celebration of the sacrament remained Calvin's norm for what constituted Sunday worship. The separation of the two—so that preaching alone has become normative—has been tragic for the Reformed tradition. It has reduced much worship to a cerebral didactic occasion instead of a joyful celebration of the crucified and risen Christ in the Spirit. Nicholas Wolterstorff is correct:

> One of the major results of Vatican II has been that the Catholic church has taken a giant step in its liturgy in the direction of Protestantism. Next to the Swiss Reform, the liturgical reform of Vatican II is the greatest in the history of the church. I am profoundly convinced that we Protestants must now take an equally large step in the direction of Catholicism—or rather, in the direction of our common ancient tradition—by reinstituting the Lord's Supper as a regular part of the church's liturgy.[102]

If we may take one further step it must now be said that the most significant liturgical reform that has built on Vatican II is the integration of eucharistic worship into the struggle for justice and liberation in the world. One of the remarkable by-

---

100. See McDonnell, *John Calvin, the Church and the Eucharist*, p. 379.

101. *Institutes of the Christian Religion, 1536 Edition*, pp. 112-13.

102. Wolterstorff, *Until Justice and Peace Embrace* (Grand Rapids: Eerdmans, 1983), p. 161.

products of this development is, moreover, a discovery of some of the insights of the Reformation. As Catholic and Reformed believers focus not on the eucharistic doctrines that have traditionally divided their understanding, but on the presence of Christ through the Spirit seeking to renew and transform the church in its service of the world, then the Eucharist becomes once again a sign of Christian unity within the church and solidarity with those who are poor and oppressed. It becomes a means of liberating grace within the world. At the same time, it is more clearly seen that what divides the church is not so much eucharistic doctrine but the kind of life and faithfulness which its celebration fosters. The relationship between eucharistic practice and social praxis becomes crucial.

The efficacy of the sacrament is not simply whether or not it is correctly celebrated but whether or not it is a means of grace within the historical experience and struggle of people for life, for justice, for peace.[103] This insight from Catholic liberation theology is remarkable given the traditional Catholic teaching on the *ex opera operato* efficacy of the Mass. For the Reformed tradition, the efficacy of the Eucharist has never been contingent upon its correct celebration by a priest ordained for that purpose, but upon the promise of the Word and the presence of the Spirit within the life of the community of faith. But it is also related to the renewal of life and to obedience to the gospel in the world.

Wolterstorff reminds us that for Calvin "reality was drenched with sacrality," and that therefore it is precisely in the sacramental life of the church that its commitment to the world and the whole of creation is most strongly affirmed.[104] Thus, there was for Calvin, as there must be for the Reformed tradition, a close connection between the Eucharist and economic sharing.[105] In fact, the true celebration of the supper of the Lord is the rejection of idolatry at its deepest level, for the "breaking of

103. See Juan Luis Segundo, *The Sacraments Today* (New York: Orbis, 1968), pp. 54-55.
104. Wolterstorff, *Until Justice and Peace Embrace*, p. 160.
105. André Biéler, *The Social Humanism of Calvin* (Richmond: John Knox Press, 1964), pp. 37-38.

bread" and the sharing of bread with the hungry are a rejection of human greed and covetousness.[106] Calvin put it in these words in his *Institutes:*

> We shall benefit very much from the Sacrament if this thought is impressed and engraved upon our minds: that none of the brethren can be injured, despised, rejected, abused, or in any way offended by us, without at the same time, injuring, despising, and abusing Christ by wrongs we do; that we cannot disagree with our brethren without at the same time disagreeing with Christ; that we cannot love Christ without loving him in the brethren; that we ought to take the same care of our brethren's bodies as we take care of our own; for they are members of our body.[107]

However important ethics is for a true understanding of eucharistic worship, the ultimate focus is not upon the call to faithfulness but upon the grace and worship of God. Worship without ethical obedience becomes idolatry, but ethics alone is not worship and can so easily degenerate into self-righteous legalism without it. We recognize the need for worship to find expression in social witness, but for Christians "a similar liturgical condition" must be "placed on the authenticity of the struggle for justice and peace."[108] Worship without the struggle against injustice is unacceptable to God, but what about social activism that does not lead to worship? Wolterstorff rightly perceives that we all have a great deal to learn at this point from the Orthodox tradition, with its profound sense of doxology as the heart of theology and ethics. For theology to become doxology, Calvin insisted, it first had to be iconoclastic. But iconoclasm is by no means the end of theology—it is only the prelude to true worship in which the praise of God becomes the all in all. Reformed and liberation theology, when they are truly theology, find each other not only in ethical obedience, but in ethical obedience grounded in doxology.

106. See Leith, *John Calvin's Doctrine of the Christian Life*, p. 197.
107. *Institutes*, 4.17.38.
108. Wolterstorff, *Until Justice and Peace Embrace*, p. 157.

6. Theology Framed by Politics

Between the years 1688 and 1689 two hundred French Huguenots arrived in Cape Town and became part of the settler farming community in the Western Cape. They had initially fled to the Netherlands after the Edict of Nantes was revoked, an act that had stripped away the last vestiges of toleration enjoyed by Protestants in France. The Dutch East India Company had decided to send French refugees to the Cape to help develop the farming so necessary for its trading ships and its resident personnel. They were particularly interested in sending out people who could cultivate the fruit of the vine, a skill in which they excelled admirably. The provisos were that they should be under oath of allegiance to the Prince of Orange and the Company, take with them "a member of their consistory who can testify to their honesty," and be of the Reformed faith.[1]

Within a short time the Huguenots were integrated into the life of the Dutch community at the Cape, and they became members of the Dutch Reformed Church. Through the succeeding centuries their descendents contributed greatly to the development of the country, and the ancestry of many leading

1. Randolph Vigne, "The Rev. Pierre Simond: 'Lost Leader' of the Huguenots at the Cape," *Journal of Theology for Southern Africa* 65 (December 1988): 15.

Afrikaner families today can be traced back to them. Thus it was that in 1988 celebrations were held to mark the tercentenary of their arrival. In a public address to mark the occasion, President P. W. Botha stressed the fact that the Huguenots came to the Cape in search of religious freedom. Strictly speaking, this was not altogether accurate, because, as we have noted, they were sent out by the Dutch authorities to become farmers and had to sacrifice their identity as *French* Calvinists in the process. Yet it remains true that they, as part of the Huguenot community, originally had to leave France because of their faith.

What President Botha did not mention, however, was that in the process of the struggle for religious freedom in France, and in particular in response to the massacre on St. Bartholomew's Night in 1572, the Huguenots developed a theology and praxis of resistance to an unjust state.[2] Theology, of course, was not the sole motivation, for there were economic and class issues at work fomenting resistance. But, using Calvin's theology as a point of departure, they took a decisive step beyond it in response to a new historical situation of political tyranny. The fact that President Botha did not refer to the Calvinist doctrine of resistance is not surprising. Ruling authorities, especially those whose legitimacy is as much under attack as the government of South Africa, do not make a habit of legitimating such subversive doctrines.

The celebration of the Huguenots' struggle for religious freedom came at a time, however, when the freedom of the church and its resistance to the state in South Africa was a matter of much controversy. It followed the government's clampdown on seventeen extra-parliamentary opposition political organizations and the banning of eighteen community leaders on February 24, 1988. In response to this action by the government several church leaders, including Archbishop Desmond Tutu, Dr. Allan Boesak, Catholic Archbishop Stephen

2. See A. A. van Schelven's introduction to Theodore Beza, *Concerning the Rights of Rulers over Their Subjects and the Duty of Subjects towards Their Rulers*, ed. A. H. Murray (Cape Town: H.A.U.M., 1956), p. 11.

Naidoo, and the Reverend Frank Chikane, general secretary of the South African Council of Churches (SACC), had issued a strong statement in which they committed themselves to exploring every possible avenue for continuing "to carry on the activities which have been banned in so far as we believe they are mandated by the gospel."[3]

Church and State in Conflict

An emergency meeting of leaders belonging to the member churches of the SACC was convened in Johannesburg on Monday, February 29. The meeting prepared a petition to be personally delivered by them to the state president the following day in Cape Town. After a service of worship in St. George's Cathedral on Tuesday, March 1, twenty-five denominational leaders processed to the Houses of Parliament nearby. The procession was halted by the police at the outer precincts of Parliament and the leaders were all arrested, though shortly thereafter they were released. In their two-page petition the church leaders expressed their strongest protest against recent state action. "We believe," they stated, "that the Government, in its actions over recent years but especially by last week's action, has chosen a path for the future which will lead to violence, bloodshed and instability." Referring to the church, they reiterated that the activities which had been prohibited were "central to the proclamation of the gospel" and that they would "explore every possible avenue for continuing the activities" which other organizations had been prohibited from undertaking. They then listed these activities:

> We will not be stopped from campaigning for the release of prisoners, from calling for clemency for those under sentence of death, from calling for the unbanning of politi-

3. This and the extracts that follow will be found in full in "Documentation" in the *Journal of Theology for Southern Africa* 63 (June 1988).

cal organizations, from calling for the release of political leaders to negotiate the transfer of power to all the people of our country, from commemorating significant events in the life of our nation, from commemorating those who have died in what you call "riots," or from calling on the international community to apply pressure to force you to the negotiating table.

In a political address shortly after the church leaders' protest march, the state president roundly condemned the march as an act of civil disobedience.[4] The same theme was echoed on South African television, in the government-oriented press, and in statements issued by the leadership of the Dutch Reformed Church. Severe personal verbal attacks were made on Archbishop Tutu and Dr. Boesak.

The next encounter in the growing conflict involved the impending execution on March 19 of the "Sharpeville Six" who had been found guilty of murdering a fellow-black town councillor. In an attempt to prevent the execution at the last moment, Archbishop Tutu met with President Botha on Wednesday, March 16. While the archbishop stated his case for a reprieve, the meeting went smoothly. But once that had been dealt with the president presented the archbishop with a letter responding to the church leaders' petition. The president then severely admonished Tutu for his role in the illegal march on Parliament, angrily accusing him of supporting terrorism. "You owe all Christians an explanation of your exact standpoint," Botha wrote in his letter, "for we are all adults, and the time for bluffing and games is long past. The question must be posed: Are you acting on behalf of the kingdom of God, or the kingdom promised by the ANC [i.e., the African National Congress] and the SACP [i.e., South African Communist Party]? If it is the latter, say so, but do not then hide behind the structures and the cloth of the Christian church, because Christianity and Marxism are irreconcilable opposites." The letter concluded

4. South African law denied the right of such public protest, especially within the vicinity of Parliament.

with the president questioning the right of the church to become involved in "secular power-play." After a heated exchange of words, Tutu left, but the verbal attacks on him and other church leaders continued. The leaders of the Dutch Reformed Church also issued a statement condemning the actions of Archbishop Tutu and Dr. Boesak.

The following day a gathering of Anglican bishops made a statement in which they insisted that Tutu's actions were in accord with Anglican church policy and not dictated by the ANC or SACP. On the contrary, they argued, the totalitarian and dictatorial actions of the state in banning political organizations promoted "Marxism and revolution." Taking the strongest exception to "Mr. Botha's abuse of Archbishop Desmond at their meeting," the bishops stated that if the authorities took "action against Desmond Tutu and Allan Boesak for their witness to the gospel, it will be an attack on the Church of Christ and it will precipitate a major State-Church confrontation."

A subsequent meeting on March 22 of all the Anglican bishops came out with a clear statement of support for their archbishop and the other church leaders. The bishops questioned "the right of the State President to arrogate to himself, as we believe he has done, the right to define what is spiritual or to decide what is valid Christian witness. . . . *The Church has a spiritual responsibility not only to individual Christians but to the lives of nations and we shall endeavour to meet that responsibility.*" Affirming their commitment to oppose apartheid, they rejected the alternatives the state president had put to Tutu:

> The State President would have it that South Africans must choose between the Government's programme and atheistic Marxism. We reject this definition of the choice and reaffirm our commitment to a just, democratic and sharing society reflecting the values of the Kingdom of God.[5]

This tense encounter between church and state during the first few months of 1989 stands in sharp contrast to the situation

5. *Journal of Theology for Southern Africa* 63 (June 1988): 76. Emphasis added.

240

that developed within the next few months, following the election of F. W. de Klerk, a descendent of the Huguenots, to the state presidency. In rapid succession, especially given the length of the struggle against apartheid, seven black nationalist leaders were released from prison, the ANC, the Pan African Congress (PAC), and the South African Communist Party, and many other antiapartheid organizations were unbanned, the death penalty for political offences was suspended, and, on February 11, 1990, Mr. Nelson Mandela was released from prison after twenty-seven years. All of this paved the way for the return of political exiles and for the beginning of discussions to prepare the way for negotiations for a new constitution. The end to apartheid had not arrived, but it certainly appeared to be the beginning of the end.

This dramatic turn of events suddenly meant that the role of the church in South Africa as the representative of banned organizations and the spokesperson for political leaders in prison as well as the oppressed more generally had to be reconsidered. Archbishop Tutu was the first to acknowledge that while he would continue to be concerned and involved in social and political issues, his role and that of the church would now have to change. No longer was it the church's role to be in the forefront of political protest and resistance; its task now was one of critical but pastoral solidarity with all who were committed to ending apartheid through negotiation and enabling the birth of a new nonracial democratic nation. What such critical and pastoral solidarity might mean was soon demonstrated when the Anglican bishops, after commending President de Klerk for his courageous steps, met with Mr. Mandela to express their joy at his release and their solidarity with the ongoing struggle against apartheid. They also, contrary to Mr. Mandela's own position, called on the ANC to suspend the armed struggle as a necessary step towards negotiation.

This case study in church-state conflict illustrates a series of complex yet urgent issues and problems with regard to the role of the church within the political arena, and concomitantly, the relationship between theology and politics. The decision by the church leaders to carry on the activities of banned political

241

organizations was nothing new. Apartheid, having excluded the black majority from participation in parliamentary politics, had forced the churches over the years, especially those belonging to the SACC, often against their will, to fulfill a political role that has not normally belonged to the church. But once the political situation had begun to change it became necessary for the churches and church leaders to reassess their political role.

A theology of politics that takes each historical context seriously will not result in a static formulation of church-state relations, but a formulation which enables the church to fulfill its evangelical, prophetic, and pastoral calling. The precise role of the church cannot be the same in a post-apartheid South African society as it was, of necessity, in the struggle against apartheid. Yet certain elements must remain constant, though they might be expressed in different ways. For one thing, the end of apartheid will not mean the end of racism or other forms of oppression such as economic and gender. The church will continue to have a critical and prophetic role but it will no longer have to function on behalf of political organizations and parties, nor will its central thrust necessarily be one of protest and resistance. Yet its role will be no less important. In fact, in periods of transition and change new dangers and problems have to be faced and overcome that could otherwise prevent the birth and development of a just society.

In other historical examples the role of the church has changed from prophetic resistance to critical solidarity. In our first chapter we reflected on the role of Calvinism as an ideology of transition in the revolutionary developments of post-Reformation Europe. We recall, too, the way in which some churches in post–World War II Eastern Europe developed a relationship of critical partnership with Marxist governments. Sometimes this has unfortunately meant that churches have so identified with those who come to power that they have forgotten their calling to be prophetic. That was the tragedy of Afrikaner Calvinism and it is the temptation facing those churches that have shared in the struggle against apartheid now that a post-apartheid society is emerging. The need for a critical theology addressing the church is never more necessary than in such transitional moments, in order to prevent the church from either withdrawing from its public responsibility or attempting to act in a triumphalist way. This danger faces not only those churches that have identified with the struggle against apartheid, but also others like the Dutch Reformed Church that have generally supported government policy. In this connection it is interesting to note that as Afrikaner politics began to change in the late 1970s and early eighties, with the concomitant fragmentation of Afrikanerdom, so the Dutch Reformed Church itself began to define its own political role in more neutral terms. With Afrikaner nationalism divided, it no longer could give unequivocal support to the National Party and therefore it had to opt out of taking political positions, quite a contrast from its role in the heyday of Afrikaner nationalist ascendency.[6]

In the light of this let us turn to examine the basic structure and content of Calvin's political thought as a basis for developing a Reformed theology of politics. Such a theology, to be truly Reformed and liberating, must avoid the dangers both of imperial Calvinism and of pious withdrawal from the public arena. It must enable a Christian presence and witness that contributes to the just transformation of society irrespective of who is in power. In focusing on this we have come full circle. In our first chapter we placed Reformed theology within the context of political struggle and change; we then discussed at length the catholic substance and evangelical center of Calvin's theology; and now we return again in conclusion to the public and prophetic responsibility of the church and to some reflections on a Reformed theology of politics. Our discussion of Reformed theology has thus, like that of Calvin himself, been framed by politics.

6. For an account of this shift see Charles Villa-Vicencio, "Theology in the Service of the State: The Steyn and Eloff Commissions," in *Resistance and Hope*, ed. Charles Villa-Vicencio and John W. de Gruchy (Grand Rapids: Eerdmans, 1985), pp. 112ff.

243

Politics as Religious Vocation

A cursory reading of Calvin's *Institutes* might suggest that because the Reformer only deals with political matters in his final chapter, it is simply an afterthought or an appendix attached to his theology. A more careful reading will indicate that the *Institutes* have a "political frame" beginning with Calvin's letter to Francis I, king of France, and ending with its warning to political tyrants. "At the heart of Calvin's thought," comments Ford Lewis Battles, "was the relation between the King and the King of Kings, between the providential rule of our Heavenly Father and the sometimes capricious and cruel rule of him who should be the father of his country."[7]

As significant as Calvin's theology was in its own right, the fact that he wrote as one who was a key participant in the interplay between theology and social and political action of his day, particularly in Geneva, is of considerable importance.[8] Calvin's theology was worked out within the context of political concerns and struggle, and it related to political philosophy in the same way as it related to philosophy more generally— positively, yet critically. Calvin did not confuse theology and politics, but neither did he separate them into watertight dualistic compartments—both were part of the same reality over which God reigned. In any case, as a trained lawyer and humanist it was impossible for him to engage in theology unrelated to human and social existence. Indeed, his very first treatise, a commentary on the Latin jurist Seneca, was "a plea for merciful rule by those who have power."[9]

Calvin was acutely aware that the reform of the church could not be pursued in isolation from its social context. He

7. Battles' introduction to the *Institutes of the Christian Religion, 1536 Edition*, rev. ed., trans. Ford Lewis Battles (Grand Rapids: Eerdmans, 1986), p. xxv. See also Ford Lewis Battles, *Analysis of the Institutes of the Christian Religion of John Calvin* (Grand Rapids: Baker Book House, 1980), p. 18.

8. William C. Innes, *Social Concern in Calvin's Geneva* (Allison Park, Pa.: Pickwick Publications, 1983), p. 295.

9. Ronald S. Wallace, *Calvin, Geneva, and the Reformation* (Edinburgh: Scottish Academic Press, 1988), p. 5.

also knew that the ferment of the gospel required not only the transformation of the church but also the transformation of society. But Calvin did not leave this at the level of vague generalizations. He was deeply involved in developing social and political structures that would enable human life to flourish to the glory of God.[10] For Calvin, as Biéler reminds us, "if a real church is not there constantly to remind the state of its mission, the very state becomes a factor of disorder."[11]

The classical statement of Calvin's position in the final chapter of the *Institutes* illustrates, as John T. McNeill has put it, this "vital contact of Calvin's thought with the world of political action."[12] The very fact that for Calvin "there can be no decisive separation between state and church," which derives from his insistence that "Christ as the Head of his Church is precisely the Lord of this world,"[13] indicates how in principle his theology and his political thought are bonded together. Thus, while Calvin did not regard himself as a "change agent," he "set in motion movements that did change society because he *united his own theology and its peculiar emphases* with an awareness of the modern world."[14] In order to keep Calvin's understanding of politics clearly in mind, let us briefly summarize his teaching, beginning with his observations on the relationship between church and state.

Calvin begins by distinguishing clearly between Christ's "spiritual kingdom" and "civil government." The two are not the same and thus there is a clear separation between church and state. The church is responsible for the preaching of the gospel; the state is responsible for enabling the church to fulfill its task and for governing society in such a way that justice,

10. See Ernst Troeltsch, *The Social Teaching of the Christian Churches*, vol. 2 (London: George Allen & Unwin, 1956), p. 591.

11. André Biéler, *The Social Humanism of Calvin* (Richmond: John Knox Press, 1964), p. 24.

12. John T. McNeill, introduction to Calvin's *Institutes*, p. lxv.

13. Wilhelm Niesel, *The Theology of Calvin* (Philadelphia: Westminster Press, 1956), p. 230.

14. John Leith, *Introduction to the Reformed Tradition* (Atlanta: John Knox Press, 1978), p. 77. Emphasis added.

peace, and tranquility flourish. But having stressed this distinction, Calvin insists that the two kingdoms are not at variance with one another. In fact, they are integrally related because both are in the service of the kingdom of God.[15] Thus, immediately, the radical dualism that separates the spiritual and the political is bridged. The only question is how they are to be related, and, more especially, what happens when church and state are at variance with each other.

The first part of the answer is for all citizens, both rulers and ruled, to recognize that the state is derived from God and that the calling of those who exercise this responsibility (i.e., in Calvin's situation the "magistrates") is to be honored as "a calling, not only holy and lawful before God, but also the most sacred and by far the most honorable of all callings in the whole life of mortal men." For Calvin, as for most Protestants, political office became a religious vocation.[16]

This meant, however, that those who govern should recognize that their authority is from God and that they do not have the right to govern as they will. On the contrary, they "should submit to Christ the power with which they have been invested that he alone may tower over all." They are, after all, God's deputies and should submit to his sovereign purposes. In sum, "if they remember that they are vicars of God, they should watch with all care, earnestness and diligence, to represent in themselves to men some image of divine providence, protection, goodness, benevolence, and justice."[17] Indeed, in the opening letter of the *Institutes* Calvin reminded Francis I that a "king who in ruling over his realm does not serve God's glory exercises not kingly rule but brigandage."[18]

The particular form of the state is not God-ordained, but God holds the state responsible for his worship and the well-

15. *Institutes*, 4.20.1-2.
16. *Institutes*, 4.20.4. See also Michael Walzer, *The Revolution of the Saints* (Cambridge, Mass.: Harvard University Press, 1965), p. 60.
17. *Institutes*, 4.20.3-7.
18. *Institutes of the Christian Religion, 1536 Edition*, p. 3. The same statement is retained in the final 1559 edition; see *Institutes*, pp. 11-12.

being of society. In this connection, Calvin stresses the responsibility of the authorities to protect the freedom of all subjects
"from being in any way diminished, far less violated"; to help
and not hinder genuine piety; to "give justice to the poor and
needy, rescue the destitute and needy, and deliver the poor and
needy from the hand of the oppressor"; and "to embrace, to
protect, vindicate, and free the innocent." Governments have
the right to use force in maintaining justice as well as to wage
a "just war," but all must be done with restraint, humanely, and
out of a genuine concern for people.[19]

The laws the state adopts and by which it governs are not
immutable but must be appropriate to each situation. However,
the laws of any nation, Calvin insists, "must be in conformity to
that perpetual rule of love."[20] In this regard, Calvin holds up the
principle of equity as the foundation of any legal constitution:

> Equity, because it is natural, cannot but be the same for all,
> and therefore, this same purpose ought to apply to all laws,
> whatever their object. Constitutions have certain circum-
> stances upon which they in part depend. It therefore does
> not matter that they are different, provided all equally press
> toward the same goal of equity. . . . This equity alone must
> be the goal and rule and limit of all laws."[21]

Here we are at the heart of Calvin's political agenda. The way
in which love is structured in society is through just and equitable laws and government. Without that, true order and peace
are not possible.

Between Tyranny and Anarchy

Calvin had a keen sense of what Reinhold Niebuhr much later
described as the human "will to power." His understanding of

19. *Institutes*, 4.20.8-12.
20. *Institutes*, 4.20.15.
21. *Institutes*, 4.20.16.

human sin as all-pervasive also made him aware of the way in which power corrupts, whether it be the power of rulers or the power of the people. Thus, Calvin sought a middle way between aristocratic and democratic government, an option which, he argued, would have the best chance of preventing both tyranny and anarchy.[22] This led him to his choice of constitutional government, rule by magistrates elected by the people, a "system compounded of aristocracy and democracy."[23] Such a government enabled the necessary combination of skills and expertise, on the one hand, and a means of checking the abuse of power for selfish interest, on the other. For Calvin, however, the important factor was not the type of government, for this could vary from place to place, but its ability to protect the freedom and liberty of the people. Rulers who fail to protect their subjects' freedom are "faithless in office, and traitors to their country."[24]

In spite of Calvin's strong insistence upon obedience even to tyrannical government, in the final two sections of his *Institutes* he opens the door for opposition to and rejection of tyrannical rulers. This is a critical passage because it qualifies Calvin's position in a way that has enabled those within the Reformed tradition to sanction not only civil disobedience but even tyrannicide and revolution. Indeed, for some it became a *duty* to resist, a duty both to God and to fellow human beings.[25] Calvin himself, however, always drew back from the brink of legitimating revolution out of a genuine fear of anarchy, especially the "anarchy of pious endeavour."[26] In fact, Calvin is something of a paradox. Just when he seems to be reactionary he becomes quite radical, but sometimes just when he takes a radical step he cautiously qualifies it! This comes out, for ex-

22. Paul Lehmann, *The Transfiguration of Politics* (New York: Harper & Row, 1975), p. 41.

23. *Institutes*, 4.20.8.

24. Ibid.

25. Quentin Skinner, *The Foundations of Modern Political Thought*, vol. 2 (New York: Cambridge University Press, 1978), pp. 190-91.

26. Walzer, *The Revolution of the Saints*, p. 59.

ample, in his teaching on the Fifth Commandment where children are enjoined to honor their parents.[27] But it is also true of his theology of politics. Calvin takes us to the brink of revolution, but does not provide justification for anarchy, as though any individual could rebel against authority. The princes had to fear God, not a revolutionary movement of the people![28]

The question that must be posed, of course, is whether God could and does bring tyrants to their knees through some kind of peasant uprising. Calvin did not support this idea, most probably for fear of inciting popular insurrection. God's actions in history—whereby tyrants are overthrown—were beyond the dictates and control of the people. The people had to obey, suffer, and pray, but not resist.[29] But Calvin does call upon the elected representatives of the people—i.e., the "magistrates"—to defend the rights and freedom of the people. As representatives of the people they did have the right to resist tyranny, to ensure that obedience to authority must never become disobedience to God, "to whose will the desires of all kings ought to be subject, to whose decrees all their commands ought to yield, to whose majesty their scepters ought to be submitted."[30]

In other words, when authority usurps the role of God and claims absolute power, then it has "exceeded its limits" and the Christian has not only the right but also the duty to disobey.[31] This applied to parents as much as to the state. In his commentary on Daniel 6:22, Calvin, again in the context of paying respect to authority, went so far as to say:

> For earthly princes lay aside their power when they rise up against God, and are unworthy to be reckoned among the number of mankind. We ought, rather, utterly to defy

27. On the Fifth Commandment, compare Calvin's *Institutes*, 2.8.36 with par. 38; on politics compare 4.20.9 with pars. 15 and 32.
28. *Institutes*, 4.20.31.
29. Ibid.
30. *Institutes*, 4.20.32.
31. *Institutes*, 4.20.30-32.

them than obey them whenever they are so restive and wish to spoil God of his rights.[32]

In similar words, Calvin comments on Acts 4:19:

> Whatever title then men may hold, they are to be listened to only on the condition that they do not lead us away from obeying God. So we must examine all their traditions by the rule of the Word of God. We must obey princes and others who are in authority, but only in so far as they do not deny to God His rightful authority as the supreme King, Father, and Lord.[33]

For precisely this reason, Calvin, as he brings his argument in the *Institutes* to a close, warns "intolerable governments," and with a rhetorical flourish declares: "Let the princes hear and be afraid." For God will not tolerate "unbridled despotism" for too long.[34]

If this is Calvin's political theology, what about the role of the church within it? Whatever influence Calvin exerted in Geneva—and it was considerable in his later years—he was quite clear that the church's role was not to govern but to exercise moral authority. At the same time, its responsibility was far more than what may be narrowly conceived as the "spiritual realm." It had a diaconal responsibility to ensure that the poor and needy, the old and infirm, widows and orphans, and exiles and refugees were cared for and the young educated. Moreover, the church had an important role to play in helping to shape public policy, not least that of ensuring a just distribution of wealth. Calvin himself was deeply concerned about and involved in the economic and labor issues affecting society,

32. Calvin, *Commentaries on the Book of the Prophet Daniel*, vol. 1 (Grand Rapids: Eerdmans, 1948), p. 382.

33. Calvin, *The Acts of the Apostles, 1-13*, trans. John W. Fraser and W. J. G. McDonald, Calvin's New Testament Commentaries, vol. 6 (Grand Rapids: Eerdmans, 1965), p. 120.

34. *Institutes*, 4.20.31.

adopting a position we would today refer to as a "mixed economy" in which there is scope for individual initiative as well as state intervention and control. Calvin would have supported the redistribution of wealth, not through revolutionary upheaval but through a system of taxation that favored social victims and the poor.[35] The church's diaconal responsibility was not intended, then, to let the state off the hook; on the contrary, the proclamation of the gospel and the commandment of God within the public sphere was intended to remind those in authority about their responsibility under God to those in their political care.

Central to this responsibility, and thus the substance of many of Calvin's sermons, was the conviction that a just and well-regulated government will be distinguished for maintaining the rights of the poor and afflicted.[36] Calvin stressed the responsibility those in authority have for the powerless and especially the poor in society. But he also insisted on the need for the church to speak out clearly on their behalf in protest against injustice done to them. In a sermon on Deuteronomy 22:1-4 Calvin declared:

> If the poor souls that have bestowed their labour and travail and spent their sweat and blood for you be not paid their wages as they ought to be, not succoured and sustained by you as they should be—if they ask vengeance against you at God's hand, who shall be your spokesman or advocate to rid you out of his hands?[37]

35. See David Little, "Economic Justice and the Grounds for a Theory of Progressive Taxation in Calvin's Thought," in *Reformed Faith and Economics*, ed. Robert L. Stivers (New York: University Press of America, 1989), p. 69; see also Biéler, *The Social Humanism of Calvin*; W. Fred Graham, *The Constructive Revolutionary: John Calvin and His Socio-Economic Impact* (Atlanta: John Knox Press, 1971); Innes, *Social Concern in Calvin's Geneva*.

36. Calvin, *Commentary on the Book of Psalms*, vol. 3, trans. James Anderson (Grand Rapids: Eerdmans, 1949), p. 332. See also *Institutes*, 4.20.9.

37. Calvin, *Opera quae supersunt Omnia*, ed. G. Baum, E. Cunnitz, and E. Reuss (Brunswick, 1863-1900), vol. 28, 11, sermon 125 on Deuteronomy 22:1-4.

In a similar and equally powerful way Calvin comments on the prophet Habakkuk's expression of God losing patience with the extortion of the poor by the rich (Hab. 2:6):

> When anyone disturbs the whole world by his ambition and avarice, or everywhere commits plunders, or oppresses miserable nations, when he distresses the innocent, all cry out, How long? And this cry, proceeding as it does from the feeling of nature and the dictate of justice, is at length heard by the Lord.

In fact, Calvin goes on to say, this passionate feeling of wrong, of injustice, of tyranny, is "implanted in us by the Lord."[38]

This being so, it is not surprising that if the "magistrates" fail in their duty towards the poor and the oppressed, then it is the church's responsibility to minister to their needs and to take their side in the struggle for justice. Christians, Kuyper insisted, have to take their stand with Jesus Christ against the powerful and wealthy and alongside and on behalf of the poor and oppressed in society.[39] Hence the necessary freedom of the church to fulfill its political responsibility was derived from the gospel rather than from the state because it often required the church to speak out against the interests of those in power, including the magistrates, on behalf of the poor and oppressed. It was prophetic freedom that sought the transformation of the whole of life according to the Word of God. From this stemmed "the determination to place the whole of public life under the command of God, an ethic which extends its critical scrutiny beyond the private morality of individuals into culture and economy, and, finally, the readiness for political resistance to tyranny."[40]

---

38. *Commentaries on the Twelve Minor Prophets, Habakkuk, Zephaniah, Haggai*, vol. 4, trans. John Owen (Grand Rapids: Eerdmans, 1950), pp. 93-94.

39. Abraham Kuyper, *Christianity and the Class Struggle* (Grand Rapids: Piet Hein, 1950), p. 50.

40. Jürgen Moltmann, "The Ethic of Calvinism," in *The Experiment Hope* (London: SCM, 1975), p. 120.

From Firebrands to Quietists

Calvin did not provide us with an inflexible blueprint for church-state relations or Christian political responsibility that would suit every situation. His theology—and subsequently, in principle if not always in fact, Reformed political theology—was and remains flexible and contextual. On the one hand there has been an attempt to remain faithful to Calvin's ideas, but on the other there has been a remarkable political pragmatism.[41] One important consequence of this contextual character of Reformed political theology has been the variety of ways in which it has been adapted and developed, some conservative and others quite radical and even revolutionary. Calvin's successors, as Höpfl puts it, "ranged in their politics from firebrands to quietists, without consciousness of the least deviation from orthodoxy."[42] Political events in France and Scotland were responsible for the fact that soon after Calvin's death the Reformer's cautious endorsement of resistance to tyrannical authority was exploited to the full. "The pressure of an unbearable external situation," wrote Karl Holl, "forced Calvinism beyond the limits set by Calvin."[43] St. Bartholomew's Night, 1572, when the French king ordered the massacre of the Huguenots, ushered in a new era in the development of Calvinism. "Psychological shock, consternation, the physical need to defend life and property swept away all restraint. This was a real revolution not only in the theses propounded, but also in mentality and outlook."[44]

Calvin's immediate successors, starting with Theodore Beza in Geneva and the leaders of the Huguenots—Francis Hotman, Hubert Languet, and Philip du Plessis-Mornay[45]—and

41. See Myriam Yardeni, "French Calvinist Political Thought," in *International Calvinism 1541-1715*, ed. Menna Prestwich (Oxford: Clarendon Press, 1985), p. 315.

42. Harro Höpfl, *The Christian Polity of John Calvin* (London: Cambridge University Press, 1982), p. 217.

43. Karl Holl, *The Cultural Significance of the Reformation* (New York: Meridian, 1959), p. 67.

44. Yardeni, "French Calvinist Political Thought," p. 320.

45. See editorial comment, *Institutes*, 4.20.31.

with John Knox and George Buchanan in Scotland,[46] developed the popular right to resist tyranny as a sacred duty.[47] This is reflected, for example, in the Scots Confession of 1560 as well as the Heidelberg Catechism.[48] From this perspective, not to resist tyranny is traitorous towards God and the nation.[49] In his famous volume *Concerning the Rights of Rulers*, Beza declares:

> My purpose with these arguments is not to tighten the conscience of men by means of the civil laws or the pronouncements of philosophers as if by most reliable rules, but only to show as clearly as may be how unjust is the opinion of those who would leave men no means at all by which they may avail themselves to break the onset of imminent or openly aggressive tyranny, however cruel and unjust the latter might be.[50]

In response to the question, "But what if the tyrant forbids what God commands?" Beza responds: "You should not at all judge that you have performed your duty if you have merely refused to obey the tyrant, unless at the same time you obey the command of God."[51]

For Beza, "what God commands" did not simply refer to true worship. It referred also to the service of others, those things "which every man in accordance with his calling either public or private is in charity bound to render to his neighbor."[52] This is a development of Calvin's notion that civil disobedience and resistance should really be confined to matters

46. See Richard L. Greaves, *Theology and Revolution in the Scottish Reformation: Studies in the Thought of John Knox* (Grand Rapids: Eerdmans, 1980).

47. On the development of resistance ideas after St. Bartholomew's Night, see Robert M. Kingdon, *Myths about the St. Bartholomew's Massacres, 1572-1576* (Cambridge, Mass.: Harvard University Press, 1988).

48. See Allan Verhey, *Living the Heidelberg* (Grand Rapids: Christian Reformed Church Publications, 1986).

49. Theodore Beza, *Concerning the Rights of Rulers*, p. 69.

50. Ibid., p. 67.

51. Ibid., p. 27.

52. Ibid., p. 25.

affecting the true but formal worship of God. The logic of Calvin's position is that true worship implies doing justice; otherwise it is sheer hypocrisy (Amos 5:21-22).[53] John Leith is right in asking the rhetorical question: "Is not the abuse of human beings made in the image of God an act against God as well as the prohibition of the worship of God?"[54] In fact, do they not belong intrinsically together?

Commenting on Romans 13, Beza acknowledges the need to respect authority, but he immediately qualifies this by refusing to admit that this means completely subjecting oneself to the will of those in power. On the contrary, Beza writes: "I boldly maintain that he suffers no injustice if he is constrained to his duty and if, when no further room is left for [an appeal to his] reason, an even more drastic procedure against him is followed."[55] In passing, we may well note that we are not very far here from the position adopted by *The Kairos Document*. It is interesting to note how already with Beza something akin to the conditions laid down for a "just war" are applied to a "just revolution":

a. Not all tyrannicides can be condemned without distinction;

b. An unjust usurper may be transformed into a lawful ruler;

c. Nothing should be done recklessly;

d. Nothing should be done by way of insurrection, but in due order and a disciplined way;

e. The magistrates have a crucial role;

f. Action is not for the sake of stirring up rebellion but rather to avoid it.[56]

53. *Institutes*, 3.7.1; 3.8.7.
54. Leith, *John Calvin's Doctrine of the Christian Life* (Louisville: Westminster/John Knox Press, 1989), p. 206.
55. Beza, *Concerning the Rights of Rulers*, p. 81.
56. Ibid., p. 43.

Thus began a tradition within Calvinism which endorsed revolution insofar as it arose out of obedience to God, and this was measured by whether or not government was serving the true interests of those governed. All this contributed to the overthrow of the monarchy in England and to the revolutionary impulses that led to the American Revolution, and, some would argue, to the French as well. Indeed, it has been argued that there is an intrinsic connection between what Calvin initiated in Geneva in the sixteenth century and what Jean-Jacques Rousseau and others initiated in France at the close of the eighteenth.[57] Calvin, Fred Graham argues,

> would have understood many of these revolutionary people. Like him, they have little sentiment for the past or for people who stand in the way of the future. Like him, they speak longingly of justice and mercy, if not (as he did) about walking humbly with God. Like him, they are apt to become impatient with followers who turn reformation disorder into personal profit. The difference between Calvin and many of these revolutionaries is that they want these goals reached at any price. The horrors of the French Directory, and Cromwell's massacre of the Irish—these are lost on people who know no history but the personal history of their own maltreatment and the misery of the oppressed.[58]

But a stronger pull within the Reformed tradition has led to a conservative reaction against revolutions not founded on obedience to God, but, as with the French Revolution, on quite the opposite. Second- and third-generation Reformed confessions reflected this more conservative position, largely because in many instances the earlier political goals had been achieved. So the role of the church in a postrevolutionary situation was regarded as different from what it had been in the struggle against tyranny. This is precisely what happened to Afrikaner Calvinism in South Africa after it shared in the victory against

57. Graham, *The Constructive Revolutionary,* pp. 17-18.
58. Ibid., p. 26.

British imperialism. It is also the issue facing the "church against apartheid" as it anticipates the post-apartheid era. Hence, John Mulder's observation is pertinent that Calvinism has "worked fairly well as a theology of politics as long as it combatted political power, as long as it remained outside the arena of actual power."[59] But then it has too often fallen prey to imperialism, and if not to imperialism then to an uncritical quietism.

The distinction between the two types of revolution, the one justified and the other to be opposed, comes out very clearly in Abraham Kuyper. While Kuyper can describe the victories of William of Orange and Oliver Cromwell as "glorious," the French Revolution and all subsequent revolutions based on atheism are anti-Christian.[60] The one was regarded as a victory for Reformed faith and liberty against Catholic repression and tyranny; the other was a victory of libertinism and licence, human emancipation from a moral responsibility based on Christian values and commitments. Without doubt, the latter view has prevailed within the Reformed tradition until the twentieth century. But largely through the challenge of Barth, the rediscovery of the political significance of eschatology, and more recently that of liberation theology, Reformed theologians have begun to reassess their tradition and to find, along with liberation theologians, a trajectory not only affirming the need for social transformation but also acknowledging that in some extreme situations armed struggle might be inevitable and even legitimate, though never unproblematic and without qualification. Even those whose cause is righteous remain affected by sin.

Original Sin, Political Realism, and Power

Both the more conservative and the more progressive Reformed views have been grounded theologically in the doctrine of orig-

59. John M. Mulder, "Calvinism, Politics, and the Ironies of History," *Religion in Life* 42 (Summer 1978): 159.
60. Kuyper, *Anti-revolutionaire Staatkunde* (Kampen: Kok, 1916).

inal sin, but with different emphasis. For the conservative, original sin in the political arena has been read to mean that whoever rules, whether prince or people, is a potential oppressor and therefore the changing of one government for another is no guarantee for the establishment of justice. God alone can, and in his own time and way will, bring that about. Thus the classic seventeenth-century Calvinist confessions emphasize God's providential rule in and over history and require in the interim that the oppressed wait in patience and trust. In effect, the traditional Reformed confessions give priority to the maintenance of law and order over justice and social transformation. For the progressive, as we shall see, precisely the same argument leads to a different conclusion. Thus André Biéler argues that while Calvin rejects the use of violent revolution as illegitimate, he also "confirms that God often uses the disobedience of workingmen as a means of judging and chastising exploiters."[61]

While the doctrine of original sin is usually understood in individualistic terms, biblically and especially within the Augustinian tradition sin is understood as endemic to social reality. For precisely this reason Luther argued that the state has become necessary because of the Fall, and Calvinists like Kuyper agreed. While Calvin himself understood the state more positively, he was no less adamant that sin required the state to maintain order and prevent anarchy. In this way the doctrine of original sin has functioned to justify coercive power, authority, and control.

A complementary implication of human sinfulness, however, is that social structures and institutions are themselves part of fallen humanity and prone to corruption. Indeed, Calvin was fully aware of what we today call "structural violence," or what he called "unrighteous violence"—that is, the violence built into the structures of society by authority, or the excessive force used by them to maintain unjust social structures.[62] Wolterstorff reminds us that "the most profound of all breaches between the

---

61. Biéler, *The Social Humanism of Calvin*, p. 49.
62. Little, "Economic Justice," p. 80.

Calvinist and the medieval vision" is the conviction, based on the Word of God, that "we live in a fallen, corrupted society: the structures of our social world are structures which in good measure do not serve the common good."[63] The state, in fact, is most prone to claim absolute power, a claim strongly resisted by Calvinism whenever it has been true to its prophetic roots:

> Calvinism protests against state-omnipotence; against the horrible conception that no right exists above and beyond existing laws; and against the pride of absolutism which recognises no constitutional rights, except as the result of princely favour.[64]

It is not therefore as surprising as it might first seem to discover that Friedrich Engels, who was himself the product of a Calvinist home in Germany, regarded Calvinism as an ally in the fight against kings and aristocratic lords.[65] But it is also an ally in the fight against any totalitarianism, any attempt by the state to become a law unto itself, to become, in other words, a god determining our lives.

A profound awareness of the social reality of sin means that the Reformed tradition is also acutely aware of the underlying conflict endemic to society. José Míguez Bonino reminds us that it was not Marx who first discovered the reality of class struggle, but Calvin. "With keen realism" Calvin "describes the economic and social realms, under the sway of sin, as a battlefield in which greed and self-seeking have destroyed the original community of justice and introduced exploitation, injustice and disorder."[66] In like manner, Kuyper's analysis of society strikes a similar Marxian note when he describes the untena-

---

63. Wolterstorff, *Until Justice and Peace Embrace* (Grand Rapids: Eerdmans, 1983), p. 16.

64. Kuyper, *Lectures on Calvinism* (Grand Rapids: Eerdmans, 1931), p. 98.

65. See Karl Marx and Friedrich Engels, *On Religion* (New York: Schocken Books, 1964), pp. 299-300.

66. José Míguez Bonino, *Revolutionary Theology Comes of Age* (London: SPCK, 1975), p. 119.

bility of the present social order as something fundamental to the nature of society. "For one who does not acknowledge this," he argues, "and who thinks that the evil can be exorcised through an increase of piety, through friendlier treatment or kindlier charity, there exists possibly a religious question and possibly a philanthropic question, but not a social question." Only critical social analysis and a genuinely political strategy can lead to social change.[67]

The doctrine of original sin thus functions as a "hermeneutic of suspicion." Sin not only affects those who are ruled; it also affects those who rule, those who have the power to shape the structures of society, and, indeed, those who may seek to overthrow present governments through revolutionary action. "Far from neglecting sin and the Fall, Christians who seek to follow the God of justice," writes Kenneth Leech, "have a higher doctrine of sin than their critics."[68]

This awareness of the reality of sin injects into Reformed political thinking the critical realism that found its expression so powerfully in the writings of Reinhold Niebuhr.[69] In turn it demands, and finds in its doctrine of God's sovereignty, the basis for an ongoing critique of political structures, ideologies, and processes. Calvin's letter to Francis I, king of France, which forms the preface to the *Institutes*, gives "startling evidence that Calvin and his followers regarded all rulers as subject to criticism from the standpoint of scriptural religion."[70] Calvin, Bouwsma reminds us, "particularly abhorred the abuse of religion for legitimation and social control and was revolted by

67. Kuyper, *Christianity and the Class Struggle*, p. 40. See Wolterstorff, *Until Justice and Peace Embrace*, pp. 80-81.

68. Leech, *Experiencing God* (San Francisco: Harper & Row, 1985), p. 380.

69. See especially Reinhold Niebuhr, *Moral Man and Immoral Society* (New York: Scribner's, 1932); *The Nature and Destiny of Man*, vol. 1 (New York: Scribner's, 1941). For a critique of liberation theology from a "Niebuhrian" perspective, see Dennis McCann, *Christian Realism and Liberation Theology: Practical Theologies in Conflict* (New York: Orbis, 1981).

70. Calvin, *On God and Political Duty*, ed. John T. McNeill (New York: Bobbs-Merrill, 1956), p. x.

its hypocrisy. 'Today,' he noted, 'rulers, in presenting their titles, describe themselves as kings, dukes, and counts by the grace of God; but how many falsely use God's name only to claim supreme power for themselves! What is the value of that phrase 'by the grace of God' but to avoid acknowledging any superior at all?' If kings can 'retain the people in obedience and duty, any kind of worship and any way of worshipping God is the same to them.' Calvin and Machiavelli were alike in their realism; but what Machiavelli was prepared to accept for its utility, Calvin hoped to abolish."[71]

But Calvin and his followers did not only confront rulers regarding the abuse of power; they also confronted the comfortable middle-class merchants who governed Geneva but whose economic practices were immoral and unjust. R. H. Tawney provides a vivid description of this conflict in which Beza is accused "of stirring up class hatred against the rich."[72] This was as much a smoke screen to protect selfish interest then as similar accusations are today against liberation theologians and Christian activists in general. Those in authority should rule for the good of all, but the doctrine of "original sin" suggests that they have a predilection to put their own interests above those they govern, and to do so in the name of God.

This pessimistic (or better, realistic) understanding of human nature, whether personal or corporate, indicates to the Calvinist that just social change inevitably assumes or even requires some degree of social conflict. The biblical record, from beginning to end, shows how God's purposes in history are worked out in situations of conflict. "Conflict is basic to the prophetic tradition and indeed the entire Christian tradition of social action."[73] This, as Gregory Baum indicates, must not be reduced to viewing the class struggle as the driving

71. William J. Bouwsma, *John Calvin* (New York: Oxford University Press, 1988), p. 55.
72. R. H. Tawney, *Religion and the Rise of Capitalism* (West Drayton, Middlesex: Penguin Books, 1948), p. 131.
73. Leech, *Experiencing God*, p. 391.

force of history, nor as an encouragement to hatred and violence.[74] Rather, conflict indicates that state corruption and absolutism is being held in check in the interests of human liberty. Thus, for Kuyper, conflict between the state and the church—as well as between the state and other social spheres—generates human rights and constitutional law and government.[75]

Such conflict is not normally or necessarily violent or revolutionary, but it is inevitable because society represents a conflict of interests. If the conflict is not managed through appropriate democratic means, then revolution is likely, if not inevitable. Hence, Calvin's theology opens the door for a more democratic form of government, but it also permits resistance against tyranny as a last resort. If Calvin's political theology achieved nothing else it helped foster the struggle for democratic government, and thus, as Karl Holl noted, placed "a solid barrier in the path of the spread of absolutism in Europe."[76] In the same way it also prevents the church from accepting other forms of totalitarian tyranny, whether fascist or Marxist.

The church itself is not immune to the corruption of original sin and the "will to power" of which Reinhold Niebuhr spoke. This was fundamental to Calvin's critique of the papacy and its involvement in temporal affairs, and thus to the struggle for the true church and its separation from state control. The church struggle is always in some measure or respect a reflection of the broader struggle within society. However, precisely because the Calvinist goal is not just for personal redemption but for the renewal of society as a whole on the basis of God's justice and righteousness revealed in the Word of God,[77] Calvinists were equally prone to become themselves absolutist in opposi-

74. Gregory Baum, *Theology and Society* (Mahwah, N.J.: Paulist Press, 1987), p. 32.

75. Kuyper, *Lectures on Calvinism*, p. 94.

76. Holl, *The Cultural Significance of the Reformation*, p. 68.

77. See Kuyper, *Lectures on Calvinism*, but also Biéler, *The Social Humanism of Calvin*.

tion to absolutism.[78] In order to speak the prophetic word, the prophet and the prophetic community need to speak with conviction and authority. But this can so easily result in the Calvinist imperialism of which we previously spoke, unless the church is itself continually sensitive to the need for rigorous and critical analysis of its own social position, interests, and praxis.

The church is not an infallible interpreter of the Word of God, but its fragile servant. Prophetic witness requires as a precondition, then, that the prophetic community is the first to hear and experience the judgment of God. The church is always itself in a state of conflict between its own self-interests and those of the gospel. It can only fulfill its political role if it is always in the process of reformation. Moreover, it will generally fulfill its political role better through the instrumentality of its members engaged in politics than as an institution claiming political rights and authority, even if the latter be in the service of justice.

The Reformed model of church involvement in the political arena is thus in the first place an iconoclastic model derived from the "second use of the law." It refuses to allow human beings or human institutions, including the church, to usurp the role of God. The church is not called to establish theocratic rule. At the same time, the church is called to enable the reform of society so that society may approximate God's purposes as closely as possible within a fallen world—purposes consonant with the perspective and vision of the kingdom of God, God's righteous rule revealed in Jesus Christ. Thus, Reformed political theology goes beyond ideological critique and contributes to the construction of society on the basis of the "third use of the law." This has led Jaroslav Pelikan to comment that the "most characteristic difference between Lutheran and Calvinist views of obedience to the word and will of God

> lay outside the area of church dogma, in what has been called, with reference to Bucer, his "Christocracy": the

78. See Georgia Harkness, *John Calvin: The Man and His Ethics* (Nashville: Abingdon, 1958), pp. 66-67.

question of whether, and how, the law of God revealed in the Bible, as distinguished from the natural law accessible through reason, was to be obeyed in the political and social order.

But the crucial link between obedience to the will of God revealed in Jesus Christ and the political process lay in the development of the Old Testament notion of the covenant. As Pelikan rightly goes on to say, it was the combination of obedience to God in Christ combined with "the doctrine of the covenant and applied to the life of nations" which had "far-reaching political significance, for it decisively affected the political and social evolution of lands that came under the sway of Calvinist churchmanship and preaching."[79]

Covenant, Accountability, and Legitimacy

The title of James Michener's popular historical novel, *The Covenant*, highlights the role which the Day of the Vow, December 16, 1839, has played in the self-understanding and legitimation of Afrikaner nationalism. Indeed, "the covenant" made between the Trekkers and God before the Battle of Blood River became the most sacred of symbols for Afrikaner nationalism, providing it with a theological rationale which has always seemed eminently Calvinistic. With "the covenant" we thus arrive at the point where Afrikaner nationalism and Afrikaner Calvinism have blended most clearly and potently to form a "civil religion" not unlike the one that emerged in the United States through the interaction of Puritan religion and the struggles and aspirations of the nation's founding fathers. The political use of the covenantal idea is, in fact, the way in which Calvinists applied their theology to the public arena, but in Afrikaner Calvinism it has taken on a particular significance.

79. Jaroslav Pelikan, *The Christian Tradition*, vol. 4: *Reformation of Church and Dogma* (Chicago: University of Chicago Press, 1984), p. 217; see also pp. 232-33.

The story of the Trekkers' covenant is well known. With their leader Piet Retief murdered by the Zulu chief Dingaan (Afrikaner and Zulu interpretations of the event differ), and thus having failed in their attempt to obtain land rights in Natal, the Trekkers, encamped in their laager on the banks of a river, were warned that a Zulu attack was imminent. Faced with overwhelming odds the Voortrekkers made a vow to God:

> Brothers and fellow-countrymen, we stand here before the Holy God of Heaven and Earth to make a vow that, if he will be with us and protect us and give the foe into our hands, we shall forever celebrate the day and date as a Day of Thanksgiving like the Sabbath in his honour. We shall enjoin our children that they must take part in all this, for a remembrance even for our prosperity. For the honour of God shall herein be glorified, and to him shall be given the fame and the honour of the victory.[80]

Opinions vary on how the Trekkers themselves understood their vow. But there can be no doubting the fact that later Afrikaner ideologists made it the hermeneutical key for interpreting Afrikaner history as the history of a people chosen and preserved by God for a divine mission in South Africa. The sacredness of the covenant for Afrikanerdom can be ascertained from the fact that any attempt to demythologize the event or critically examine the words of the vow, especially by Afrikaners, is regarded to this day as treasonous by more conservative Afrikaners. Hence the "feathering and tarring" of a doyen of Afrikaner historians, F. A. van Jaarsveld, by members of the Afrikaner Weerstands Beweging during a public lecture in which he was raising some critical questions.[81]

80. The text is to be found in T. Dunbar Moodie, *The Rise of Afrikanerdom* (Berkeley: University of California Press, 1975), p. 179.
81. The lecture was being presented as the opening address at a conference on the interpretation of South African history, held at the University of South Africa, Pretoria, in March 1979. See F. A. van Jaarsveld, "A Historical Mirror of Blood River," in A. Konig and H. Keane, *The Meaning of History* (Pretoria: UNISA, 1980).

The idea of a covenant between God and a nation has its origin in the Old Testament, where Yahweh entered into a covenant relationship with the people of Israel through the patriarch Abraham. For Calvin, as for Christians generally, this covenant was made anew in the death and resurrection of Jesus Christ on behalf of humanity as a whole, and the church, elect from every nation, was the people of the new covenant called to witness to the gospel. As such, God's covenant of grace in Jesus Christ had no direct political significance.

Calvin would have fully understood the piety that led the Trekkers to make their vow to God. Who would not, given their circumstances. But Calvin would have had great difficulty in regarding it as a covenant in the biblical sense, whether this was how the Trekkers understood it or only the way it was later interpreted within Afrikaner Calvinism. Not only would he have disapproved of the contractual nature of the covenant, which meant that a bargain was struck with God, he would also have disapproved of the identification of the Trekkers with Israel or the church. To them the covenant made national self-preservation the focal point rather than God's grace and justice for all. In turn, this inevitably led to the conviction that the Afrikaner nation as it came to be was an elect people, chosen by God to exercise rule and authority in southern Africa.

Such notions were by no means confined to Afrikaners. Oliver Cromwell and John Milton,[82] along with Puritan divines in seventeenth-century England, regarded the English nation as covenanted to God and in existence as a people with a divine calling—a notion later used to legitimize British colonial policy and to justify exclusive policies based on race, culture, gender, and class.[83] Indeed, the political use of the covenantal idea profoundly affected the political history of nations influenced by Calvinism in a way that was distinct

82. See, for example, William Haller, *The Rise of Puritanism* (New York: Harper, 1957), pp. 346ff.
83. See Preston Williams, "Calvinism, Racism and Economic Institutions," in Stivers, *Reformed Faith and Economics*, pp. 51, 58-59.

from Lutheran lands.[84] How was it, then, that this idea of the covenant came to play such a dubious role?

The origins of relating the covenant directly to politics and law within the Reformed tradition may be traced to Zwingli and especially his successor in Zurich, Heinrich Bullinger. For Bullinger, the covenant was not only the hermeneutical key which unlocked the Scriptures, but it did so in such a way that covenant provided the key for understanding human history as a whole.[85] The idea of the covenant as a political instrument, however, enters the political arena largely through the French Huguenots and John Knox. As James Torrance describes it,

> situations emerged in France and Scotland where the Protestant reformers, even if in a minority, as in France, were prepared to use force in the defence of religious and civil liberty, but they wanted to do it lawfully and constitutionally. It was here that they appealed to the concept of covenant between the king and people to safeguard both the rights of the king and the rights of the people — a contract of government, based on the law of nature and enshrined in civil law.[86]

For both Bullinger and Knox, as in the Old Testament, the covenant relationship affected not only the church but also the nation. It was not a covenant of grace alone but also one of obligations and works. God's promise of grace was conditional upon human obedience. For them, as for Calvin, there was, indeed, only one covenant of grace, but there were also other covenants made between God and his people in the Old Testament. God would bless and protect Israel if Israel obeyed God. Otherwise divine punishment would follow.

---

84. See H. Richard Niebuhr, "The Idea of Covenant and American Democracy," *Church History* 23 (1954); Pelikan, *Reformation of Church and Dogma*, pp. 217, 232-33.

85. Edward A. Dowey, "Covenant and History in the Thought of Heinrich Bullinger," unpublished paper, Princeton Theological Seminary, 1975.

86. James B. Torrance, "The Covenant Concept in Scottish Theology and Politics and Its Legacy," *Scottish Journal of Theology* 34 (1981): 323.

The doctrine of the covenant with its contractual obligations thus became the link between Calvin's theology of politics
and later Calvinist political theology. It provided the basis for
determining the grounds upon which a ruler could be regarded
as tyrannical and therefore justly overthrown by the people in
the name of God; but it also, by the same token, provided the
basis for the genuine exercise of power through necessary
checks and balances acceptable to the people, and thus the
means for building a postrevolutionary society.

Previously, piety required submission on the part of the
people to the authority of rulers, but the covenant turned that
on its head. Now not only were rulers accountable to the
people, but the people could even decide that particular rulers
were tyrants and that therefore their rule was illegitimate, in
terms of the covenant. God's blessing was thus dependent
upon the rulers fulfilling their contractual obligations to both
God and the people.

In modern parlance, rulers became democratically accountable. The "divine right of kings" had been replaced by
the "divine right of the people." Rulers were accountable to the
people because they were accountable to God. In his treatise
*Concerning the Rights of Rulers over Their Subjects and the Duty of
Subjects towards Their Rulers,* Theodore Beza made it clear that
"peoples were not created for the sake of rulers, but on the
contrary rulers for the sake of the people."[87] He went on to
insist that "those who possess authority to elect a king will also
have the right to dethrone him."[88] Indeed, "the covenant was
an idea with awesome political potency,"[89] for it related, as
Pelikan reminds us, "the will of God" to the political process.
The covenant was not a way of controlling God or limiting his
sovereignty, but of activating the people. "What the covenant
did was to suggest a disciplined and methodical response to
grace, a new, active and willing obedience to command."[90]

87. Beza, *Concerning the Rights of Rulers*, p. 30.
88. Ibid., p. 64.
89. Greaves, *Theology and Revolution*, pp. 124-25.
90. Walzer, *The Revolution of the Saints*, p. 167.

From a Reformed theological perspective the prophetic message of Scripture requires some equivalent of the covenant relationship if it is to relate to the political process. After all, the prophets in their proclamation of God's justice were declaring that God would not bless Israel unless she obeyed God's will by keeping the commandments. The prophetic message presupposed a covenant relationship. In order for prophetic theology to exercise its critical function in society, it is necessary that it is able to appeal to some norm or set of values regarded as binding upon society. For Christians, and especially those within the Reformed tradition, such values derive from the biblical message of the kingdom of God. It is God's reign over all reality, a reign of justice and love, that provides the basis for human rights and responsibilities. Here is, in fact, the basis for later secular versions of the doctrine of human rights. Thus, while Christians would still want to insist on the theological basis for human rights as expressed in the covenantal idea, within secular societies which are inevitably religiously pluralistic, the crucial consideration is the upholding of those rights. For this a constitution with a clearly articulated bill of rights is very important. Every state, if it is to be governed justly and equitably, requires that those who rule and those who are governed should be committed to a shared set of values that derive from those norms.

Thus, just as Calvinism provided a vital stepping stone towards democratic government,[91] its vision for society, its understanding of a nation's covenantal responsibilities, and its prophetic commitment to justice and equity indicate the role that Reformed theology and those ecclesial communities influenced by it can still play in the shaping of a nation's public life. Under certain circumstances, where a government is neither representative of the people nor concerned about the welfare of all citizens, especially the poor, or where it is downright oppressive, then Reformed theology must raise the question of its illegitimacy. For at the very least the idea of the covenant

91. See the debate on this issue in *Calvin and Calvinism: Sources of Democracy?* ed. Robert M. Kingdon and Robert D. Linder (D. C. Heath and Co., 1970).

insists that the legitimacy of the government (as distinct from the state) depends upon its pursuance of justice based on equity. This in turn will lead Reformed theology to recognize and support—indeed even call for—protest and resistance, including civil disobedience.[92] The intention is not anarchy, but the restoration of order based on justice and equity.

So Reformed theology is ultimately concerned about the establishment of true government, a government that is legitimate before God and the people, and therefore one accountable to God. This is where a common acceptance of and commitment to covenantal obligations, a bill of rights, or a constitution become fundamental to the well-being of society and a crucial element in the negotiations required for resolving political conflict. But a further dimension to this process derives from an understanding of the covenant. The validity of a bill of rights and its implementation is ultimately to be gauged from the way it relates to the victims of society.

It is noteworthy that in recent times liberation theologians in Latin America have shifted the emphasis of their praxis from one of revolutionary to one of democratic struggle.[93] For ultimately an "armed struggle," unless it can bring a speedy end to oppression, must lead to a total devastation contrary to the self-interest of all concerned. At some point negotiation becomes inevitable and essential. But this, in turn, requires that all the people, and especially those who have been oppressed, become an integral part of the process. Precisely here liberation theology once again finds an important point of contact with the Reformed tradition, while at the same time presenting it with a further challenge. In the process a profounder understanding of the liberating significance of covenantal theology becomes possible.

92. See the application of this to the South African situation in Charles Villa-Vicencio, *Civil Disobedience and Beyond: Law, Resistance and Religion in South Africa* (Grand Rapids: Eerdmans, 1990), esp. p. 71.

93. See Paul E. Sigmund, *Liberation Theology at the Crossroads* (New York: Crossroads, 1990), pp. 176-77.

If it is true that God's election indicates a special concern for the poor, then it means that God's covenant has a special regard and relevance for the victims of society and their struggle against oppression. It is not a covenant that leads to the striking of a bargain with God in favor of self-preservation and nationalist self-interest; it is a "strategic covenant" of liberating grace God makes with the poor and other social victims in their struggle for justice.[94] This means that the test of good government, and ultimately its legitimacy, is dependent on its treatment of those who are socially disadvantaged or oppressed. Its accountability before God is no longer simply to be understood in terms of its accountability to "the people," those who may have the power of privilege, numbers, or arms to elect or depose a government. Its accountability before God has to do with the way in which it acts towards the powerless, those relegated to the periphery of social existence, whether they be urban squatters, farm laborers, peasant women, the physically or mentally disabled, or a particular group of people like the Jews in Nazi Germany—that is, any of those whom Jesus defined as the least of his brothers and sisters (Matt. 25:40). This provides, then, the focal point for the church's prophetic and pastoral ministry, the test of its own obedience and freedom.

A Prophetic and Free Church

The theological focus of the altercation between State President Botha and the church leaders with which we began this chapter was the question of the freedom of the church and its role in politics. However much President Botha may have been influenced by the rhetoric of the contemporary religious right—for

94. Victorio Araya, "The God of the Strategic Covenant," in Pablo Richard et al., *The Idols of Death and the God of Life* (New York: Orbis, 1983), p. 104.

whom any kind of socialist state, whether democratic or not, meant the death of religious freedom—the position he adopted reflected the Constantinian position within dominant Western Christian tradition as it has been interpreted since the Reformation.

According to this tradition, the freedom of the church, and therefore its public role, has to do with the "spiritual realm," not the political. This is particularly true of Luther's doctrine of the "two kingdoms," the kingdom of the spirit and the kingdom of the sword, as interpreted within mainstream Lutheranism. While this may protect the formal freedom of the church by making the state its guardian, in effect it makes it part of the civil service, thus destroying its true freedom and ability to engage in prophetic social critique and action against the dominant culture. The disastrous consequences of the doctrine were most clearly demonstrated in Nazi Germany. But neo-Calvinism, especially as interpreted in South Africa, has had a similar effect, through its doctrine of the sovereignty of separate spheres, in preventing the church from prophetically challenging the government.[95]

All of this must be kept in mind in seeking to understand the way the church leaders in South Africa responded to President Botha as described at the beginning of this chapter. They were reluctantly forced to accept political responsibilities because of a failure of government, and they were of necessity adopting a role that in normal circumstances would be beyond their mandate. In the same way church leaders in Brazil acted as surrogates for political groups in the late 1960s and through the 1970s.[96] If they surrendered this responsibility they would not be fulfilling their duty both to the nation and to its victims, and they would, as a consequence, have surrendered their freedom for the sake of some breathing space from the state. The

95. See de Gruchy, *Bonhoeffer and South Africa* (Grand Rapids: Eerdmans, 1984), pp. 106-7.
96. See Arthur F. McGovern, *Liberation Theology and Its Critics* (New York: Orbis, 1989), p. 209.

church leaders understood the freedom of the church not as a possibility given to it by the state but as an evangelical necessity that had to be exercised. More recently, in April 1990, the leaders of the South African Council of Churches found it necessary to decline an invitation from President de Klerk to participate in a government-sponsored conference on the church's participation in the building of a new South Africa. Their fear, justified in the light of church history, was the surrendering of the church's freedom to be truly prophetic.

The fact of the matter is that since the Reformation and within a Constantinian framework the traditional ways of relating church and state have become increasingly problematic for the church when it seeks to take its gospel mandate seriously in the form of prophetic and social action.[97] Indeed, it is a seriously flawed understanding of the freedom of the church if we regard it as something given and guaranteed by a constitution. This does not mean that the statutory separation of church and state or the constitutional defense of religious liberty—formal as they may be in some places, absent or curtailed in others—are no longer important. On the contrary, the safeguarding of a proper formal and legal relationship between church and state and the safeguarding of religious liberty for all faiths are of great importance. But these formal arrangements do not constitute the freedom of the church to proclaim the gospel in its fullness. "They can help us to describe the ideal conditions for the witness of the church. But the witness itself stems from another source."[98] It is a gift and task derived from the gospel—hence Kuyper's very Calvinistic dictum that it is the privilege of the church and not the state "to determine her own characteristics as the true church, and to proclaim her own confession as the confession of truth."[99]

The Constantinian understanding of church and state was

97. See *Church and State: Opening a New Ecumenical Discussion* (Geneva: WCC, 1978), pp. 7-8.
98. Ibid., p. 15.
99. Kuyper, *Lectures on Calvinism*, p. 106.

challenged at the time of the Reformation by the Anabaptists. Indeed, it was partly as a result of the Anabaptist protest, as much as if not more than the role of Calvinism, that many of the constitutional liberties now enjoyed by churches in the West were won. The Anabaptist protest against Constantinianism is, however, not simply something of the past; it is a constant challenge to the way in which the Reformed tradition relates to the public sphere. For precisely that reason Reformed theology continually has to face the critical challenge presented by Anabaptism. James Gustafson has acknowledged that the Anabaptist witness "represents the sharpest challenge to any theology and theological ethics that desires to claim some backing from the particularities of the Christian tradition while moving in quite another direction."[100]

This challenge has to be faced at the level of both the social location of the church and its adopted strategies in relating to society and culture. For whenever there has been an alliance between the heirs of the magisterial Reformers and the dominant culture it has led to a social witness not informed by the gospel. Luther's siding with the princes against the peasants, and the way in which Calvinism developed its power base within the city councils and among the urban middle-classes, ensured that the churches of the Reformation would not be churches of the poor. Churches of martyrs, exiles, persecuted, refugees, yes, but often churches seeking political alliances with those in authority to their own advantage rather than for the sake of the oppressed and poor as such.

Nevertheless, there were some good reasons why the Reformed tradition refused to follow the Anabaptist withdrawal from direct political involvement. Central to these reasons was the conviction that the exercise of political power was a Christian calling and not something to be left to the devil. Thus, while we must stress the need for the Reformed tradition to cut its ties with Constantinianism, we must equally insist that it does not

100. James M. Gustafson, *Theology and Ethics* (Chicago: University of Chicago Press, 1981), p. 75.

lose its "passionate desire to reshape the social world,"[101] as long as it does so on behalf of the poor and oppressed. This is fundamental to the challenge liberation theology presents to the Reformed tradition. Thus, like the Anabaptists in the sixteenth century and their more prophetic heirs today, liberation theology has radically challenged the Constantinian captivity of the church, especially its alliance with oppressive governments in Latin America and elsewhere. In this respect liberation theology is in continuity with the Radical Reformation.

Yet, clearly Anabaptists and liberation theologians do not take the same stance. For the Anabaptists, the break with Christendom was complete because it was a rejection of any attempt to exercise political power; for liberation theologians the break with Christendom is no less complete—insofar as Christendom is the realm of the powerful, the oppressor, and the privileged—but it is not a surrender of the legitimate use of power by Christians.[102] Liberation theology confronts the Reformed tradition's alliance with oppressive power, as in imperial or colonial Calvinism, but it also challenges any attempt to be "neutral," to withdraw from public responsibility in the struggle for justice and liberation in the world. The challenge of liberation theology comes, therefore, in terms of the Reformed tradition's own Constantinian heritage, only from the other side. The break with Constantinianism is not a withdrawal from the political arena—for the Reformed tradition that is not an option. Power has to be exercised, but in solidarity with the powerless.

Thus, while the Reformed tradition can respond to the challenge of the heirs of the Radical Reformation with a certain historical and theological confidence, any sense of complacency it may have is more seriously disturbed by liberation theology's challenge to exercise that responsibility not from the side of the powerful, nor from the sidelines of history, but on the side of its victims. This is precisely the challenge that both the Belhar

101. Wolterstorff, *Until Justice and Peace Embrace*, p. 21.
102. See Laverne A. Rutschman, "Latin American Liberation Theology and Radical Anabaptism," *Journal for Ecumenical Studies* 19 (Winter 1982): 53.

Confession and *The Kairos Document* present to those churches and Christians in South Africa who support the status quo on the grounds that Christians should be neutral or only concerned about the "spiritual realm." Neutrality is necessary in the sense that the church should not align itself with a particular political party or organization. It is not legitimate when it comes to taking sides with and supporting the cause of those who are the victims of injustice.

The challenge of liberation theology goes beyond calling a privileged church to identify with the poor and oppressed. It calls the privileged church to recognize that the church in South Africa and probably in most of the world today is by and large the church of the poor and oppressed. *The Kairos Document* makes this point:

> To say that the Church must now take sides unequivocally and consistently with the oppressed is to overlook the fact that the majority of Christians in South Africa have already done so. By far the greater part of the Church in South Africa is poor and oppressed. . . . This fact needs to be appropriated and confirmed by the Church as a whole.[103]

The question we then face is whether the Reformed tradition is open to this possibility of a shift from a Constantinian defense of power and privilege, through legitimation or neutrality, to a political commitment to those who are poor and oppressed and all who struggle for justice and liberation. Only in this way will its tendency to imperialism be countered and overcome without it also losing its passionate commitment to shaping a just society. When the church does this it becomes truly prophetic and free to be the church.

The Politics of Hope and Love

Despite Calvin's passion for affirming and shaping the world to the glory of God, it remained fundamental to his theology

103. *The Kairos Document*, 5.1.

that the Christian's ultimate citizenship was not on earth but in heaven. The Christian life was not only one of self-denial and crossbearing, but also one of anticipation of eternal life. For Calvin, the "cry for life" could never have been reduced to a concern for this world's goods, no matter how important. The "cry for life" went deeper. It arose out of the depths of human existence, it was the human quest for ultimate meaning, for hope beyond despair, for life beyond death. The final restoration of God's image in humankind and creation as a whole lay in the ultimate, not the penultimate.

Calvin's eschatology thus remained focused on the eternal destiny of the individual Christian. His understanding of the kingdom of God predates the major advances in biblical scholarship that have enabled us to rediscover the full significance of God's reign for our lives here and now. Yet for Calvin "meditation on eternal life" and hope for the life to come impinged directly on this life. Personal salvation found its goal in the completion of God's total redemptive work, the final coming of God's kingdom of justice and peace. For the promise of eternal life was grounded in the victory of Christ over sin and death, a victory that enabled the Christian to live in this life with courage and faith knowing that God's purposes could not be defeated. Within this tension—between living fully on earth, yet anticipating heaven—lies much of the dynamic of Calvin's ethics. "It is this eschatology," writes John Leith, "which enabled the Calvinists to be brave in the face of danger and active in the work of the Lord." He continues:

> No matter how much the evils of life may have tormented them they knew that these evils would be eliminated in the life which awaited them beyond history. No matter how insignificant the task which they performed for the Lord on earth, they knew that God would carry it on to fulfillment.[104]

Indeed, it is precisely this hope of eternal life, evoked through meditation on the victory of Christ and the promise of future

104. Leith, *John Calvin's Doctrine of the Christian Life*, pp. 161-62.

life, that enables Christians to give their very lives in the service of the gospel.

The fact that Calvin's eschatology was not a way of escape from engagement in the world but rather a motivating source for witness and struggle sets him apart from much traditional Christian piety. Just as for Bonhoeffer, so for Calvin the penultimate and ultimate were integrally related: justice in this world and justification in the world to come. Eternal life was not contingent upon human effort. It was a gift of grace, but one that called forth human response in this life, for this was precisely how eternal life was appropriated.

In a previous chapter we noted a major shift in recent years in the confessional position of many churches within the Reformed family. The shift came about not through a jettisoning of the tradition but by reworking it on a new eschatological foundation. "The priority for stability and patience," we heard, "has been replaced by the urgency of the coming of the kingdom of God. The poor must not be made to wait and the captives must no longer be kept in prison." This found expression, for example, in the Song of Hope of the Reformed Church in America in 1974,[105] and indicated something of the impact that theologies of hope and liberation have begun to have on the tradition.

It is clearly significant that liberation theology followed closely on the heels of political theologies of hope and drew heavily on the fresh insights of biblical eschatology.[106] God's covenant with the poor and oppressed is a promise that their hopes will be fulfilled. It is a promise that is both ultimate and historical; it is a promise of God's ultimate gift, but also a calling to participate in those struggles which, like John the Baptist, prepare the way for the coming of the messianic kingdom. "A poorly understood spiritualization has often made us forget the human consequences of the eschatological promises and the power to transform unjust social structures which they imply."

105. Song of Hope, published in *Reformed Witness Today*, ed. Lukas Vischer (Bern: Evangelische Arbeitsstelle Oekumene Schweiz, 1982), pp. 222-23.

106. See Gutiérrez, *A Theology of Liberation*, rev. ed. (New York: Orbis, 1988), pp. 91-92.

But, continues Gutiérrez, "The elimination of misery and exploitation is a sign of the coming of the Kingdom."[107] In fact, "without liberating historical events there would be no growth of the Kingdom."[108]

Part of the church's political responsibility is thus to participate in the struggle for social transformation as a witness to the coming of God's kingdom. It is a costly witness because it arises out of struggle and finds expression in suffering. It is a witness of crossbearing, a witness to the saving grace of Christ's death that liberates and gives life. That is why martyrdom, the death of those who in struggling for the gospel of the kingdom are put to death for their faith and commitment, keeps hope alive. Such a witness unto death demonstrates, moreover, the integral relationship between life beyond death and life here and now, between the penultimate signs of the kingdom of God's justice and the ultimate fulfillment of God's reign in Christ. It is also here that hope and love come together in a way that is liberating and transforming. Thus Sobrino says:

> Martyrdom is the expression and product of love. Therefore it generates hope. Again we confront the great paradox: the cross generates hope. It does so not in virtue of its negative element, but in virtue of the fact that it is the maximal expression of love. So many are the martyrs of our lands today, such a "cloud of witnesses" (cf. Heb. 12:1) surrounds the poor, that it is no wonder their faith does not falter. But the martyrs also make it possible for the poor to maintain their hope. It is a "hope against hope," surely. But it is a genuine hope, arising, in the last analysis, from the unshakeable conviction that nothing is more real, nothing more fruitful, than love.[109]

The political task of the church is always to point beyond the politics of the possible to the possibilities that reside in God's promise of a "new heaven and a new earth." For the

107. Ibid., p. 97.
108. Ibid., p. 104.
109. Sobrino, *Spirituality of Liberation* (New York: Orbis, 1988), p. 168.

church, witnessing to the kingdom means that the end of the struggle for liberation has not yet occurred. For when that happens then the kingdom has come—justice and peace have arrived in their fullness. What the church does is to celebrate liberating grace and hope in Word and sacrament, keeping hope and love alive in the struggle for justice and the sacrifice this entails, and pointing beyond the present to what is yet to be revealed. Present liberatory events, significant as they are, are not and cannot be the whole of salvation. That always remains beyond human achievement; that is always a gracious, surprising gift that finally comes and transforms all of reality into the image of God, thus revealing God's glory in the liberation of the whole created order. Archbishop Romero told his Salvadorean congregation:

> As Christians formed in the gospel, you have the right to organize and, inspired by the gospel, to make concrete decisions. But be careful not to betray those evangelical, Christian, supernatural convictions in the company of those who seek other liberations that can be merely economic, temporal, political. Even though working alone with those who hold other ideologies, Christians must cling to their original liberation.[110]

This brings us back to the evangelical foundation of human liberation. Liberating grace, the evangelical core of Reformed theology, remains at the center of the ferment created by the gospel; it remains the motivating power for prophetic witness and struggle. It does so because it provides the way beyond ideological absolutism, and therefore idolatry, to a truly humanized society. That is, it shows that the true motivation for the struggle for justice and its implementation in the structures of society is love. Once again Míguez Bonino helps us to see the connection. "Love is thus the inner meaning of politics, just as politics is the outward form of love. When this relation

110. Oscar Romero, *The Violence of Love*, trans. and ed. James R. Brockman (London: Collins, 1989), p. 4.

is made operative in the struggle for liberation, there is both the flexibility necessary for humanizing the struggle and the freedom necessary for humanizing the result of the struggle."[111] We have returned, then, to Calvin's insistence that the laws of every nation, and therefore the exercise of justice, must conform to the "perpetual rule of love,"[112] a rule central to the hermeneutics and praxis of Reformed, Catholic, and liberation theology.

Max Weber and Ernst Troeltsch were correct in discerning that there is something restless about the true Calvinist or Reformed Christian. It is not, however, a restlessness that comes from anxiety about the state of one's soul, for even though there are no grounds for complacency in that regard, God's grace is far greater than human sin and failure. No, the restlessness of which we speak derives from a deep concern for the redemption of the world, its liberation from oppression in all its dimensions. It is not the restlessness that comes from lack of faith or hope or love, but the restlessness such faith creates, hope sustains, and love directs. For the world is God's, yet it is not as God the creator intends—it neither mirrors God's goodness nor reflects God's image as it should. Therefore the Christian, not in competition with others but alongside them, is called to respond in faith, active in hope and love, to God's redemptive activity, so that the whole of creation can be liberated by grace from the bondage of sin and oppression and can be restored to full life in Jesus Christ, through the Spirit, to the glory of God.

111. José Míguez Bonino, *Toward a Christian Political Ethics* (Philadelphia: Fortress, 1983), p. 114.
112. *Institutes*, 4.20.15.

Index of Names

282

Index of Subjects